The Master Musicians

EDITED BY

FREDERICK J. CROWEST

Mendelssohn

Mendelssohn

By

Stephen S. Stratton

With
Illustrations and Portraits

London : J. M. Dent & Co.
New York : E. P. Dutton & Co.
1901

58473
Mrs. Lilian Shuman Dreyfus

PRINTED BY
WILLIAM CLOWES AND SONS, LIMITED,
LONDON AND BECCLES.

Preface

ALTHOUGH so much has been written concerning Mendelssohn, the chief part lies in the "Recollections" or "Reminiscences" of this or that individual; therefore, the reader desirous of studying the subject of Mendelssohn and his works must gather together a small library for the purpose. The present is an attempt to exhibit the whole in a concise form, with a close adherence to facts, rather than the portrayal of an ideal. I am indebted to almost the whole of the Mendelssohn literature, as detailed in the Bibliography, the quotations in every case being from the English editions. Dates—those milestones of history—have been verified by reference to periodicals of the time, and in this respect the present publication may be found useful. Messrs. Breitkopf and Härtel of Leipzig have kindly given permission to reproduce the drawings of the exterior of the Old Gewandhaus, and the interior of the Concert-room, with the orchestra arranged as in

Mendelssohn's day. Concerning the *facsimile* of a page of the MS. of *Elijah*, the following story may be told here. At the Jubilee performance of *Elijah* given in the Town Hall, Birmingham, on October 8th, 1896, Mr. William Pountney, a well-known local bass singer, took part in the quartet, "Cast thy burden upon the Lord." This gentleman sang in the chorus at the first performance in 1846, and that fact was brought to the notice of Mrs. Benecke, Mendelssohn's daughter, who had intended to be present at the Jubilee performance. Mrs. Benecke sent Mr. Pountney the photograph of a page of the MS., with the following inscription :—

"Photographed from the original MS. of *Elijah*, in the possession of, and presented to Mr. William Pountney by, Marie Benecke, *née* Mendelssohn-Bartholdy, December, 1896."

STEPHEN S. STRATTON.

BIRMINGHAM, 1901.

Contents

Contents

Contents

Contents

Contents

Contents

List of Illustrations

Mendelssohn

CHAPTER I

The Mendelssohn family—Heredity—State of the Jews in Germany in the eighteenth century—Mendel of Dessau—Moses Mendelssohn—Days of poverty and struggle—Fame and happiness—The family of Moses Mendelssohn—Abraham Mendelssohn—His marriage—Leah Salomon—The family remove to Berlin—Received into the Lutheran Church—The Mendelssohn family a rare example of domestic happiness—Abraham Mendelssohn's remarkable musical insight.

THE Artist is the Child of his Age; he is also the product and outcome of the preceding Age. In the life of Felix Mendelssohn—a career of incessant activity, of restless work, though his circumstances were so favourable for ease and leisurely art-product—a career that ended ere the short span of thirty-nine years was reached, there is much that can only be explained by heredity, those qualities transmitted from generation to generation. Before entering upon the main subject of this work, it will be well to devote a little attention to the earlier members of the Mendelssohn family, to whose name Felix added fresh lustre. It is beyond the purpose of this work to enter into details of the condition of the Jews in Germany in the early part of the eighteenth century. They were a people deteriorated and paralyzed by ill-treatment and oppression; a people cruelly neglected, and impolitically excluded from the emporiums of polite learning and useful knowledge.[1] Under Frederick William I. the Jews of Berlin were obliged to buy the wild boars killed at the royal hunting-parties, and under Frederic the Great every Jew had to purchase, on the occasion of his marriage, a certain amount of china from the newly established royal china factory in Berlin, and that not according to his own choice, but that of the manager of the factory, who made use of the opportunity to get rid of things otherwise unsaleable.[2] From a people so unhappily situated sprang Moses Mendelssohn, the great Jewish philosopher, known as "The Modern Plato." His father was a poor Jew, of Dessau, by name Mendel, whose occupation was that of a *Sopher*, or transcriber of the *Pentateuch*. He also kept a Hebrew day-school, but both occupations were of a humble and precarious description at that period. Moses was born on the 6th of September, 1729, and derived the name Mendelssohn, *i.e.* the son of Mendel, from the Jewish custom of forming surnames.

Jews in Germany

Mendel of Dessau

Moses Mendelssohn

His father, a scholar as the times went, began the

[1] "Memoirs of Moses Mendelssohn" (Samuels).

[2] "Mendelssohn Family," vol. i. p. 1.

boy's education almost from infancy. He would make him rise at three or four o'clock on winter mornings, and after giving him a cup of tea, carry him wrapped in a cloak to the public seminary, his teacher being a learned Jew, Rabbi David Frankel (or Fränkel). Consumed by the spirit of inquiry, the boy resolved to make Scripture his principal study, and set himself to acquire a grammatical knowledge of Hebrew, and before his tenth year he had composed Hebrew verses. Soon afterwards Maimonides' "The Guide of the Perplexed" fell into his hands, and he meditated on it day and night, impairing his health, and bringing on a nervous disorder, the neglect of which produced deformity of the spine, and ruined his health for life. "*Maimonides*," he once remarked, "is the cause of my deformity; he spoiled my figure, and ruined my constitution: but still I doat on him, for many hours of dejection which he has converted into those of rapture. And if he have, unwittingly, weakened my body, has he not made ample atonement, by invigorating my soul with his sublime instructions?"

To a character of such determination few things were impossible. So we find him following his teacher Frankel to Berlin, and increasing his store of learning, while undergoing extreme hardship, notching his loaf, not according to his appetite, but in keeping with the state of his finances. He found a friend in one Hyam Bamberg,[1] who allowed him an attic to sleep in, and

[1] Or Hermann Bamberger, "Mendelssohn Family," vol. i. p. 4.

gave him two days' weekly board. He studied German—a dangerous proceeding, as that language was forbidden the Jews—and acquired a fair knowledge of English and French. Latin, too, he tried, and even translated into that tongue Locke's "Essay on the Human Understanding."

In 1750 he was admitted as tutor into the house of an opulent Jew named Bernhard, his improved circumstances enabling him to buy books, and to take lessons in Greek. From obscurity he rose to be the first scholar of his day; sustained a famous controversy with Lavater, became the close friend of Lessing, and the centre of a circle of the best intellect in the Prussian capital. His chief work, "Phædon, or the Immortality of the Soul," has been translated into every European language, and the "Ritual Laws of the Jews" was written and published (1778) by authority of Frederick II. In 1762, Moses Mendelssohn married Fromet, daughter of Abraham Gugenheim, or Gaugenheim, of Hamburg. His later years were tranquil and happy, and he died at Berlin, January 4, 1786.

Professor Rammler erected to his memory a monument bearing this inscription—

MOSES MENDELSSOHN,
BORN AT DESSAU, OF HEBREW PARENTS.
A SAGE LIKE SOCRATES,
FAITHFUL TO THE ANCIENT CREED,
TEACHING IMMORTALITY,
HIMSELF IMMORTAL.

Family

According to that grotesque and insulting law of Frederick the Great, Moses Mendelssohn became possessed, on his marriage, of twenty life-sized china apes. These afterwards were highly prized as family heirlooms.

Moses Mendelssohn left a family of three sons and three daughters. Joseph, the eldest son, had a small banking business in Berlin, and lived there with his widowed mother until 1804, when the family moved to Hamburg. He died on November 25, 1848. Nathan, the youngest son, held a government appointment. He outlived all his brothers and sisters, dying in 1852, at Berlin. Dorothea, the eldest daughter, was born in Berlin in 1765. She married a Jewish merchant, Simon Veil, from whom she was judicially separated in 1798, and afterwards she married Friedrich von Schlegel, so well known as the translator of Shakespeare's plays, and as a critical writer. Henrietta—playfully spoken of as "Tante Jette"—was unmarried. For many years she was governess to the daughter of General Sebastiani in Paris, where she had a school, carried on in the garden of the Foulds' house. Recha, the second daughter, was married to one Meyer, Hof-Agent at Mecklenburg. The union was unhappy, and ultimately dissolved. Dorothea and Henrietta eventually became Roman Catholics. Joseph and Nathan died in the Jewish faith.

The second son of Moses Mendelssohn, Abraham, born in Berlin, December 11, 1776, demands fuller notice here, though his life was so closely bound up with that of his son Felix that constant reference to him will have to be made. Of his early years nothing seems to be known. He was sent to Paris, and in 1803 became cashier in the banking establishment of M. Fould (his sister Henrietta's school adjoining the premises). The next year he resigned his office, and joined his brother at Hamburg, the bank at Berlin being also carried on. It is supposed that he met the lady who became his wife on the journey from Paris to Berlin. The marriage with Leah Salomon took place December 26, 1804, and the pair lived in the same house with Joseph Mendelssohn and his widowed mother at Hamburg. Leah Salomon, born March 26, 1777, came of a wealthy Jewish family resident in Berlin. She was a woman of great accomplishments, played and sang with expression and grace, but seldom, and only for her friends; she drew exquisitely; she spoke and read French, English, Italian, and—secretly—Homer, in the original language.[1] Wealthy, she was simple in dress and manner, and allowed her mother a liberal income, while she carefully kept house for her. Abraham Mendelssohn was a fortunate man to secure such a woman for his wife. In Hamburg there were born to the pair, first, a daughter, Fanny Cäcilie, November 14, 1805; next a son, Jakob Ludwig Felix, February 3, 1809; then a daughter, Rebecka, April 11, 1811. For some time Abraham Mendelssohn lived outside the

Abraham Mendelssohn

[1] "Mendelssohn Family," vol. i. p. 62.

town, in "a pretty little cottage with a balcony! situated on the Elbe, close to the Neumühlen."[1] Soon after the birth of Rebecka, Hamburg was occupied by the French, and life there was so unendurable that the family escaped in disguise to Berlin. Things were not much better there at first. In 1813, Abraham Mendelssohn at his own cost equipped several volunteers, and his services were acknowledged by his election as Stadtrath.[2]

On October 30, 1813, the last child, Paul, was born.

Leah Salomon's brother had become a Christian, and had adopted the name of Bartholdy, after the former proprietor of the garden belonging to the family. This garden, it may here be added, subsequently belonged to Abraham Mendelssohn. Salomon Bartholdy was an accomplished art-critic, and in his later years resided at Rome as Prussian consul-general. He urged upon his brother-in-law the necessity of bringing up his children in the Christian faith, and advised him to add the name of Bartholdy to his own, as a distinction from the other Mendelssohns, adding that this would give him much pleasure as a means of preserving his memory in the family. Abraham took the advice, and the children were baptized according to the rites of the Lutheran Church. The change was kept secret, from a desire to spare the feelings of Madame Salomon, a

[1] "Mendelssohn Family," vol. i. p. 73.

[2] Ibid., p. 74.

Jewess of rigid orthodoxy, who had cursed and cast oft her son on his conversion. Some time later Abraham and his wife were received into the Christian Church at Frankfort. Leah took the additional names of Felicia Paulina in allusion to her sons, and the whole family adopted the double-surname of Mendelssohn-Bartholdy.

Parents become Christians

But with all this diversity in religious conviction, there was unity in affection ; and perhaps no more beautiful picture of domestic love and happiness is on record than that presented by the various members of the Mendelssohn family. Even Madame Salomon was softened in process of time, and, through the instrumentality of the little Fanny Mendelssohn, forgave and was reconciled to her son. Salomon Bartholdy died in 1827, and left his fortune to his sister Leah.

Abraham Mendelssohn-Bartholdy, occupying a central place between two men of genius, was, if not exactly a genius, a very remarkable man. He used to describe himself thus : "Formerly I was the son of my father ; now I am the father of my son." His method of education was severe, and in his character there was more than a little of the old Jewish despotism. His judgment was, however, tempered by affection ; and though he ruled his children with strictness, he treated them as his friends and equals. For a non-musician, his insight into the art was simply wonderful. He detected at once the weak spot—did one exist—in his son's compositions at a first hearing. "I often cannot understand," wrote Felix, "how it is possible for you to have so acute a judgment with regard to music, without being technically musical; and if I could express what I feel with as much clearness and intuitive perception as you do, as soon as you enter on the subject, I never would make another obscure speech all my life long."[1]

But he read his son's character and disposition as well as his music; and to the last he was the best friend and adviser that Felix could have had or desired to have.

[1] "Mendelssohn Family," vol. i. p. 88.

CHAPTER II

Felix Mendelssohn—Birth and childhood—The house in the Neue Promenade, Berlin—Fanny and Felix begin their musical studies—Visit to Paris—Return to Berlin—The children kept hard at work—Felix appears in public as a pianist—Enters the Berlin Singakademie—Early compositions—The father's appreciation and advice.

Birth of Felix

JAKOB LUDWIG FELIX, elder son and second child of Abraham and Leah Mendelssohn, was born, as already stated, at Hamburg, on the 3rd of February, 1809. The day was Friday, and the birth-house was No. 14, Grosse Michaelisstrasse, at the corner of the Brunnenstrasse. The house is now marked by a mural tablet, the loving tribute of the artist pair, Madame Lind-Goldschmidt and her husband. By a strange coincidence, Ferdinand David, afterwards to be so closely associated with Mendelssohn's work at Leipzig, was born in the same house less than a year later—January 19, 1810. On the removal of the Mendelssohn family to Berlin in 1811, they all lived together in a large house in the Neue Promenade, a retired street with buildings only on one side, and a canal bordered by trees on the other. Here the little Felix found a playground, and, as late as 1820, Eduard Devrient saw him playing there with other boys at

F. MENDELSSOHN-BARTHOLDY'S GEBURTSHAUS IN HAMBURG.

marbles or touchwood. The house belonged to the widow Fromet, and there she died, in 1812, at a very happy old age. The banking business had extended, and Abraham Mendelssohn separated from his brother Joseph and started on his own account. The musical education of the elder children now began. Their first teacher was their mother, who commenced with daily lessons of five minutes' duration, and long afterwards superintended their practice. Fanny showed exceptional talent, and, according to her mother's fanciful idea, was born with "Bach Fugue fingers."

First musical studies

In 1816, Joseph and Abraham Mendelssohn went to Paris on business connected with the war indemnity to be paid by France to Prussia.[1] Abraham took his family with him, and Fanny and Felix were placed under Madame Marie Bigot for instruction in pianoforte playing. On the return to Berlin the systematic education of the children began. Heyse, father of the novelist, undertook the general work; Rosel taught drawing; Ludwig Berger was the pianoforte instructor; Carl Zelter gave the children harmony lessons; and Carl Wilhelm Henning taught the violin. The whole was under the strict supervision of the parents, who kept the children closely to their work. Abraham Mendelssohn did not believe he had done enough when

[1] In "Mendelssohn Family," vol. i. p. 89, it is stated that Abraham went to Paris on this particular business in 1819, and that he went alone.

he provided teachers ; neither did he consider his children, even when grown up, too old for his discipline and correction. Aunt Henrietta reminded him that his children's talent wanted direction, not forcing. No wonder Felix, in recalling these early days, said how glad he was when Sunday came round, as then he did not have to get up to work at five o'clock in the morning. His childish experiences were a repetition of those of his grandfather so far as work was concerned.

Parental discipline

The little Felix was nine years old before he made his first appearance in public as a pianist. This event took place on October 24, 1818, at a concert given by Joseph Gugel, a *virtuoso* on the horn. It is probable that his brother Heinrich, also a celebrated horn-player, took part in the concert, as Felix was the pianist in a trio by Joseph Woelfl for pianoforte and two horns. It is said that the juvenile artist was much applauded. The next event was his entering the Singakademie when in his eleventh year. He sang alto, and Devrient noticed him at the Friday practices, "in his child's dress—a tight-fitting jacket, cut very low at the neck, and over which the wide trousers were buttoned ; into the slanting pockets of these the little fellow liked to thrust his hands, rocking his curly head from side to side, and shifting restlessly from one foot to the other."[1] His joining the Berlin

First public appearance

Enters the Singakademie

[1] "Recollections of Felix Mendelssohn" (Devrient).

Singakademie was destined to lead to results which no one then could have anticipated.

Early compositions

Felix began composition during this year, 1819, and applied to his father, who was in Paris, for some music-paper. In a letter to Fanny, from Paris, dated July 2, 1819, Abraham Mendelssohn added a few lines to his boys. To Felix he wrote: "You, my dear Felix, must state exactly what kind of music-paper you wish to have—ruled or not ruled; and if the former, you must say distinctly how it is to be ruled. When I went into a shop the other day to buy some, I found that I did not know myself what I wanted to have. Read over your letter before you send it off, and ascertain whether, if addressed to yourself, you could fully understand it and execute the commission contained in it." Evidently Felix had not then mastered the art of clear verbal expression.

Up to 1820 it is computed that Felix had written from fifty to sixty complete movements. These included a trio for pianoforte and strings; a sonata for pianoforte and violin; a sonata for pianoforte; four pieces for the organ; songs; a little comedy in three scenes; and a cantata, "In rührend feierlichen Tönen." The earliest date is that attached to the cantata, January 13, 1820. These MSS. form part of the collection of forty-four volumes, now in the Royal Library, Berlin. From the first the wonderful neatness of Mendelssohn's penmanship is evident, and most of the pieces are headed by the letters L. e. g. G., or H. d. m., the meaning of which still remains a mystery. Some of the compositions of both Fanny and Felix were sent to their father in Paris, who refers to the songs of the former, and to Felix's last fugue, which a certain M. Leo played to him—very imperfectly. He wrote of it: "I like it well; it is a great thing. I should not have expected him to set to work in such good earnest so soon, for such a fugue requires reflection and perseverance." Then follow remarks on the musical occupations of the two. For Felix music may become a profession; but for Fanny it can and must only be an ornament. In Abraham Mendelssohn's opinion a girl's only avocation was that of a housewife, and though he admired Fanny's musical talent, he never encouraged the idea that she should devote her chief attention to the art. In one letter he refers to the deplorable condition of poor Madame Bigot, who died of consumption in September, 1820.[1]

In 1820 Fanny Mendelssohn was confirmed, and a quotation from a letter addressed to her on the occasion by her father, still in Paris, may fitly close this chapter, as it so clearly conveys the writer's views on life, and on the relations between parents and children. "By pronouncing your confession of faith you have fulfilled the claims of *society* on you, and obtained the *name* of a Christian. Now *be* what your duty as a human being demands of you, *true*, *faithful*, *good*; obedient and

[1] "Mendelssohn Family," vol. i. pp. 78–82.

devoted till death to your mother, and I may also say to your father, unremittingly attentive to the voice of your conscience, which may be suppressed but never silenced, and you will gain the highest happiness that is to be found on earth, harmony and contentedness with yourself."

CHAPTER III

Weber in Berlin—Felix and Benedict—The latter's description of Felix—The Quartet in C minor, Op. 1—Felix's memory for music—More compositions—Visit to Weimar—Goethe and Mendelssohn—Letters from Weimar—The young musician as a letter-writer—Description of Goethe—Felix plays before the Court—His extempore performances—The value placed upon his early correspondence.

NOTWITHSTANDING his many occupations and unceasing round of study, Felix was a bright, merry boy. In the spring of 1821 Carl Maria von Weber visited Berlin in connection with the production of *Der Freischütz* at the new opera-house. Benedict had only recently become Weber's pupil, and joined him at Berlin in May. The meeting with Felix must be told in Benedict's own words: "It was in the beginning of May, 1821, when, walking in the streets of Berlin with my master and friend, Carl Maria von Weber, he directed my attention to a boy, apparently about eleven or twelve years old, who, on perceiving the author of *Freyschütz*, ran towards him, giving him a most hearty and friendly greeting. ''Tis Felix Mendelssohn,' said Weber, introducing me at once to the prodigious child, of whose marvellous talent and execution I had already heard so much at Dresden. I

Weber

Benedict meets Mendelssohn

shall never forget the impression of that day on beholding that beautiful youth, with his auburn hair clustering in ringlets round his shoulders, the look of his brilliant clear eyes, and the smile of innocence and candour on his lips. He would have it that we should go with him at once to his father's house; but as Weber had to attend a rehearsal, he took me by the hand, and made me run a race till we reached his home. Up he went briskly to the drawing-room, where, finding his mother, he exclaimed, 'Here is a pupil of Weber's, who knows a great deal of his music of the new opera. Pray, mamma, ask him to play it for us;' and so, with an irresistible impetuosity, he pushed me to the pianoforte, and made me remain there until I had exhausted all the store of my recollections.

Quartet in C minor, Op. 1

"On my next visit I found him seated on a footstool, before a small table, writing with great earnestness some music. On my asking him what he was about, he replied, gravely, 'I am finishing my new Quartet for piano and stringed instruments.' I could not resist my own boyish curiosity to examine this composition, and, looking over his shoulder, saw as beautiful a score as if it had been written by the most skilful copyist. It was his first Quartet in C minor, published afterwards as Opus 1."[1] Then Felix jumps from his seat, runs to the pianoforte, plays

Musical memory

[1] "Sketch of the Life and Works of the late Felix Mendelssohn-Bartholdy" (Benedict), p. 7.

from memory everything Benedict had done on his previous visit, and finishes up by rushing into the garden, "clearing high hedges with a leap, running, singing, or climbing up the trees like a squirrel—the very image of health and happiness."

More compositions

The compositions of 1821 included five symphonies for quartet of strings; nine fugues for strings; several pieces for pianoforte, and songs; and two operettas.

Visits Goethe

The great event of the year 1821 was the journey to Weimar, to visit the poet Goethe. This was the first time Felix had left home without his parents. The rugged, good-hearted Carl Zelter, the friend of Goethe, was desirous of introducing his brilliant pupil to the poet, and in November they arrived at Weimar, and spent a fortnight under the poet's roof. His mother, writing to Aunt Henrietta, says: "Just fancy, that the little wretch is to have the good luck of going to Weimar with Zelter for a short time. He wants to show him to Goethe. You can imagine what it costs me to part from the dear child, even for a few weeks. But I consider it such an advantage for him to be introduced to Goethe, to live under the same roof with him, and receive the blessing of so great a man. I am also glad of this little journey as a change for him; for his impulsiveness sometimes makes him work harder than he ought to at his age."[1] Much loving counsel did Felix

[1] "Goethe and Mendelssohn," p. 4.

receive from his parents concerning his behaviour at Weimar, and his sister Fanny wrote: "When you are with Goethe, I advise you to open your eyes and ears wide; and after you come home, if you can't repeat every word that fell from his mouth, I will have nothing more to do with you."

The "little wretch" was not long in communicating with the family at home. His letter from Weimar, November 6, 1821, the earliest that has appeared in print, shows already some of the facility and style that was afterwards to characterize this prince of letter-writers. "Now, stop and listen, all of you," he writes. "To-day is Tuesday. On Saturday, the Sun of Weimar, Goethe, arrived. We went to church in the morning, and heard half of Händel's 100th Psalm. (The organ is large, but weak; the Marien-organ,[1] small as it is, is much more powerful. This one has fifty stops.)

"After this I went to the 'Elephant,' where I sketched the house of Lucas Cranach. Two hours afterwards, Professor Zelter came and said, 'Goethe has come,—the old gentleman's come!' and in a minute we were down the steps and in Goethe's house. He was in the garden, and was just coming round a corner. Isn't it strange, dear father? that was exactly how you met him. He is very kind, but I don't think any of the pictures are like him."[2]

Felix played to the poet, and even improvised, an

[1] In the Marien-Kirche at Berlin.

[2] "Goethe and Mendelssohn," p. 6.

art he had recently begun to practise. Goethe tested his powers of sight-reading by placing before him manuscripts of Mozart and Beethoven, and was delighted with his talent. Felix, quite at home, was very happy with the aged poet. He writes : "Every morning I get a kiss from the author of *Faust* and *Werther*, and every afternoon two kisses from my friend and father Goethe. Think of that !" He was not unmindful of his sister's compositions, and told her he had taken her songs to Frau von Goethe, who had a pretty voice. "She is going to sing them to the old gentleman." Felix soon caught up Zelter's expression. His teacher was "Professor Zelter," while the famous poet was "the old gentleman." O Felix !

As showing the boy's powers of observation and description, a further quotation from the Weimar letters may be given. Writing of Goethe, he says, "It does not strike me that his figure is imposing ; he is not much taller than father ; but his look, his language, his name, they are imposing. The amount of sound in his voice is wonderful, and he can shout like ten thousand warriors. His hair is not yet white, his step is firm, his way of speaking mild." This, from a boy of eleven, is good.

Goethe

During his stay at Weimar, Felix played to the Grand Duke and Duchess, and improvised before the Court, and in the presence of Hummel. His Sonata in G minor, just completed, was much praised. His proud mother sent his letters to Tante Jette at Paris, who wrote in reply :

Mendelssohn

"If God spare him, his letters will in long, long years to come create the deepest interest. Take care of them as of a holy relic—indeed, they are sacred already as the effusion of so pure, childlike a mind." Mendelssohn's letters, indeed, belong to literature, and that of a very high description. They will outlive some of his musical compositions.

CHAPTER IV

Mendelssohn's second appearance in public—Tour in Switzerland—Meeting with Ferdinand Hiller—Second visit to Goethe at Weimar—Compositions of 1822—Third public appearance—Mention of Mendelssohn in English papers—Musical literature in England—Home music—As a conductor—Gives Berner a theme for treatment at Breslau—Performance of "The Two Nephews"—Felix admitted into the brotherhood of musicians—The close of his boyhood.

FELIX played for the second time in public, March 31, 1822, at Aloys Schmitt's concert, taking part, with the concert-giver, in a performance of a duo for two pianos, by Dussek.

In the summer of 1822 the Mendelssohn family made a tour in Switzerland, leaving Berlin on July 6. The very first day Felix was left behind at Potsdam, each party thinking him in the carriage of the other. However, the boy marched after them, and was met by the tutor, Heyse, so all ended well. At Cassel they met Spohr, and at Frankfort Aloys Schmitt gave them a musical entertainment, and his favourite pupil, Ferdinand Hiller,—"the little pianoforte-player with the long hair,"—then and there began an acquaintance that ripened into a lifelong friendship. Hiller heard

Tour in Switzerland

Hiller

Felix's compositions, but was especially struck with the fine playing of Fanny, who at this time was in advance of Felix as an executant.[1]

From Frankfort the party went, by way of Darmstadt and Stuttgart, to Schaffhausen, and then on to Interlaken, Vevey, and Chamounix. On the return journey the party again stopped at Frankfort, to make the acquaintance of Johann Nepomuk Schelble, founder and director of the celebrated Cäcilien-Verein in that town. Felix fairly astonished Schelble by his improvisations on themes from Bach. Eduard Devrient, who early this year had become personally acquainted with the Mendelssohns, and had assisted at the rehearsal of Felix's operettas, *Die Beiden Pedagogen*, and *Die wandernden Virtuosen*,—Devrient was in Frankfort at this time, and refers to the changed appearance of Felix. "The pretty brown curls were cut short to the neck, the child's dress had given place to the boy's suit,—an open jacket over a waistcoat. The alteration was suited to his age, but I could not but regret his former unique appearance."[2]

A further stay was made at Weimar, to make the acquaintance of the Goethe family. Goethe was never tired of listening to Felix when he was at the piano, and with the father talked almost exclusively about him. To Felix himself he said one day when something had happened to annoy him, "I am Saul, and you are my

[1] "Mendelssohn" (Hiller), p. 4.

[2] "Recollections of Felix Mendelssonn" (Devrient), p. 10.

David; when I am sad and dreary, come to me and cheer me with your music."[1]

The compositions for 1822 were very numerous, and testify to the increasing activity of the young artist. The following is the list given in "The Mendelssohn Family:" Psalm 66, for three female voices; Concerto in A minor, pianoforte; two songs for male voices; three songs; three fugues for pianoforte; quartet for pianoforte and strings; symphonies for strings; one act of the opera "The Two Nephews;" *Jube Domine* (C major), for Schelble's Cäcilien-Verein at Frankfort; a violin concerto (for Rietz); *Magnificat*, and *Glöria*, for chorus and orchestra.

On December 5 Felix again appeared in public, at a concert given by Madame Milder-Hauptmann, when he played a concerto of his own—conjectured to be that in A minor just mentioned. This occasion was of great interest, inasmuch as it received a notice in an English periodical.

Musical literature in England

Here a brief digression may be permitted. At this date there was but one paper in England devoted to music. That was the *Quarterly Musical Magazine and Review*, edited by Richard Mackenzie Bacon, and started in 1818. The nineteenth number contains an article on the "State of Music on the Continent." Under the heading "Berlin, December, 1822," it reads: "At this, as well as the other capitals of Germany, concerts

[1] "Mendelssohn Family," vol. i. p. 113.

appear to be very frequent. On the 5th, Madame Anna Milder, a celebrated singer, gave one. She was assisted by Mesdames Seidler and Türrschmidt. The young Felix Mendelssohn performed a concerto, composed by himself, on the pianoforte." The same article, in describing M. Moser's concert of April 26, 1823, says, "A symphony by the gifted young Mendelssohn Bartholdy deserves notice; its rich invention, unity of design, and attentive study of effect, promises much for his future works." As England was to be the scene of Mendelssohn's greatest triumphs, it will be best here to give all the references to him previous to his visit to London in 1829. Some topics will necessarily be anticipated, but that is of small moment. The same magazine, in the number for September, 1825, has a long extract from a German paper referring to the German pianists in the French capital in the spring of 1825. It mentions a remarkable performance at a concert given by Moscheles at the Académie Royal de Musique —an arrangement, by Moscheles, of Weber's overture to *Der Freischütz* for three pianofortes and twelve hands, which was executed by himself, Pixis, Schunke, Henry Hertz (*sic*), Felix Mendelssohn Bartholdy, and Camille Pleyel. Reference is also made to the piano quartets of Feliz, and his brilliant style as a pianist. A second periodical, *The Harmonicon*, was started in 1823, with William Ayrton as editor. This publication was distinguished for the inclusion of foreign news, and it contains several allusions to the compositions of

Mendelssohn. In the report from Berlin, 1825, mention is made of the publication of his Sonata, Opus 4, for pianoforte and violin. "This production of the grandson of the celebrated philosopher of the same name, is hailed by the amateurs of the Continent as a presage of great musical excellence." The performance of a *Kyrie* by the Cäcilien-Verein, Frankfort, is noted in the number for August, 1826—probably the one written in Paris in 1825, and supposed by Sir George Grove to be among the lost MSS. The number for November mentions the publication of another work—*Capriccio per il Pianoforte, composta dal Felix Mendelssohn Bartholdy, Op.* 5. The German critics, it appeared, made fun of the "mongrel tongue" of the title-page, but the report goes on to say, "With respect to the composition itself, it contains some things not unworthy of the rising reputation of this youthful artist, but as a whole it is considered as unequal." The Berlin correspondent, in the number for June, 1827, announces the publication of the Pianoforte Sonata in E, Op. 6, but without comment. The next number contains quite a long account of the production, at the *Königliche Theater*, of the comic opera *Die Hochzeit des Camacho* (but misspelt Gamacho). It speaks of the work as the great novelty of the day, and that its appearance was looked for by the *cognoscenti* with more than common interest. The music is spoken of in very favourable terms, as "a specimen of early talent which justifies the highest hopes." In February, 1827, Mendelssohn went to

Stettin to conduct a performance of his overture to "A Midsummer Night's Dream." It speaks volumes for the leisurely way in which reporting was done in those days, for the account of the concert appears in the *Harmonicon* for December, 1827! But better late than never, though the critic was not greatly taken with the music. At this concert Felix took part, with Karl Gottfried Loewe, in his concerto for two pianos (which of the two is not stated), "a subject of much beauty and power, and more within the limits of his talent." There were then, as now, critics of various degrees of purblindness. The appearance in print of his Seven Characteristic Pieces, Op. 7, is noted in the number for January, 1828. The August number contains a short account of the Albert Dürer commemoration held in Berlin the previous April. "On this occasion were produced a new symphony (or more properly overture[1]), and a new cantata, from the pen of Felix Mendelssohn Bartholdy, a young composer of great promise, and nephew (*sic*) of the celebrated philosopher Mendelssohn. Both compositions are in a good style, abounding with melody and expression, and were admirably performed." The *Harmonicon* for January, 1829, has a notice of the musical *soirée* given by the celebrated traveller Alexander von Humboldt to a congress of scientists at Berlin, in September, 1828. For this function Felix composed the music to a cantata

[1] The "Trumpet Overture," published posthumously as Opus 101.

written by Rellstab. This excited general admiration. The *soirée* was private, and, according to Grove, the German musical paper gave no account of the performance. Finally, according to the leisurely manner of those days, two months after Mendelssohn's arrival in London, there is a brief reference to the revival of Bach's *Passion Music* under his conductorship.

These may seem small matters, and they have been overlooked by all Mendelssohn's biographers; but they throw interesting side-lights on his career, and go to prove that when Mendelssohn came to England for the first time, in 1829, neither himself nor his works were altogether unknown to English people interested in music. His friend Moscheles, who went to live in London in 1821, would do his best to spread the fame of the young composer.

Sunday music

It was about the year 1822 that meetings were held at the Mendelssohns' house on alternate Sunday mornings for the practice of concerted music. It was for these meetings that Felix wrote his symphonies and other pieces. The children thus became accustomed to playing before an audience, and Felix had the advantage of hearing outside opinions upon his compositions. Musicians of distinction, passing through Berlin, requested permission to attend these *matinées*. Devrient says that, despite the wealth attributed to Abraham Mendelssohn, the house gave an impression of studied plainness. "The singers sat round the large dining-table, and close to the grand piano, raised on a high cushion, sat Felix, grave and unembarrassed, directing us with an ardour as if it had been a game he was playing with his comrades."[1] Among the visitors, in 1823, was Kalkbrenner, about whom Fanny wrote: "He heard a good many of Felix's compositions, praised with taste, and blamed candidly and amiably."[2] In this year, 1823, Abraham took his sons on a journey to Silesia. At Breslau Felix wrote, showing that he knew his Homer—

Visits Berner

"'Ημος δ' ἠριγένεια φάνηῥοδοδάκτυλος ἠώς.

"We all went to the church to hear Berner play. First he took off his coat and put on a light one instead, then he asked me to write down a theme for him, and then he began. He took the low C in the pedal, and then threw himself with all his might upon the manual, and after some runs began a theme on the manual. I had no idea that it could be played on the pedals, for it was as follows:—

Felix writes a theme for Berner

But he soon began with his feet, and carried it out with both manual and pedals. After he had thoroughly developed it, he began my theme on the pedals, carried

[1] "Recollections of Felix Mendelssohn" (Devrient), p. 3.
[2] "Mendelssohn Family," vol. i. p. 118.

it out for a short time, then took it on the pedals in augmentation, put a fine counter subject with it, and then worked up both themes splendidly. He has wonderful execution on the pedals."[1] This was a lesson not lost upon the future improvisator on the organ. At Reinerz Felix played at a charity concert, extemporizing on themes from Mozart and Weber, and on leaving the town received a nosegay from a pretty girl.

To this year belong the symphonies, Nos. 9 to 12, which were in advance of those preceding. The *Scherzi* of two of them had parts for triangle, cymbals, and drums, in addition to the string quintet. A *Kyrie* for two choirs; a Psalm, and various songs, pianoforte pieces, and other compositions, were also written at this time, and the comic opera, "The Two Nephews," was completed.

"The Two Nephews"

On February 3, 1824, Felix attained his fifteenth year, and his opera was rehearsed for the first time with orchestra. At the supper which followed, the health of Felix was proposed, and old Zelter, taking his hand, and placing him in front of the company, said, "My dear boy, from this day you are no longer an apprentice, but an independent member of the brotherhood of musicians. I proclaim you independent in the name of Mozart, Haydn, and old father Bach." The opera was afterwards acted with success in the parents' house. About this time Felix was confirmed, and his boyhood, one

[1] "Mendelssohn Family," vol. i. p. 119.

of the most beautiful in the records of musical art, was brought to a close. It only lacked one element—repose. With less call upon his vital powers, Mendelssohn might have lived longer; but it was in the blood, this unceasing energy and devouring passion for work, and the spark of life burnt itself out before ripe manhood was reached. It was an heritage from his grandfather.

CHAPTER V

1824 an eventful year—The Symphony in C minor—Meeting of Moscheles and Mendelssohn—A musical evening—Moscheles' opinion of Felix Mendelssohn—Spohr in Berlin—Second visit of Felix to Paris—Cherubini—Unsatisfactory state of music in Paris—Goethe and the B minor Quartet, Op. 3—Removal of the Mendelssohn family to Leipziger Strasse, No. 3—The Garden House—An ideal family—Music and friends—Felix at the Berlin University—Shakesperian studies and their outcome—Overture to "A Midsummer Night's Dream"—"The Wedding of Camacho"—Felix's first trial—Bears it manfully—Thibaut—Klingemann in London—Compositions to 1828.

C minor Symphony

THE year 1824 was an eventful one for Felix. The chief composition of that time was the Symphony in C minor, the thirteenth of that order in his juvenile efforts, but hereafter to count as No. 1, and to bring him before the world in a manner not experienced before. It was the year in which he first beheld the sea—his father taking him and his sister Rebecka to Dobberan, on the Baltic. There he wrote for the military band at the baths the overture, afterwards published as Op. 24. Above all, in 1824, Moscheles, then in the full tide of artistic success, visited Berlin, and soon became an intimate friend of the Mendelssohn family,

Moscheles

and exercised a great influence on the future of the young composer. It was on the 31st of October, 1824, that Moscheles, on his way from Vienna, arrived at Berlin. During the following month he gave three concerts for charitable institutions, and at the first concert, apparently, played his pianoforte concerto in E flat. Hummel was present, and so was "a boy of fifteen, who, in breathless excitement, followed every passage and every note. His handsome face was flushed, his dark eyes sparkled with enthusiasm. It was Felix Mendelssohn."[1] After the concert there was a supper-party at the Mendelssohns', Moscheles and Hummel being among the guests. Felix, after consulting his father, raised his glass, and proposed the health of the composer of the E flat concerto! Then there was music. Zelter sang, and Ludwig Berger, Moscheles, and Hummel played, the last named extemporizing on a theme by Mozart. Felix, who had stood motionless beside the piano, taking in everything, was then suddenly called upon by Zelter to play something, and, to the surprise of all, refused. Zelter reproached him for his timidity; but his banter was of no effect. Had not Felix played at grand concerts, and even before Goethe? Zelter asked. "Oh! at that time I did not rightly know what I was doing," answered Felix, in a faltering voice; "but now I can only say that, after those two there" (glancing with swimming eyes at Hummel and Moscheles), "I neither can nor ought to

[1] "Reminiscences of Mendelssohn" (Polko), p. 3.

play"—and, bursting into a flood of tears, he rushed out of the room.[1]

Next morning Moscheles received a charming note from Madame Mendelssohn, with the request that he would, during his stay in Berlin, take Felix and Fanny as pupils, and further begging him to lend the copy of the concerto to Felix, who longed to try it. The MS. was sent forthwith, and on the 22nd of November Moscheles gave Felix his first lesson. What Moscheles thought of the family may be gathered from the entries in his diary. He writes: "This is a family the like of which I have never known. Felix, a boy of fifteen, is a phenomenon. What are all prodigies as compared with him? Gifted children, but nothing else. This Felix Mendelssohn is already a mature artist, and yet but fifteen years old! We at once settled down together for several hours, for I was obliged to play a great deal, when really I wanted to hear him and see his compositions, for Felix had to show me a Concerto in C minor, a double concerto, and several motets; and all so full of genius, and at the same time so correct and thorough! His elder sister Fanny, also extraordinarily gifted, played by heart, and with admirable precision, Fugues and Passacailles by Bach. I think one may well call her a thorough 'Mus. Doc.' (*guter Musiker*). Both parents give one the impression of being people of the highest refinement. They are far from overrating their children's talents; in fact, they are anxious about

[1] "Reminiscences of Mendelssohn" (Polko), p. 7.

Felix's future, and to know whether his gift will prove sufficient to lead to a noble and truly great career."[1] Again, when referring to the lessons, Moscheles says he never loses sight of the fact that he is sitting beside a master, not a pupil. The delightful intercourse with the family continued until December 15, when Moscheles left Berlin.

Spohr's opera *Jessonda* was to be brought out in Berlin, in February, 1825, and the composer went there to superintend the rehearsals. The acquaintance at Cassel in 1822 was renewed, the young artist deriving benefit from the visits of the famous violin *virtuoso* and composer. Spohr, in his Autobiography, makes no mention of the Mendelssohns at this time; he was too much taken up with the obstacles thrown in his way by Spontini.

Spohr

In March, 1825, Abraham Mendelssohn undertook a journey to Paris, for the purpose of bringing his sister Henrietta back to Germany. Felix accompanied his father, and they arrived on the evening of the 22nd. Here Felix came in contact with many musicians of eminence, and some of his performances have already been described. He had just finished his third Quartet for pianoforte and strings (in B minor), and after a performance of the work, and by no means a good one, Cherubini went up to the young composer, smiling and nodding. "He then turned to the bystanders and said, 'Ce garçon est riche; il fera

Cherubini

[1] "Life of Moscheles" (Coleridge), vol. i. p. 98.

bien ; il fait même déjà bien, mais il dépense trop de son argent, il met trop d'étoffe dans son habit.'"[1] Halévy, who was not present, when told of it, absolutely refused to believe that Cherubini could have been so civil to a young musician. Felix seems to have got on very well with Cherubini, whom he compared to an extinct volcano, still throwing out occasional flashes and sparks, but quite covered with ashes and stones. He wrote for him a *Kyrie* for five voices and orchestra. "In bulk it surpasses anything I have yet written," said the composer, in a letter. Felix went to the Théâtre Feydeau, where he heard Auber's *Léocadie*. This he slashes up in merciless style in a letter to his sister Fanny. Poor Auber ! He had not then written *La Muette de Portici*, which might have mollified this terrible young critic. Felix was not happy in the musical atmosphere of Paris ; he missed the sincerity of German art, and was horrified at the ignorance of the French musicians, who knew nothing of the masterpieces of the great Germans, and believed Bach to be a mere old-fashioned wig stuffed with learning.

The Mendelssohns, with Aunt Henrietta, left Paris on the 19th of May, stopping at Weimar for a short visit to Goethe. Felix played the B Minor Quartet, which he dedicated to the poet, who, in acknowledgment, sent him what Zelter called a "beautiful love-letter :"

"You have given me very great pleasure, my dear Felix, by your valuable present ; which, though already

[1] "Goethe and Mendelssohn," p. 39.

announced, took me by surprise. The print, the title-page, and the splendid binding, all vie with each other to make it a magnificent gift. I regard it as the graceful embodiment of that beautiful, rich, energetic soul which so astonished me when you first made me acquainted with it. Pray accept my very best thanks, and let me hope that you will soon give me another opportunity of admiring in person the fruits of your astonishing activity. Remember me to your good parents, your equally gifted sister, and your excellent master. May a lively remembrance of me always be maintained in such a circle.

"Yours faithfully,
"J. W. GOETHE.

"Weimar, June 18, 1825."[1]

At home again, Felix applied himself with fresh vigour to the work of composition. The Capriccio, Op. 5, is dated July 23, 1825, and the opera *Die Hochzeit des Camacho* was completed in August. Other compositions of this year were the "Trumpet Overture," and the Octet for strings, Op. 20—a masterpiece; and in the *Scherzo* the revealer of an absolutely new creative faculty.

In this year the family removed to Leipziger Strasse, No. 3. Abraham Mendelssohn for some time had contemplated the purchase of this property. It lay on the confines of Berlin, by the Potsdam gate, and friends

[1] "Goethe and Mendelssohn," p. 51.

complained that Mendelssohn was moving out of the world, into regions where grass grew on the pavement. The house was large, with stately, lofty apartments; the back overlooked a court with low side-buildings, and closed by a garden-house of one story, over which could be seen the fine trees of the park, for the whole formed a small estate of some ten acres. In the house was a room most suitable for theatrical performances, and the centre of the garden-house formed a hall capable of holding several hundred persons, and here it was that the Sunday music was kept up, and assumed great artistic importance. On either side of the hall were suites of apartments. Fanny, after her marriage with Hensel the painter, lived on one side, and for a time Eduard Devrient and his wife lived in the other suite. The house had belonged to the family of Von der Reck, the garden adjoined the grounds of Prince Albrecht, and in Frederick the Great's time it had been a part of the Thiergarten, and was rich in beautiful old trees. "In this house and garden arose a singularly beautiful, poetic life. The circle of friends then formed, with few exceptions, remained in personal intercourse, or correspondence, until death, one by one, called them off. The Hanoverian Klingemann, a diplomatist, a very refined, poetic nature, author of the text of 'Son and Stranger,' was one of the most prominent and most faithful of the circle. The ties of friendship which united him to the family were strengthened by Felix's and

Happy home life

Friends

Hensel's frequent visits to London, where Klingemann was attached to the Hanoverian legation, and by a constant animated correspondence. Louis Heydemann and his brother, Wilhelm Horn, son of a famous physician, and himself one likewise, Eduard Rietz the violinist, and for a long time especially Marx, then editor of the Berlin *Musikalische Zeitung*, were Felix's more intimate friends. Marx, a man of great genius, was the champion of a new school in music, which rallied round the flag of Beethoven, and contributed not a little to make the works of that great master known. He was truly fond of Felix, and the two endeavoured in their enthusiasm to approach each other by exchanging opinions, which at first differed widely."[1]

The house remained in the possession of the Mendelssohn family until after the death of Felix, when it was sold to the State. The street front remained unchanged, but the garden-house was pulled down to make room for the session-chamber of the Prussian House of Lords. The happiest time in the life of the whole Mendelssohn family was passed in the Leipziger Strasse, No. 3. Felix began gymnastics, in which he became a great proficient. In the summer-houses writing materials were provided, and Felix edited a newspaper, called in the summer, "The Garden Times," and in the winter, "The Snow and Tea Times." To this all comers were invited to contribute, and the young people were joined in their fun by their elders, including

[1] "Mendelssohn Family," vol. i. p. 123.

such distinguished personages as Humboldt and Zelter. It was probably in 1826 (Zelter says 1827) that Felix entered the University of Berlin, where his tutor, Heyse, was now a professor. His matriculation essay was a translation in verse of Terence's "Andria," which scholars have pronounced to be meritorious. Zelter says, however, that Felix gave the piece to Heyse as a birthday present.[1] Felix attended the lectures of Gans, Ritter, Lichtenstein, and Hegel, the last giving a course of lectures on music. He took great interest in Ritte's discourses on geography, and his notes, dated 1827 and 1828, still exist. He did not take any degree.

Enters Berlin University

All this time Felix was adding to his list of musical compositions. To the year 1826 belong the string Quintet in A (Op. 18), the Sonata in E (Op. 6), some minor pieces, and the overture to Shakespeare's "A Midsummer Night's Dream." This was evidently inspired by the Shakesperian studies of Fanny and Felix in 1826, when the translations of Schlegel and Tieck fell into their hands. The overture, of which more later, was first written as a pianoforte duet, and in that form Moscheles heard it played by Fanny and Felix, in November. It was afterwards given with orchestra in the Garden House, before a crowded audience, and had its first public performance, as already noticed, at Stettin, in February, 1827.

"Midsummer Night's Dream" overture

[1] "Goethe and Mendelssohn," p. 51.

His opera, "Camacho's Wedding," had been submitted to Spontini, as General Music Director of the Royal Opera, by Felix himself, in 1826. According to Devrient, motherly fondness yearned to witness the son's great success. Count Brühl, the General Director, was favourably disposed towards the young composer, but Spontini was jealous of every one likely to be taken into public favour. He criticized the score, which rumour said he had little ability to read, and, leading Felix to the window, which was opposite to the dome of the Jewish Church, said, "Mon ami, il vous faut des idées grandes, grandes comme cette coupole." After many difficulties and delays, rehearsals were commenced, and then Blum, the tenor, fell ill, and the opera was only produced on April 29, 1827, the very end of Blum's stay in Berlin, and precluding a repetition. The performance took place—not in the opera-house, but in the smaller theatre, as being more suitable to the piece. The house was crowded, the applause was great, and the composer was called for; but he had left the theatre, and Devrient had to appear for him. Blum became convalescent, but objections were raised against a repetition, though it was asked for. Felix became indifferent; he had outgrown the music, and it was not heard again in his lifetime. The music need not be discussed in this place, but it may be mentioned as rather a curious thing, that the first complete stage performance of "Camacho's Wedding," since

"The Wedding of Camacho"

1827, took place at Boston, U.S.A., March 19, 1885. Mendelssohn felt keenly the hostile criticism of an obscure paper in the production of his opera, and altogether the affair upset him very much. Moreover, this spring he had been deeply affected by the death of a dear young friend, August Hanstein, by whose bedside he composed the Fugue in E minor, Op. 35, No. 1, in which, Schubring says, he marked the progress of the disease as it gradually destroyed the sufferer, until he made it culminate in the Choral of Release in E major.[1]

At Whitsuntide he spent some days at Sakrow, an estate belonging to the Magnus family, and situate near Potsdam. There he wrote the song "Ist es wahr?" which became the theme of the string quartet in A minor, Op. 13. In the summer he made a holiday excursion with some friends to the Harz Mountains, visiting Baden-Baden, Heidelberg, Frankfort, and Cologne. That he had fully recovered his spirits is shown by his letter, dated Heidelberg, September 20, 1827. "'O Heidelberg, beautiful town, where it rains the whole day,' is the snobbish saying; but what does a student, a jolly fellow like me, care about the rain? There are grapes left, instrument-makers, journals, inns, Thibauts—no, that is saying too much; there is but *one* Thibaut, but he is worth six. What a man!" Felix acknowledges to learning much from Thibaut, who revealed to him the merits of Italian music, and warmed him with

Meets Thibaut

[1] *Musical World*, 1866, p. 318.

his enthusiasm for it. *Per contra*, Felix had to tell that inasmuch as he knew little of Bach, he was yet unacquainted with the fountain-head and most important things in music, because all that was comprised in Sebastian. At parting, Thibaut said, "Farewell, and we will build our friendship on Luis de Vittoria and Sebastian Bach, like two lovers who promise each other to look at the moon, and then fancy they are near each other."

While on his holiday tour, Felix began the five-part chorus, *Tu es Petrus*, which was a birthday present to his sister Fanny. In a letter to Klingemann—who had gone to London in the autumn as secretary to the Hanoverian Legation—Fanny mentions this work, as also a children's symphony, scored after that of Haydn, and a motet, *Christe, du Lamm Gottes*. Klingemann's letters to the Mendelssohns contain some droll remarks on English taste in music. "It is quite touching to see how fond the good people are of music, and what a stomach they have for listening! Like ostriches, they swallow pebbles or sweetmeats as it happens. And everything is so long here! I believe Beethoven must have been an Englishman."

Klingemann on music in London

In the winter of 1827, Felix got together a small chorus of sixteen voices, and held weekly rehearsals of Bach's *Passion*. This originated in the desire of Felix to convert to his own views his friend Pastor Schubring, who had said that he found it difficult to conceive

Bach's music as aught but a dry arithmetical sum. As early as 1823, Felix had become possessed of a MS. score of the *Matthew Passion* music, written, by permission of Zelter, by Eduard Rietz, and forming a Christmas present from Felix's grandmother. Eduard Devrient and his wife assisted as soloists. This was the seed-sowing; the harvest was to be reaped in 1829.

In April, 1828, the Dürer Festival was held, and the cantata of Felix was given by the Singakademie; in September occurred the Humboldt *soirée*, when a second cantata was performed. This was written for men's voices, wind instruments, and string basses. Both performances have already received notice. In the summer of 1828, Felix was busy on his overture to Goethe's "Calm Sea and Prosperous Voyage," and during the year he finished a great *Antiphona* and *Responsorium*, *Hora est*, for four choirs. This, with some pianoforte pieces—one "A Song without Words" —formed the next birthday present for Fanny. She wrote: "The academy is going to sing it." A correspondent, signing himself J. T., in the *Harmonicon* for January, 1830, gives an account of the performance, but without date. He writes:

Hora est

"Among other pieces, there was one to which I listened with intense interest and delight, a 'Hora est,' in sixteen parts, by M. Mendelssohn, written by him in his sixteenth year! (Was this correct?) It opens with a chorus in eight parts for tenors and basses, in a grave and solemn manner: at the allegro maestoso, the whole sixteen burst in with prodigious effect; and then lead off a fugue which is wrought up with fire and grandeur." This communication is headed "Notes of a Musical Tourist," and is dated from Edinburgh, November 23, 1829. The continuation of the article in a later number contains a great deal of interesting information concerning the Mendelssohn family.

For Christmas, 1828, Felix wrote a second Kindersymphonie, and, soon afterwards, the Variations in D, Op. 17, for violoncello and pianoforte, dedicated to his brother Paul, who was above the average of amateur violoncellists. Rebecka, the younger sister, sang very well, so that the whole family were musical.

CHAPTER VI

The year 1829 an epoch in the history of music—Betrothal of Fanny Mendelssohn—Revival of Bach's "Passion according to St. Matthew"—Devrient's share in the preparation of the work—Felix pays his first visit to London—His impressions of the metropolis—Felix makes his English *début*—The musical press on his C minor Symphony—The "Midsummer Night's Dream" Overture—Fétis on the state of music in London—Felix involved in a criticism of Purcell's *Te Deum* in D—Letter to the newspaper—Tour in Scotland—In Wales—Felix and national music—A pleasant home in Flintshire—Accident to Felix—Recovery and return to Berlin—The silver wedding of his parents—Performance of "Son and Stranger."

Fanny Mendelssohn, writing to Klingemann under date December 27, 1828, and referring to the projected performance of the "Passion Music," went on to say: "At the same time the work will appear at Schlesinger's, a number of plates are already finished, and the year 1829 is likely to form an epoch in the annals of music." [1]

Fanny Mendelssohn was right; the year 1829 *did* form an epoch in the annals of music, as well as of the Mendelssohn family. Felix had finished his University course; his formal musical education ceased still

[1] "Mendelssohn Family," vol. i. p. 165.

earlier, though as a true artist he remained a student to the end of his life. The time had come for him to choose a profession. His uncle Bartholdy was dead against music, and plainly told Felix's father so. Abraham Mendelssohn for some time was undecided in the matter. He is said to have consulted Cherubini, when in Paris in 1825; and in the intercourse with Moscheles the subject was discussed. So far, Mendelssohn had done all his work without pecuniary reward; but now, if he adopted the art seriously, he was to live by it. But previous to his decision an event occurred that must be noticed. This was the betrothal of Fanny Mendelssohn and Wilhelm Hensel. Born in 1794, Hensel had made some reputation as a painter before he met the Mendelssohns. It was not long before friendship ripened into love when Hensel and Fanny came to understand each other. The mother with quick intuition saw how matters were going, and would allow no formal engagement before he went to Rome for further study. During the five years of his absence Hensel had to be content with letters from the mother, when he would have given all he was worth for a line from the daughter. Fears were entertained of his conversion to the Roman Catholic faith, but they were unfounded. In October, 1828, Hensel returned to Berlin, and in January, 1829, he was formally accepted as Fanny's betrothed.

Fanny Mendelssohn's betrothal

Then there were the preparations for the performance

of Bach's "*Matthew*" Passion Music. The rehearsals had filled every one with such enthusiasm that nothing less than a performance by the Singakademie would satisfy those who had studied the work. Felix apparently knew it by heart, and was, of course, fixed upon as the conductor. But Zelter first of all had to be approached and propitiated. Devrient was the bolder in the negotiations, as Felix, with his excessively sensitive nature, was fearful of a rebuff. There were many difficulties to overcome, but eventually Zelter gave way, and details were soon arranged. Devrient tells how he and Felix went round to invite the co-operation of the solo singers from the Opera. For the occasion they were dressed exactly alike—a whim of Felix—and, what Devrient called this "Bach uniform," consisted of blue coats, white waistcoats, black neckties, black trousers, and yellow chamois-leather gloves! Devrient gives many interesting particulars of the full rehearsals, from which it was clear that Felix Mendelssohn was master of every detail of the work. Zelter attended the orchestral rehearsals, and became quite interested in the proceedings. The orchestra was made up chiefly of amateurs, with principals in the strings and wind from the Royal band, and the chorus consisted of over three hundred voices. Eduard Rietz was orchestral leader, and played the violin *obbligato* parts in the solos. The vocal principals were Stümer, who took the part of the Evangelist, and also sang the air "With Jesus I will watch and pray." Bader was the other tenor.

The soprano was Madame Milder-Hauptmann, and the contralto, Fräulein von Schätzel. Devrient himself delivered the words of Jesus. The performance took place March 11, 1829, and created an extraordinary sensation. The concert-room was crammed, and hundreds of people were turned from the doors. Even before the first performance there was a demand for a second. This, Spontini—the recipient of two of the six free tickets issued—tried to prevent; but an order from the Crown Prince settled the matter, and the second performance took place on March 21st—Bach's birthday—with the greatest success. There was even a third, after the departure of Felix, under Zelter, on Good Friday, April 17th. These performances led to the great Bach revival, the effects of which have been felt throughout the civilized world. The share taken in the work by Devrient must not be overlooked. He was a thorough enthusiast for Bach, and it is hardly too much to say that, but for his insistence, Felix would have succumbed to the obstacles thrown in his way. As it was, Felix said—referring for the only time to his descent—"To think that it should be an actor and a Jew that give back to the people the greatest of Christian works."[1] It was supposed at the time, and for long after, that these performances were the first since the death of the famous Leipzig Cantor; but Spitta has shown that

Bach's "Matthew Passion"

Bach revival

[1] "Recollections of Felix Mendelssohn" (Devrient), p. 57.

the *Matthew Passion* music continued to be given at St. Thomas's Church up to the end of the eighteenth century.[1] Paganini made his first appearance in Berlin in March of this year, and was soon a guest at the house in the Leipziger Strasse. Heine, too, was in Berlin, and, among the frequenters of the house of the Mendelssohns, were Ludwig Robert, the poet, and his wife, Hegel, Madame Milder-Hauptmann, and others.

With all his work and artistic zeal, Felix Mendelssohn was not in the happiest position in Berlin at this time, and when Moscheles, in reply to a letter from Abraham Mendelssohn, counselled a visit to London, the idea was soon taken up. This was part of a larger plan, designed by the father, in order that experience might be gained, and reputation acquired, before finally fixing upon the scene of his future artistic activity. This important step was an epoch in the life of the young musician. The decision to visit London first was a compliment to England, a country that—whatever her treatment of her own artist children—has always extended the hand of friendship to the stranger landing upon her shores.

Visits London

Felix left Berlin on the 10th of April. He was accompanied as far as Hamburg by his father and his sister Rebecka, and to that place Fanny sent him a farewell letter. The boat left on Saturday, the 17th, and did not reach London until Tuesday, the 21st. Directly he landed at

[1] "Johann Sebastian Bach" (Spitta), vol. ii, pp. 518, 568.

the Custom House, Felix sent off the tidings of his safe arrival. He was very unhappy on the voyage, had fainting-fits, and cursed the sea, and his "Meeresstille"—a misnomer for the nonce—and scolded the waiter.[1] He was met by his friend Klingemann, and by Moscheles, who had secured him a lodging at 103, Great Portland Street. In a letter dated April 25, Felix writes: "It is fearful! It is maddening! I am quite giddy and confused. London is the grandest and most complicated monster on the face of the earth. How can I compress into one letter what I have been three days seeing? I hardly remember the chief events, and yet I must not keep a diary, for then I should see less of life, and that must not be. On the contrary, I want to catch hold of whatever offers itself to me. Things roll and whirl round me, and carry me along as in a vortex." And this was the London of 1829! A London without a railway station, a hansom cab, or many other external features of to-day; a London that was a village to what it is now; but then, as now, a place to strike the visitor with something like awe. Mendelssohn arrived at the height of the musical season, and had much to say of the performances at the opera. He was taken about by Madame Moscheles in her carriage. "Think of me," he writes, "in a cabriolet, taking a drive with a lady!—me, in my new suit, of course." He went to see Kemble in *Hamlet*, and was not altogether well pleased; complained of the "cuts,"

[1] Mendelssohnian for steward.

and ends by saying, "There is little poetry in England. Really!" On the other hand, in writing to Devrient, he says: "The people here like me for the sake of my music, and respect me for it, and this delights me immensely." Again: "Were I this minute to play my 'Calm Sea,' etc., to the public, they would comprehend it far better than the cultivated circle in our drawing-room. Yet they understand nothing about music, which here is bad and at the worst. Then how is it? Alas, by Jove, I play better here than in Berlin, and why is that? Because the people have more pleasure in listening." So, this gifted youth, as a critical free lance, rattles on to his friends; but he meant no harm.

Appearance in England

Mendelssohn's first public appearance in England was at the Philharmonic Concert of May 25, 1829, the seventh of the season. Felix gives a delightful account of the rehearsal, at which there were about two hundred listeners, chiefly ladies. "I mounted the orchestra," he writes, "and pulled out my white stick, which I have had made on purpose (the maker took me for an alderman, and would insist on decorating it with a crown). The first violin, François Cramer, showed me how the orchestra was placed—the furthest rows had to get up so that I could see them—and introduced me to them all, and we bowed to each other; some perhaps laughed a little, that this small fellow with the stick should now take the place of their regular powdered and bewigged conductor."[1] The symphony went well; the directors were pleased, and the composer had to shake hands with the performers. "It was one of the happiest moments within my recollection, for one half-hour had transformed all those strangers into friends and acquaintances. But the success at the concert last night was beyond what I could ever have dreamed." J. B. Cramer, the conductor for the evening, led Mendelssohn to the pianoforte, "as if he were a young lady," and he was received with immense applause. The concert opened with the symphony. Instead of giving Mendelssohn's own account of the performance, it will be more interesting to quote the critiques of the musical papers—the first direct personal notices the composer received in this country. Both papers begin with references to Mendelssohn himself, but these may be passed over. "This Symphony has at once obtained for him a reception and reared a name more than sufficient to gratify that proud ambition and that devoted ardour which have led him to cultivate the science with such laborious perseverance and such singular success. It contains an allegro—an andante—a scherzo, trio, and finale. Among these, so excellent in all the qualities of graceful, soothing, sweet, airy, and fanciful melody, sustained with an unfailing energy throughout, it may almost be thought superfluous to give a preference. But the scherzo is admitted by the best judges to be pre-eminent to a degree that perhaps

C minor Symphony

[1] "Mendelssohn Family," vol. i. p. 184.

has never been equalled, certainly never exceeded. The originality of conception which is displayed in the novel effects, not less than in the diversity of the means, declares the composer's genius and resources. The whole was received with acclamation, and the scherzo and trio encored. The author conducted his work, and was overwhelmed by the gratulations of the audience."[1] The other account is equally favourable: "Fertility of invention and novelty of effect, are what first strike the hearers of M. Mendelssohn's symphony; but at the same time, the melodiousness of its subjects, the vigour with which these are supported, the gracefulness of the slow movement, the playfulness of some parts, and the energy of others, are all felt; though from a first hearing, and without some previous knowledge of the score, it were in vain to attempt any analysis of the work which we can now only describe in general terms, but hope ere long to be able to enter upon its details. The author conducted it in person, and it was received with acclamations. The audience wished the adagio to be repeated, but M. Mendelssohn did not construe the continued applause as an encore. The scherzo and trio, however, were instantly called for a second time, and the band seemed most happy to comply with the demand."[2] Then follow remarks on the excellent qualities of the band, and how Mendelssohn expressed his satisfaction with it. The concert took place in the Argyll Rooms.

[1] *Quarterly Musical Magazine and Review*, vol. x. p. 298.

[2] *Harmonicon*, vol. vii. p. 173.

Sir George Smart conducted a second performance of the symphony at Mr. Charles Nicholson's concert, held in the same rooms, on June 10th, when it went "with great spirit, accuracy, and effect." The scherzo, which was so much admired, was taken from the Octet, and substituted for the original minuet and trio.

And now, Felix Mendelssohn had, through the Philharmonic Society, been placed before the world in a manner worthy of his genius. He felt the kindly recognition of this famous artistic body most keenly, and expressed his thanks in a letter to the Society.[1] The symphony was published the same year, with a dedication to the Society, and at the general meeting, held on November 29th, Mendelssohn was unanimously elected an honorary member.

Felix played in public for the first time in London at a concert in the Argyll Rooms on May 30th. He went early to the rooms to try the new Clementi pianoforte, but it was locked; however, he seated himself at an old instrument, and was soon lost in improvisation, and was only roused from his abstraction by the arrival of the audience. The hour for the concert, a *matinée*, had almost come, and he had to hurry off to dress—"very long white trousers, brown silk waistcoat, black neck-tie, and blue dress coat," as he described his toilet in a letter to the Mendelssohn family. He played the solo in Weber's "Concertstück," without notes—a thing then very remarkable. On June 24th, he performed at the

[1] "History of the Philharmonic Society" (Hogarth), p. 51.

concert of Louis Drouet the flutist. He played, for the first time, in England, Beethoven's Concerto in E flat (the "Emperor"). By a happy coincidence this midsummer night witnessed the production in London of Mendelssohn's "Midsummer Night's Dream" overture. The overture was heard again on July 13th, and Felix and Moscheles played the former's Concerto in E, for two pianos and orchestra. This concert was given, at Mendelssohn's instigation, by Madame Sontag for the relief of the sufferers by the floods in Silesia. Felix, writing about it, said it was splendid; the best of the season. The Argyll Rooms were crowded, and ladies might be seen among the double-basses, between the bassoons and horns, and one seated on a kettledrum! The scene recalled that witnessed at Moscheles' concert in the same place a year before, when it was punningly remarked that "there were more *belles* than *bows* in the orchestra."

First performance in England of Beethoven's Concerto in E flat

Overture to "A Midsummer Night's Dream"

London life suited Felix exactly, so he said. He brought influential letters of introduction, and the doors of Devonshire House and Lansdowne House were open to him; and he attended parties innumerable. After a grand dinner at the Prussian Ambassador's (Von Bülow), Felix, and his friends Rosen and Mühlenfels, on their way home passed a very enticing sausage shop, in which "German sausages, twopence each," were laid out for show.

Gastronomic patriotism

Overcome by patriotism, each bought a sausage, and turning into Portland Street, devoured it, to an accompaniment of German part-songs and laughter.[1]

Felix's great friend was, of course, Carl Klingemann, but he was indebted to Moscheles and his wife for many delightful days in London. It was at the house of Moscheles that Felix met the Chevalier Sigismund Neukomm. The two were very friendly, apart from music. Felix, never backward in passing judgment, said, "If only that excellent man Neukomm would write better music! He speaks so ably, his language and letters are so choice, and yet his music—how commonplace!"[2] The outspokenness of Felix led to an incident not altogether pleasant, and as it was the cause of his "writing to the papers"—probably for the first and only time in his life—the story is worth reviving. François Joseph Fétis, intending to deliver his lectures on "La musique à la portée de tout de monde," passed three months in London in the early part of 1829. Either owing to want of support, or from the season being too far advanced, the project fell through. He was induced, however, to give a musical *matinée*, which included a short lecture, on May 29th. Instead of lecturing, Fétis wrote a series of letters to his son, on the state of music in London, which letters were published in the *Revue Musicale*. It happened that Felix attended the Festival of the Sons

Fétis in London

[1] "Mendelssohn Family," vol. i. p. 192.
[2] "Moscheles," vol. i. p. 226.

of the Clergy, at St. Paul's Cathedral, on May 14th. Fétis also was present, as he wished to hear some of Purcell's music. The *Te Deum* in D was performed, "not exactly in its original state," as a writer remarked, and not in a particularly excellent manner. Dr. Boyce's version was probably given. Fétis wrote: "I was prepared to admire when the *Te Deum* of this giant began; but what was my disappointment when I heard, instead of the chef-d'œuvre I had been promised, a long series of unmeaning phrases, ill-connected modulations, and incorrect, though ambitious harmonies. At first I thought I might be mistaken, and that I ought not to trust to my first opinion on a kind of music to which I was unacquainted. But M. Felix Mendelssohn, a young and distinguished German composer, who was near me, received exactly the same impressions." Fétis adds that Mendelssohn left before the *Jubilate*, as he had had enough.[1] A weekly paper, supposed to be the *Britannia*, took Fétis to task, and included Felix in its diatribe, calling him *unhappy* Mendelssohn—a licence more personal than poetical. This was more than Felix could endure, and so he wrote the following letter to the Editor:—[2]

Purcell's Te Deum in D

[1] *Quarterly Musical Magazine and Review*, vol. x. p. 415; *Harmonicon*, vol. vii. p. 242.

[2] Reprinted in the *Harmonicon*, vol. vii. p. 193.

103, Great Portland Street, July 8, 1829.

SIR,

Having read in your last number an article under the head of "MUSIC AND MUSICIANS," I beg to offer you some remarks, for the purpose of preventing any misconception which may arise from the article alluded to.

M. Fétis has, it appears, thought fit to drag my name before the public, by referring to some expressions which may have fallen from me in *private* conversation with him, and also to draw conclusions therefrom in corroboration of his censure on a celebrated English composer. You, Sir, have further deemed it incumbent on you, while commenting on his strictures, to identify my *alleged* observations with the *published* censure of M. Fétis. While denying the right of M. Fétis thus to quote any private and detached expressions of mine in order to support his own opinions, I must, at the same time, question the justice of your holding me up to the British public as a co-censor with that gentleman. Whatever were the words used by me on the occasion referred to, they were uttered merely to give expression to a momentary feeling, caused by a performance which, to use your own language, was "timid and unsatisfactory." Generally speaking, a single performance will, in no case, enable any one to give a public judgment on the merits of an eminent composer; and while admitting this, I must, for myself, resist that criticism which, from a detached and single expression, uttered in private, draws a general conclusion as to the opinions of the individual so uttering it.

Feeling myself deeply indebted to English "music and musicians" for enjoyments which have made my short residence in this country a bright period of my life, I must say that the allusions in your paper of Sunday last were most painful to my feelings, by their appearing calculated to create misconceptions to my prejudice among those from whom I have received so much kindness, and for whom I feel the liveliest regard.

I am, Sir,
Your most obedient Servant,
FELIX MENDELSSOHN BARTHOLDY.

It is satisfactory to learn that the letter was inserted in the paper, and accompanied by a "very polite and proper apology."

Towards the end of July, Felix and his friend Klingemann left London for Edinburgh, arriving in that city on the 28th. The letters written by Felix give a graphic account of what he has seen. Describing Holyrood, he says: "Everything around is broken and mouldering, and the bright sky shines in. I believe I found to-day in that old chapel the beginning of my Scotch symphony."

Tour in Scotland

The tour included visits to Abbotsford—just missing Sir Walter Scott—Blair Athol, the Hebrides—with a peep at Fingal's Cave—ending with Glasgow. Felix, writing on August 7th, says: "In order to make you understand how extraordinarily the Hebrides affected me, the following came into my mind there." Then he gives twenty bars which formed the opening of his "Hebrides" overture. From Glasgow the travellers went to Liverpool, and then to Holyhead, with the intention of crossing over to Ireland. Bad weather stopped this excursion, so they returned to Liverpool, and Klingemann parted from his friend and returned to London. Felix wrote from Llangollen, August 25th:

Welsh music

"No national music for me! Ten thousand devils take all nationality! Now I am in Wales, and, dear me! a harper sits in the hall of every reputed inn, playing incessantly so-called national melodies; that is to say, most infamous, vulgar, out-of-tune trash, with a hurdy-gurdy going *at the same time!*"[1] What if he had been asked to act as an adjudicator at an Eisteddfod!

From Liverpool, passing through Chester, Felix went to pay a visit to the family of Mr. John Taylor, a mining engineer (and relative of Edward Taylor, the Gresham Professor of Music[2]), living at Coed-du, near Mold, in Flintshire. There he spent a happy time, sketching, making music—and flirting. "Yes, children," he writes home, "I do nothing but flirt, and that in English!" His stay at the Taylors' he looked upon as one of those times of which he would never lose the flowery memory. There were three daughters of the

[1] "Mendelssohn Family," vol. i. p. 213.

[2] "Mendelssohn" (Rockstro), p. 41.

house, and for them he composed the three pianoforte pieces, published as Op. 16.

Felix was back in London by September 10th, and was soon at work with composition. The Quartet in E flat, Op. 12, for strings, the "Reformation" and "Scotch" symphonies, the "Hebrides" overture, and vocal music, these were all shaping themselves in his mind. But there were two works he was particularly bent upon finishing—an organ piece for Fanny's wedding, and an operetta for the celebration of the silver wedding of his parents. Then occurred an accident that upset all his plans. On September 17th he was "thrown out of a cabriolet, and very severely wounded in the leg, in consequence of the carriage first falling on him, then being dragged over his limb."[1] He was tenderly nursed by Klingemann, and received much care and attention from his musician friends Attwood and Hawes, from Sir Lewis and Lady Moller, and others. This mishap confined him to his bed for a couple of months, and he missed his sister's wedding (October 3), and the tour through Holland and Belgium with his father. In October he writes: "You cannot think how kind the English people are to me. As I cannot do justice to books, and am not allowed to eat meat, they load me with fruit and all kinds of sweets." In November he was able to get about, and he stayed some days with Attwood at his house in Upper Norwood. There, in his bedroom, was

Accident to Mendelssohn

[1] *Harmonicon*, vol. vii. p. 255.

"Old Attwood's" music cupboard, which he freely rummaged. Among other treasures, he lighted upon the full score of Weber's *Euryanthe*, and was delighted to find a certain passage scored for brass, as he had always imagined it to be. He wrote: "It seems strange to me that I should get so well acquainted with Weber's favourite work here in England, where nobody knows it nor can know it, and where they really treated him shamefully, and where he died." Here Felix is "Sir Oracle" once more.

While in London, Felix finished the opera, *Die Heimkehr aus der Fremde*, known as "The Son and Stranger." Klingemann wrote the book, and also the music to the twelfth number, the song "Die Blumenglocken," the words of which were by Mendelssohn. There were parts for Hensel, Fanny, Rebecka, and Devrient. Hensel had no ear for music, and his part in a trio was confined to one note throughout. On November 29th Felix was in Calais, and was soon at home in Berlin once more. He was still rather lame, and in walking used a stick. The operetta was rehearsed, and performed with the greatest success on December 26th; but Hensel missed his note, "though it was blown and whispered to him from every side." [1]

Die Heimkehr aus der Fremde

[1] "Recollections of Felix Mendelssohn" (Devrient).

CHAPTER VII

Felix receives a commission from Ceylon—A chair of music founded at Berlin University—Felix departs on his tour to the South—Last meeting with Goethe—Music and society in Munich—Two gifted young artists—Felix in Vienna—Arrival in Italy—Rome in 1830—Death of the Pope, and election of his successor—Holy Week and its music—The homeward journey—Switzerland—Organ-playing—Concert in Munich—Paris, 1831-32—Death of Eduard Ritz—Death of Goethe—Concerts in Paris—The Symphony in D minor—A disappointment—Second visit to London—Music and friends—Death of Zelter—The "Hebrides" overture—Publication of "Songs without Words"—Return to Berlin.

FELIX was looked upon in England as a brilliant young amateur, and his successes led to nothing more solid than social recognition and friendship. One commission he did indeed receive, but that was one he could not entertain. This is his own account of it: "I have been intrusted with a commission, and you will laugh immensely when you hear what it is. It gives me great pleasure, as it is quite unique, and possible only in London. I am to compose a festival song for a celebration which is to take place in—Ceylon! The natives some time ago were emancipated, and intend keeping the anniversary of the event, and are to sing a song on the occasion; and Sir Alexander Johnston, the Governor of Ceylon, has given me the order. It is really very mad and droll; and for two whole days I have laughed at it to myself."[1] But though no substantial result followed his first visit to London, Felix made a good foundation, and better things were to follow. His travels, moreover, were not yet at an end, and, in accordance with the plan laid down by his father, he had to visit Italy.

In the beginning of 1830 a chair of music was founded in the University of Berlin, with the view of its being filled by Mendelssohn. He declined the offer, and suggested Marx, and through his good offices Marx obtained the appointment. The date of his departure for the great southern journey was approaching when his sister Rebecka was taken ill with measles. Felix himself was soon attacked with the same malady, and it was not until May 13th that he was able to start. His father accompanied him as far as Dessau, where Felix spent a few days with his friend Schubring.

At Dessau

While there his "Meeresstille" overture was tried over by the Court orchestra,[2] and Felix extemporized at a small party at Wilhelm Karl Rust's, and also visited the Duchess of Anhalt-Dessau. He met Friedrich Schneider, too, but was not very cordially received, and this he did not like. Schneider absolutely knew nothing of the Bach "Passion Music,"

[1] "Mendelssohn Family," vol. i. p. 188.

[2] Schubring does not clearly state what rehearsal Mendelssohn attended during this visit.

and he was annoyed at hearing so much about the performance under Mendelssohn.

The next stopping-place was Weimar, and from there dates the first of those charming letters, published after his death as *Reise-Briefe*. Space will only permit of the briefest quotations of these in order to trace the course of his travels, and relate the chief incidents of his tour. He passed a fortnight in delightful intercourse with Goethe, and on leaving, was presented by the poet with a sheet of the autograph of *Faust*, with this inscription : "To my dear young friend F. M. B., the powerful and gentle master of the piano, as a remembrance of happy May days in 1830—J. W. v. GOETHE."

At Weimar

Felix quitted Weimar on the 3rd of June, and never saw Goethe again. Travelling by way of Nürnberg, Felix reached Munich on the 6th, remaining there till the end of July. There he met Josephine Lang—then a girl of fifteen, and called "Peppi" Lang; Delphine von Schauroth—"an artist, and very well educated," as Felix wrote, though she was only sixteen—and "Excellencies and Counts as thick as fowls in a poultry-yard." Felix "flirted very considerably," as he informed his sister Fanny, and was altogether in a fair way of being utterly spoilt. Marx met him at Munich, and in a letter to Fanny Hensel says: "You cannot have an idea of Felix's position here. . . . It is worth standing by and watching how he is the darling in every house, the

Visits Munich

centre of every circle. From early in the morning everything concentrates on him."[1] But he was not idle, and he sent Fanny a little "Song without Words," on the 14th of June, and another on the 26th, as a congratulatory offering on the birth of a son, this last afterwards published as Op. 30, No. 2.

Arrival at Vienna

From Munich, passing through the district of Salzkammergut, and touching Salzburg, Ischl, and Linz, Felix arrived at Vienna on August 13th. There he had as mad a time as at Munich, with music at Eskele's, billiard-playing at the Kärnther Thor, and amusements of all sorts with his friends Hauser and Merk. He had some caustic remarks to make on Czerny, and generally was not pleased with the state of music in the Austrian capital. Hauser gave him a tiny book of Luther's hymns to take with him on his travels. He set several to music later on. At the end of September Felix is in Presburg, witnessing the coronation of the Crown Prince as King of Hungary, and getting his hat smashed by a Hungarian whose view it impeded. Back to Vienna, and then on to Graz, Udine, and in Venice by October 9th.

In Italy

"Italy at last! and what I have all my life (he was twenty-one!) looked forward to as the greatest felicity, is now begun and I am basking in it."[2] Later he says in the same letter, describing the scene as he entered the Land of Song:

[1] "Mendelssohn Family," vol. i. p. 261.

[2] "Letters from Italy and Switzerland" (Wallace), p. 27.

"The whole country had such a festive air, that I seemed to feel as if I were myself a Prince making his grand entry." The young traveller certainly was on the best of terms with himself, and is charmingly egoistical throughout his wanderings. His descriptions of scenery are graphic, and he had the artist's eye for a picture. While gazing on Titian's "Martyrdom of St. Peter," in the Franciscan Church, during Divine service, he was rudely aroused by the vulgar, clap-trap stuff played by the organist. Felix stayed but a week in Venice, and, travelling by Bologna—"to have a glance at the St. Cecilia"—and Florence, where he stayed a week, he reached Rome on November 1st. "The first thing connected with music that I met with here," he wrote, "was the *Death of Christ*, by Graun, which an Abbate here, Fortunato Santini, has translated faithfully and admirably into Italian. . . . I understand that the Abbate has been long impatiently expecting me, because he hopes to obtain considerable information from me about German music, and thinks I may also have the score of Bach's *Passion*."[1] Felix became very friendly with "Old Santini," as he called him. His first stay in Rome extended to April 10, 1831, and he formed a plan of work—and play. He was not called "Felix" for nothing; happy he was here in his surroundings, working when in the mood, and with no carking care to cast a shadow on his life. This was the

In Rome

[1] "Letters from Italy and Switzerland" (Wallace), pp. 48, 49.

programme he sketched out for himself: "After breakfast I set to work and play, sing, and compose, till near noon. Then Rome in all her vast dimensions lies before me, like an interesting problem to enjoy; but I go deliberately to work, daily selecting some different historical object." He made himself familiar with the wonders of Rome; went much into society; and did not neglect composition. Among his friends were Baron Bunsen, Horace Vernet, Thorwaldsen, and some English people. He visited Santini, Baini, and saw something of Berlioz and Montfort. He satirized the German painters, and was not too partial to Berlioz. Of course there was a beautiful young lady—English, this time—with whom he fell in love. In January, 1831, he saw for the first time the frescoes in the villa where his uncle Bartholdy died in 1827.

Friends in Rome

It was at Bunsen's house in November, 1830, that Felix "first played before the Roman musicians *in corpore.*" The Papal singers had been performing Palestrina's music, and Felix felt that a brilliant piece would be unsuitable, while on the other hand they had had enough of serious music. He therefore asked Astolfi, the director, to give him a theme for improvisation. The Abbaté "lightly touched the notes with one finger thus:—

"The black-frocked Abbati pressed round me and seemed highly delighted. I observed this, and it inspired me so much that towards the end I succeeded famously; they clapped their hands like mad, and Bunsen declared that I had astounded the clergy; in short, the affair went off well."[1] Matters musical were, however, in a very unsatisfactory condition. The "so-called Philharmonic Society" gave concerts, but only with piano. There was no orchestra, and an attempt to perform Haydn's "Creation" was abandoned as an impossibility.

Music in Rome

In November Pope Pius VIII. died, and early in the next year Gregory XVI. was elected his successor. Felix gives an account of all this, and playfully appropriates to himself the ceremonial connected with the latter event, as it took place in the beginning of February. "It was all to celebrate my birthday; and the election of the Pope, and the homage, was a spectacle got up in my honour; but it was well and naturally performed, and so long as I live, I shall never forget it."[2] Then came the Carnival, and Felix entered into the fun of it. "All idea of work," he wrote, "is out of the question at present; I have only composed one little song; but when Lent comes, I intend to be more industrious." He sent his friend Zelter a most elaborate account of the music sung at the services in

[1] "Letters from Italy and Switzerland," p. 65.

[2] Ibid., p. 106.

the Sistine Chapel in Holy Week; and gave proofs of an astonishing memory in the copious notes he made of the pieces sung. Palestrina's *Improperia* and Allegri's *Miserere* excited his admiration; he also heard the *Miserere* of Bai and Baini, but the last he characterized as a composition entirely devoid of life or power. Of the Ancient Plain Song, or the Gregorian Chant, he shows himself strangely ignorant. His dislike of the music was a matter of training or temperament. But one little bit of *Canto fermo* he *did* like, though it would appear that he was unaware of its extreme antiquity, and thought it the work of the master he most revered, Sebastian Bach. He writes: "I must not omit here to make mention of my favourite point; I mean the Credo. The priest takes his place for the first time in the centre, before the altar, and after a short pause, intones in his hoarse old voice the Credo of Sebastian Bach. . . . When I for the first time heard my well-known

Holy Week music

Bach's Mass in B minor

and all the grave monks round me began to recite in loud and eager tones, I was positively startled: this is the point I still like the best of all."[1]

[1] "Letters from Italy and Switzerland," p. 127.

Felix left Rome for Naples on April 10, 1831, and there he enjoyed the *dolce far niente* until the end of May. His companions were Bendemann, Hildebrand, and Carl Sohn. Benedict was delighted when Felix called upon him, and renewed the acquaintance begun in boyhood. He gives an account of Felix's marvellous extempore playing at an evening party at the house of Madame Mainvielle-Fodor. While at Naples, Felix refers to the removal of his brother Paul to London, and adds: "That smoky nest is fated to be now and ever my favourite residence; my heart swells when I even think of it."[1] In Rome again early in June, Felix, after a short stay, set out on his homeward journey, travelling by Florence and Genoa, and staying for a week at Milan in July. This time he made the acquaintance of Madame Ertmann, and delighted her and the General her husband, by playing Beethoven's B flat Trio, singing the string parts as best he could.[2] Madame Ertmann played to him Beethoven's Sonatas in C sharp minor, and D minor. Felix also met Karl Mozart, and charmed him by playing some of his father's music. From Milan, by way of Lago Maggiore, the Simplon, Geneva, across the mountains to Interlaken, he journeyed on to Lucerne. His letters abound with fine descriptive passages. From Lucerne he wrote what proved to be his last letter to Goethe. It was dated August 28th (Goethe's birthday—and his last!). After describing a terrible

[1] "Letters from Italy and Switzerland," p. 155.
[2] Ibid., p. 199.

thunderstorm, he goes on to say: "I spent last week at Engelburg, in an Unterwald monastery several thousand feet above the sea, perfectly secluded, where I found a nice organ and pleasant monks. They had never heard of Sebastian Bach, so that a few of his fugues on the organ were a complete novelty to them; but still they were pleased, and on the Saint's day (St. Bartholomew's) I had to play the organ for them, accompany the Mass, and make the Responses. It was the first time on this journey that I had got hold of a decent organ, for in Italy I didn't find a single one in good order."[1] Continuing his journey, Felix arrived in Munich early in September. There he made a considerable stay, enjoying life and working at his music. He composed there, and dedicated to Fräulein von Schauroth, the pianoforte Concerto in G minor; gave lessons in double counterpoint and harmony to Josephine Lang, of whose genius he wrote in most enthusiastic terms; held musical picnics at his lodgings with Bärmann, Breiting, Staudacher, and others; and wound up by giving a grand concert, for the benefit of the poor. The concert took place in the Odeon Hall on October 17th. His Symphony in C minor, and "Midsummer Night's Dream" overture were performed, and he played his new pianoforte concerto and also extemporized. The King (Louis I.) gave him the theme, "Non più andrai," on which to

Plays the organ in a monastery

Concert in Munich

[1] "Goethe and Mendelssohn," p. 85.

improvise; the audience applauded, but Felix was not pleased with himself, and resolved never again to extemporize in public. Before leaving Munich Felix received, and accepted, a commission to write an opera, and went to Düsseldorf—visiting Frankfort on the way—to consult Immermann on the subject, and arranged with him for a *libretto* on "The Tempest." But nothing came of the compact.

Commission to write an opera

It has been said that Felix was not idle during his southern tour. "The 'Hebrides' is completed at last," he writes on December 30, 1830; the Psalm, *Non nobis*, dates from November; the "Italian" and "Scotch" symphonies were both well advanced; the three Motets, written for the French nuns of the church of Trinità de' Monti, though not published until 1838, were finished during the winter. The "First Walpurgis Night" was begun in Rome, and in its first form completed in Milan. Then he was busy on a version of Handel's *Solomon*, and as early as November he refers to a pianoforte concerto, that he wished to write for Paris, as beginning to float in his head. Probably the Concerto in G minor thus had its rise. Other pieces might be mentioned, but these will afford indication enough of his creative activity at this period.

Compositions, 1830–31

While in Frankfort Felix was informed of his sister Rebecka's engagement, and of the death of his aunt Henriette. In Paris, where he stayed from December to April, 1832, he was destined to hear more sad news, for his friend Edward Ritz [1] died in January, and Goethe passed away in March. These events threw a gloom over his otherwise happy life in the gay capital. He met many old friends, and his letters teem with allusions to Baillot, Herz, Hiller, Kalkbrenner, and others. Hiller gives a full account of Mendelssohn's stay in Paris, and relates how it saddened Felix to find Baillot lodging on a third floor, in reduced circumstances, and giving lessons the whole day long. Felix occasionally visited Cherubini, and met Habeneck, who became a good friend. Chopin, Liszt, Ole Bull, and Meyerbeer were all in Paris at the time, and Felix became acquainted with them all, and with Franchomme, Cuvillon, and others. Habeneck introduced Felix to the public at the concerts of the Conservatoire, where he played Beethoven's Concerto in G. His own overture, "A Midsummer Night's Dream," was performed at the same concerts on February 19th, and his Octet was played in a church at a funeral mass in commemoration of Beethoven. "I can scarcely imagine anything more absurd than a priest at the altar and my scherzo going on." [2] But the thing Felix had most set his heart upon ended in disappointment. His Symphony in D minor ("Reformation Symphony") was to be produced

Plays at the Conservatoire concerts

[1] Mendelssohn always spelt the name Ritz, though its correct form was Rietz.

[2] "Letters from Italy and Switzerland," p. 339.

by his friend Habeneck; the work was rehearsed—Felix wrote in delight about it—but the performance never took place. The orchestra did not like the music; it was "too learned, too much *fugato*, too little melody." Felix said nothing of this in his letters, but he was much hurt. The cholera was raging in Paris in 1832, and Felix had a slight attack, which delayed his journey to London. He does not seem to have composed much while in Paris, but several of his works were revised. He writes: "People now know that I exist, and that I have a purpose, and any talent I display, they are ready to approve and to accept. They have *made advances* to me here, and asked for my music, which they seldom do; as all the others, even Onslow, have been obliged to *offer* their compositions. The London Philharmonic have requested me to perform something new of my own there on the 10th of March.[1] Elsewhere Felix refers to his brother Paul's letter from London, with an invitation to visit him in the spring. The *Dilettante*, in the *Harmonicon*, as early as January, 1832, refers to the expected visit of Mendelssohn,[2] but no other details are obtainable. However, by April 23, Felix is again in his old quarters, 103, Great Portland Street, only wishing he could describe how happy he feels to be there once more. At the sixth Philharmonic Concert, May 14th, his "Hebrides," under the title "Overture to the Isles

Second visit to London

[1] "Letters from Italy and Switzerland," p. 333.

[2] *Harmonicon*, vol. x. p. 42.

of Fingal," was produced. The *Athenæum* said of it that, as descriptive music, it was decidedly a failure. At the next concert, the 28th, Felix played the G minor Concerto, and the same journal on that occasion said the concerto might be described as a dramatic scena for the pianoforte, adding that the performance, as an exhibition of pianoforte playing, was more astonishing than any the writer had yet witnessed.[1] The concerto was repeated at the next, and last concert, June 18th, when the overture "A Midsummer Night's Dream" was performed for the first time by the Philharmonic Society. The composer's relations with the orchestra, and with all musicians, were of the most cordial nature, and Mendelssohn's stay in London was very happy, though clouded for a time by the news of the death of his friend and teacher, Zelter. Felix presented the MS. score of the "Hebrides" overture to the Philharmonic Society, and by way of thanks the Society gave Mendelssohn a piece of plate. Moscheles, Klingemann, and all his old friends, Felix met again, and made new acquaintances, among them the Horsley family. Once more he stayed at the house of Thomas Attwood, Upper Norwood, where he enjoyed the English spring, smelt the lilacs, and practised his gymnastics in the garden. In London he played at several concerts, among them that of N. Mori, on May 25th, when his

"*Hebrides*" *overture*

[1] *Athenæum*, 1832, pp. 326, 356. This was before H. F. Chorley became the music critic of that paper.

Capriccio brilliante, Op. 22—only finished a week before —was produced. At Moscheles' concert, June 1st, Mozart's concerto for two pianos was performed by Felix and Moscheles. Felix inserted two long cadenzas for each performer, and of these the *Harmonicon* said: "In this (the concerto) each introduced his own cadenza, in which musical skill and powers of execution were exhibited that certainly none in the present day could surpass, and very few would dream of rivalling."[1] On June 10th Felix gave a wonderful display on the organ in St. Paul's Cathedral. His first book of *Lieder ohne Worte* was published by Novello, but with the title "Original Melodies for the Pianoforte." In July he was back again at *Leipziger Strasse*, his *Wanderjahre* were over, and the serious business of life before him.

Publication of "Songs without Words"

[1] *Harmonicon*, vol. x. p. 154.

CHAPTER VIII

Felix and the Berlin Singakademie—A disappointment—Commissions and concerts—The "Italian" Symphony—Third visit to London—Festival at Düsseldorf—Felix offered a fixed appointment—Fourth visit to London—Accident to Felix's father—Felix at work in Düsseldorf—Lights and shadows of artistic life—Felix as a librettist—Compositions, 1833–35—Presents and honours—An invitation to Leipzig—The Cologne Musical Festival—A family gathering—Gratifying testimonial from Cologne—Resignation of position at Düsseldorf—Departure for Leipzig.

THROUGH all his wanderings Felix always turned in thought to the Fatherland. He was a German artist, and to Germany must his life's work be devoted. But the particular place was not so easy to determine upon. The death of Zelter left the Singakademie without a conductor, and Felix would have accepted the post, even in conjunction with Rungenhagen, who for some time had assisted Zelter. Devrient took an active part in urging the claims of Felix, but when it came to the vote, Rungenhagen was elected by a large majority. The whole Mendelssohn family then seceded from the society, and the position of Felix in Berlin became anything but satisfactory. Nevertheless, between November, 1832, and January 1833, Felix gave four concerts in Berlin, and produced his "Walpurgisnight,"

"Reformation" Symphony, Capriccio in B minor, and concert overtures.

An oratorio

Commission from the Philharmonic Society

While in Paris, Felix received from the Cecilia Society, Frankfort-on-Main, a commission to write an oratorio, and St. Paul was the subject selected. He immediately wrote to his friend Devrient to help in compiling the text, a task Devrient felt himself not equal to, and which he had to decline. However, the oratorio was not yet to see the light. At the general meeting of the Philharmonic Society (London), November 5, 1832, the following resolution was unanimously passed :—

"That Mr. Mendelssohn Bartholdy be requested to compose a symphony, an overture, and a vocal piece for the Society, for which he be offered the sum of one hundred guineas.

"That the copyright of the above compositions shall revert to the author after the expiration of two years; the Society reserving to itself the power of performing them at all times : it being understood that Mr. Mendelssohn have the privilege of publishing any arrangement of them as soon as he may think fit after their first performance at the Philharmonic Concerts."[1]

This was the best piece of business that had yet fallen to the young composer, and his letter of acknowledgment expressed his sense of the honour paid him. Then about this time he must have received the invitation to

[1] "The Philharmonic Society of London" (Hogarth), p. 59.

conduct the Lower Rhine Festival, to be held at Düsseldorf in the spring of 1833. And here it may be well to mention that his "Midsummer Night's Dream" overture was performed at the Leipzig Gewandhaus Concerts, on February 21, 1833, and repeated in April, though the first time his name was associated with an Institution he was afterwards to raise to a position far above that yet attained was much earlier, his Symphony (in C minor?) having been performed on February 2, 1827. This appears to be revealed for the first time in the statistics published in connection with the centennial celebration of the Gewandhaus Concerts. Felix was now becoming famous, and the question how he was to live by his art seemed in a fair way of settling itself. The Symphony in A (afterwards known as the "Italian" Symphony) was finished early in 1833, and that, with two overtures—supposed to be the Meeresstille and Trumpet overtures—were placed at the disposal of the Philharmonic Society, and the vocal piece promised in a short time. But before Felix could visit London, he had to go to Düsseldorf to make the preliminary arrangements for the festival.

Third visit to London

However, on April 26th he was once more in his lodgings in Great Portland Street, and again happy in "that smoky nest." His first business was with his friend Moscheles, to whom a son was born on February 6th. Felix stood godfather to the boy, who bore his own name, Felix.[1] At the

[1] Felix Moscheles, afterwards famous as a painter.

THE EXTERIOR OF THE OLD GEWANDHAUS, LEIPZIG

Philharmonic Concert of May 13th, the "Italian" Symphony was produced. The concerts of the Society were this year, and onward, given in the Hanover Square Rooms, which had just been remodelled. The symphony made a great impression, and Felix electrified the audience by his wonderful performance of Mozart's Concerto in D minor, his cadenzas being marvels in design and execution. He had, on the 1st of May, appeared at the annual concert of Moscheles, when, in conjunction with the latter, he played Weber's Gipsy March from *Preciosa*. The work was only roughly sketched out, and was practically improvised at the performance. The notice in the *Harmonicon* was very laudatory, and said the cadenzas were of the most masterly kind, and excited the admiration of a crowded room.

Production of the "Italian" Symphony

Shortly after the Philharmonic Concert, May 13th, Mendelssohn left London for Düsseldorf, to undertake the duties of conductor of the Lower Rhine Festival. This was the most important function yet intrusted to the young musician, and his father went to Düsseldorf to witness the triumphs of his son. Handel's *Israel in Egypt* was the principal work performed, other compositions being Beethoven's "Pastoral" Symphony, and "Leonora" overture, and Mendelssohn's own "Trumpet" overture. Abraham Mendelssohn, in letters to his family, gives a most interesting account of this festival. The description of the hall in which it

Lower Rhine Festival

was held is worth quoting; it affords an opportunity for comparison with our own provincial musical festivals. The hall was in a large shady garden belonging to a restaurant; it was 135 feet long, about 70 feet broad, but only 27½ feet high; entirely without ornament, and with whitewashed walls. The room held some twelve hundred people; one-third of the space being railed off for orchestra and chorus. Though the surroundings were of so homely a character, the festival was a great thing, inspired purely by the love of music. Two points connected with it are worthy of notice: Mendelssohn, though only twenty-four, exacted implicit obedience from the forces under him, and abolished the horrible process of "tuning" on the platform; then, after the intervals, the scattered audience was called together by a "loud flourish" from the orchestra—an anticipation of the practice at Bayreuth.

A fixed appointment

The success of the festival was so marked, and the talent of "Mr. Felix"—for so he was generally called—as a conductor was so evident, that he was offered the post of "director of all the public and private musical establishments of the town for a period of three years, with a salary of 600 thalers (about £90)." The engagement to begin on October 1st, with a three months' leave of absence each year, to be taken between May and November. So at last Felix entered upon a settled sphere of action. His father wrote home: "One thing I especially like about Felix's position here is, that whilst so many others have titles without an office, he will have a real office without a title."[1]

But there was yet some time to elapse before Felix entered upon his official duties, and how better to fill up that period than by another visit to smoky London? This time Felix had the happiness of being accompanied by his father. The two arrived in London early in June. The English climate, and particularly a "fine day" in London, are amusingly hit off by Abraham Mendelssohn in his correspondence. He enjoyed his visit, however; went sight-seeing, attended Alsager's quartet parties, and heard Felix's quintet and octet performed. There is no evidence of his attending the Philharmonic Concert on June 10th, when Felix's "Trumpet" overture was performed—"the offspring of genius and knowledge," as the critic to the *Harmonicon* called it; but he went to St. Paul's Cathedral on the 23rd, and heard his son play the organ, while Klingemann and two other gentlemen filled the places of the absent bellows-blowers. Very curiously, on the very day he had fixed for his departure, Abraham Mendelssohn met with an accident. He hurt his shin-bone, and neglecting it, the injury became serious, and he was confined to his room and unable to leave London until August 25th. Felix accompanied his father to Berlin, spent a few happy days with the family, and on September 27th took up his duties at Düsseldorf.

Fourth visit to London

[1] "Mendelssohn Family," vol. i. p. 292.

All this time *St. Paul* was occupying Mendelssohn's attention, and it is evident from a letter addressed to Pastor Schubring from Berlin in 1833, that much of the music was already arranged—at least in the composer's mind. Of his Düsseldorf appointment he wrote that he was going "nominally in order to direct the church music, and the Vocal Association, and probably also a new theatre which is now being built, but in reality for the purpose of securing quiet and leisure for composition."[1] This notwithstanding, he threw himself into the work with all the ardour of his nature. The church music engaged his first attention. He said "no appropriate epithet exists for the music which has hitherto been given here." He could not find one tolerable Mass, so he went off to Elberfeld, Bonn, and Cologne, and returned with a load of music by Palestrina, Lotti, Leo, Lasso, Pergolesi, and others. Rockstro says the good Düsseldorfers showed no particular taste for these Italian masters at first.[2] At the theatre Felix was equally uncompromising. He began by arranging with Immermann for a series of "classical" performances, beginning with Mozart's *Don Juan*. The term "classical" displeased the theatre-goers, and the increased rates for admission irritated them still more. There was something like a riot the first night, and the curtain had to be lowered four times before the middle of the

Felix at work in Düsseldorf

[1] "Mendelssohn's Letters from 1833 to 1847," p. 6.

[2] "Mendelssohn" (Rockstro), p. 52.

first act. Felix was furious, and demanded a public apology before he would conduct a second performance. Ultimately the instigator of the riot complied with the request, and the second representation of the opera went off with complete success. For a time all went well, and Beethoven's *Egmont*, Cherubini's *Der Wasserträger*, with other works, were given. But there was a "rift within the lute," and Mendelssohn's relations with Immermann became strained. There was something of the autocrat about Felix, and he was impatient of restraint. He said that he had no sympathy with actual theatrical life, so he gave up his official connection with the opera, and with it his salary. His work in the concert-room was much more to his liking, and he gave excellent performances of Handel's *Messiah*, *Israel in Egypt*, and *Alexander's Feast*. Then his oratorio, *St. Paul*, was well on the way to completion. It was Felix's idea to write this oratorio for the Cecilia Society, Frankfort, conducted by his friend Schelble. For this he had already received the commission. At the outset, he and Marx each arranged to write an oratorio book for the other. Felix carried out his part of the compact, and wrote the book *Moses* for Marx; the latter threw up his task, objecting to the introduction of chorales, which he regarded as an anachronism. Moreover, he rejected Felix's book. As it happened, *St. Paul* was not to be finished yet. Felix began the selection of

Gives up the opera

Mendelssohn as a librettist

the text himself, and generally arranged the book, but his letters to Bauer, Fürst, and Schubring show his indebtedness to them for much advice and help. During his Düsseldorf period, however, Felix completed the overture *Die Schöne Melusine;* the Rondo in E flat, for pianoforte and orchestra, Op. 29; the Scena, *Infelice*, composed for the Philharmonic Society, and sung by Madame Caradori-Allan, at the concert of May 19, 1834; various songs, including *Auf Flügeln des Gesänges;* and sundry pianoforte pieces. Apart from the theatrical disputes, Mendelssohn's life at Düsseldorf was happy enough. He had a couple of pretty rooms on the ground floor of Schadow's house;[1] took lessons in water-colour drawing from Schirmer; and entered with zest into every form of social pleasure. He was much in the company of artists, and was almost one of them-selves. He also took to riding, and kept a horse, first dutifully consulting his father on the subject: "I wished to ask you whether you don't think it rather too *genteel* for me, at my years, to have a horse of my own?"[2] In the same letter to his father he mentions a pretty girl to whom he was persuaded to give a few lessons. He converted her from Herz to Mozart and Beethoven, and her grateful father, a manufacturer, sent Felix a parcel of cloth. "I could scarcely believe this at first, but the parcel really contained enough of

Compositions at Düsseldorf

1 "Mendelssohn" (Hiller), p. 38.
2 "Mendelssohn's Letters from 1833 to 1847," p. 31.

the finest black cloth to make an entire suit. This savours of the middle ages; the painters are mad with envy at my good luck." Well they might be! There was little chance for them while Felix was about!

In the spring of 1834 Mendelssohn was made a member of the Berlin Academy of Fine Arts. In May he went to the Lower Rhine Festival held at Aix-la-Chapelle, and there met his friends Hiller and Chopin. The chief work then given was Handel's *Deborah*, for which additional accompaniments were written by Hiller, who also translated the text into German. The festival ended, the friends went together to Düsseldorf, "and passed a most agreeable day there, playing and discussing music."[1] Though his official connection with the theatre was over, Felix took great interest in the approaching opera-season. The new theatre was to be opened on November 1st, and all through the summer Felix was in correspondence with Devrient, engaging singers and so forth. His holiday was mostly passed in Berlin, but he was back again in October, the first concert of the season being held on the 23rd. Soon after the new theatre was opened, matters became so intolerable to Felix that he threw the thing up altogether. "Never again in my life," he wrote to Devrient, "will I be a director, and I shall not forget those few weeks."

At the beginning of the year 1835, Felix received

[1] "Mendelssohn's Letters from 1833 to 1847," p. 36.

an invitation to accept the position of Conductor of the Gewandhaus Concerts, Leipzig. This was communicated by Dr. Conrad Schleinitz, and Mendelssohn's reply is dated January 26th. His experience has made him careful, and while acknowledging the great compliment paid him, he proceeds: "Before, then, giving a decided answer to your proposal, I must beg you to solve some doubts—namely, at whose disposal is the appointment you describe? with whom should I be in connection—with a society, or individuals, or a Board? and should I by my acceptance injure any other musician?" The last question reveals the generous, high-minded artist. The matter was not one to be settled off-hand. Felix wishes to have things made quite clear, and argues the question of salary in a very business-like manner. A benefit concert, to augment the stipend, had been mentioned, but he will have none of it. "During my musical career," he writes, "I have always resolved never to give a concert for myself (for my own benefit). You probably are aware that, personally, pecuniary considerations would be of less importance to me, were it not that my parents (and I think rightly) exact from me that I should follow my art as a profession, and gain my livelihood by means of it. I, however, reserved the power of declining certain things which, in reference to my favoured position in this respect, I will not do; for example, giving concerts or lessons. . . . In all other relations I shall gladly

New post offered to Felix

an consider myself as a musician who lives by his profession."[1]

Matters were satisfactorily arranged in the end, but there were other things to see to before the new appointment could be taken up. Mendelssohn was appointed conductor of this year's festival, to be held at Cologne. The function was held in June, and was attended by Felix's parents, the Hensels, and Dirichlets, for Rebecka Mendelssohn was married in 1832 to Gustav Dirichlet. At Cologne Mendelssohn met once more his friend Benedict, who attended a rehearsal, of which he gives an account in his sketch of the life of Mendelssohn. It goes to show the tact and humour of Felix as a conductor. The principal work performed was Handel's *Solomon*, to which Felix has given much attention when in Italy, in 1830, writing an organ part, and arranging the oratorio "with proper curtailments" for performance. A Hymn, and a "Religious March," by Cherubini, were also given, the music having been sent from Paris by Hiller, at Felix's request. The festival arrangements were on a large scale; "the orchestra consisted of 476 vocalists, and 204 instrumentalists, making a total of 680 performers."[2] There was much that was pleasant connected with this festival. Felix submitted to his relations such parts of his oratorio as were finished. "Abraham was quite satisfied, and then

Conducts the Cologne Festival

[1] "Mendelssohn's Letters from 1833 to 1847," pp. 66, 79.

[2] *The Musical Magazine*, 1835, p. 144.

Felix considered his work to have passed the ordeal of an impartial and incorruptible criticism, and confidently looked forward to its general success."[1]

Gift from Cologne

A gratifying incident was the presentation to Felix by the committee of Arnold's Edition of Handel's Works. True, he did not receive the books until after his removal to Leipzig. In a letter to his family, dated October 6, 1835, he mentions the arrival of the present: "Thirty-two great folios, bound in thick green leather, in the regular nice English fashion, and on the back, in big gold letters, the title and contents of each volume; and in the first volume, besides, there are the following words, 'To Director F. M. B., from the Committee of the Cologne Musical Festival, 1835.'" After the festival, his parents went with Felix to Düsseldorf. There his mother fell ill; and on the return to Berlin, his father was taken ill at Cassel. The resignation of his position at Düsseldorf seems to have been accomplished without difficulty, and in August Felix took up his residence in Leipzig, and busied himself in preparations for the approaching season.

[1] "Mendelssohn Family," vol. i. p. 331.

CHAPTER IX

Felix at Leipzig—*Début* at the Gewandhaus—Visitors, and social life—The last visit to his father—Death of Abraham Mendelssohn—Work and duty—Ferdinand David settles in Leipzig—University honours for Felix—Production of *St. Paul*—Sterndale Bennett in Germany—Felix at Frankfort—The family of Jeanrenaud—Felix in love—Engaged to Fräulein Cécile Jeanrenaud—*St. Paul* produced at the Liverpool Festival—Sterndale Bennett's *début* at Leipzig—Friendly reception—The Leipzigers and the betrothal of Mendelssohn—The wedding at Frankfort.

Settled at Leipzig

THE social and artistic attractions of Düsseldorf found an equivalent in the busy life of Leipzig with its commerce and its University. Then the place having been the home of Bach, Felix's idol, acquired additional charm. He was agreeably settled outside the town, in Reichel's Garden, adjoining the Promenade. Engaged as director by a free association, formed for the sole purpose of promoting good music, he was perfectly satisfied with his position. The Gewandhaus Concerts, now to enter upon their most brilliant period, dated back more than half a century, the first regular subscription concert taking place in the then new Gewandhaus, on November 25, 1781. The concerts, indeed, had a more remote origin, going back to the time of Bach himself.

INTERIOR OF THE CONCERT ROOM, GEWANDHAUS

The first concert under Mendelssohn's direction was held on October 4, 1835, and began with his overture *Meeresstille und glückliche Fahrt.* The other pieces were: an Air in E by Weber (written for Cherubini's *Lodoiska*), sung by Henriette Grabau; Spohr's Violin Concerto, No. 11, in G, played by Otto Gerke; the Introduction, *O welche Glück*, from Cherubini's *Ali Baba*, and Beethoven's Symphony No. 4. Was there not some special significance in the selection of the *Meeresstille* overture (then given for the fifth time at these concerts)? Did it indicate his feelings of relief after the stormy days of Düsseldorf, and was it another way of expressing what he said in a letter some years later—when he went to Leipzig he thought himself in Paradise? It may be so. Among his earliest visitors was Chopin, and Felix in his letter home—for so the house in the Leipziger Strasse must yet be considered—wrote that it was so pleasant for him to be once more with a thorough musician. Felix introduced Chopin to Clara Wieck, then a girl of sixteen. Then came Moscheles, and he, Felix, and the Wiecks made much music together. Moscheles gave a concert on October 9th, at which he and Felix played the duo "Hommage à Handel;" and on Sunday, the 11th, Moscheles played, at the second Gewandhaus Concert, his own Concerto in G minor. Then Moscheles, Clara Wieck, and Felix on another occasion played Bach's triple Concerto in D minor. On the 14th, the Dirichlets passed through Leipzig on their way to

Berlin, and Felix and Moscheles went with them, returning after two days. In the family circle there was happy mirth; the two famous pianists, to quote the words of Moscheles, allowed themselves "all manner of musical extravagancies," extemporizing jointly or alternately on two pianos, to the mystification and amusement of Abraham Mendelssohn, now quite blind. Fanny Hensel was induced to play her compositions, and joined with zest into the gaiety and fun. Felix returned to his work in high spirits, and was busy with his oratorio and concert business, when, like a bolt from the blue, Hensel broke in upon him with the news of his father's death. Abraham Mendelssohn, a slight cough apart, retired to rest on the night of November 18th in his usual health. Early on the following morning the family were roused with the news that he had been taken ill in the night. He was, however, quite conscious, and the doctors, who had been hastily summoned, declared there was no danger, and that Felix need not yet be sent for. About ten in the morning Abraham turned from his family, saying he would sleep a little, and in half an hour his spirit had fled. So gently and quietly he passed away, that none of those watching could say when death had come. So came to Felix the first great grief of his life. With Hensel, Felix rushed off post-haste to Berlin, and on the morning of the 22nd was with his mother. That scene of sorrow is too sacred to be dwelt upon. Felix, stunned,

Death of Abraham Mendelssohn

returned to his duties at Leipzig. "The only thing that now remains is to do one's duty" — thus he wrote to Pastor Schubring. His *St. Paul* was to have been brought out at Frankfort this month of November, but it was yet incomplete. Felix now devoted himself to that work, feeling that in doing so he was fulfilling his father's desire. Schelble's illness put a stop to the idea of producing *St. Paul* at Frankfort, but the work was accepted for the Festival of Düsseldorf in 1836, and was finished early in the spring. The concerts at Leipzig, meanwhile, were successfully carried on, the crowning effort being the magnificent performance of Beethoven's "Choral" Symphony on February 11th. Ferdinand David played at the concert of December 12, 1835, at the extra concerts of February 7th and March 24, 1836; and took his place as *Concertmeister*, on April 4th.[1] David was in every way a friend to Mendelssohn, relieving him of much of the routine work of his office. In March, 1836, the University of Leipzig conferred upon Felix the degree of Doctor of Philosophy. But none of these things could lift the load of depression from Felix's heart. At last the dreary winter was over, and in May, 1836, Felix was once more at Düsseldorf, everything being well prepared for him by Julius Rietz. The festival was held in the same long, low room as heretofore, now known as the *Rittersaal*, and began on

[1] Succeeding Heinrich August Matthäi, who died at Leipzig on November 4, 1835, a date of sad significance.

the 22nd with *St. Paul.* Hiller, who attended the festival, but could not get to the rehearsal, was not so deeply impressed as he expected to be. But then the room "was frightfully hot and close." The performers were all enthusiasm, and everything went well, though one of the "false witnesses" made a slip, which Fanny Hensel, singing among the contraltos, cleverly covered.[1] Klingemann wrote an account of the festival for the *Musical World*, from which it appeared that the orchestra consisted of 172, and the chorus of 364. Most of the instrumentalists, and all the chorus-singers, were amateurs.[2] He wrote that the performance was glorious, and that never had he heard such chorus-singing.

Production of "St. Paul"

This festival seems to have done Mendelssohn good, for Hiller says he was not only the centre-point of the whole, but a lively and agreeable host, introducing the visitors to each other, and bringing the right people together. Among the visitors to the festival was the young Sterndale Bennett, who, through the instrumentality of the firm of Broadwood, had been sent to Germany for a year to enlarge his experience. Mendelssohn had noticed the brilliant young Academy student when in London in 1833, and now a friendship began that ended only with death.

At the beginning of June Mendelssohn was in Frankfort, carrying on the work of the St. Cecilia Society

[1] "Reminiscences of F. Mendelssohn-Bartholdy" (Polko), p. 45.
[2] *Musical World*, vol. ii. p. 1.

for his sick friend Schelble, and enjoying the society of the Hiller family, friendly intercourse with Rossini, and making the acquaintance of a family one member of which was to influence the remainder of his life. In the winter of 1835–6, his sister Fanny, alarmed at his morbid condition, told Felix he must begin a new life, and marry. As he answered that he would look about him on the Rhine next summer, it seemed proof that he had a certain object in view.[1] Well, it was in the family of Madame Jeanrenaud, widow of a pastor of the French Reformed Church, that Felix met his fate. The second daughter, Cécile Charlotte Sophie, a girl of singular beauty, ten years the junior of Felix—he was now twenty-seven—entirely won his heart; but before declaring his passion, Felix put himself to the test by silently withdrawing to Scheveningen, whither he had been ordered for sea-bathing. He stayed away a month, and on the 9th of September the betrothal took place. He at once wrote to his mother to say he had been accepted. "My head is quite giddy from the events of the day; it is already late at night, and I have nothing else to say; but I must write to you. I feel so rich and happy."[2] Leaving him in the rosy halo of his new-found bliss, it is time to return to his oratorio.

Mendelssohn engaged

The success of *St. Paul* at Düsseldorf did not escape observation in England. As early as July it was proposed to give a selection at the approaching festival at

[1] "Mendelssohn Family," vol. ii. p. 1. [2] Ibid., p. 21.

Manchester,[1] but the project apparently fell through. Liverpool, however, secured the work for its festival of the same year, and in St. Peter's Church, on Friday morning, October 7, 1836, *St. Paul* was performed for the first time in England, and for the second time anywhere. Days before every ticket had been sold, and the building was crowded. Sir George Smart conducted, F. Cramer led the band, and the principal vocalists were Madame Caradori, Mrs. Joseph Wood, Mrs. Alfred Shaw, Mr. Braham, and Mr. Henry Phillips. In some recitatives and concerted numbers Mrs. Knyvett, Miss Birch, and Mr. James Bennett took part. There were some slight alterations and omissions as compared with the performance at Düsseldorf. The *Times* was lukewarm in its notice; the *Athenæum* enthusiastic. The Rev. John Edmund Cox was present at the performance, and his record of it is just and impartial.[2] To appease the appetite, real or supposed, of English music-lovers, the committee arranged for a selection from *Judas Maccabæus* to precede Mendelssohn's oratorio. The chorus-singing is described as being very fine, and the new work created the greatest interest. It was decided to give the work in London the next year, and it is worthy of note that before that performance took place, four choruses were given at one of the private concerts at the Royal Pavilion, Brighton, before Queen Adelaide, in November, 1836.[3]

"*St. Paul*" *in Liverpool*

[1] *Musical World*, vol. ii. p. 79.

[2] "Musical Recollections," vol. ii. p. 34, *et seq.*

[3] *Musical World*, vol. iii. p. 173.

Felix returned to Leipzig in time to prepare for the musical season, the first concert taking place October 2nd. At this he introduced Beethoven's "Leonora" overture, No. 1, then unknown at Leipzig. On January 19, 1837, young Bennett made his first appearance at the Gewandhaus. Felix wrote of this to Fanny: "Last week Bennett played his C minor Concerto, and was enthusiastically applauded by the Leipzigers, who have all of a sudden become his friends and admirers; indeed, he is the sole topic of conversation here now." Of course Felix's engagement soon became known, and at the concert of December 12th the directors put in the programme the second finale in *Fidelio*, the audience at once grasping the significance of *Wer ein holdes Weib errungen* ("He who has won a gentle wife"), and applauded until Felix sat down to the pianoforte and extemporized on the theme. At the Paulus-Kirche on March 16, 1837, *St. Paul* was performed, with many alterations, omissions, and some additions; and the next day Felix was off to Frankfort.

The wedding

The wedding took place at the Walloon French Reformed Church, on March 28th. As a surprise, Hiller had written a Bridal Chorus, which was sung by some young ladies, members of his private choral society, as the bride and bridegroom were returning to Madame Jeanrenaud's house by the Fahrthor. The incident touched the happy couple deeply. The honeymoon was spent at Freiburg in the duchy of Baden, and the summer was passed at Frankfort.

CHAPTER X

Mr. Moore, of the Birmingham Festival, and Mendelssohn—*St. Paul* performed in London—Mendelssohn's fifth visit to London—At the Birmingham Festival, 1837—Performances on the Town Hall organ—Production of *St. Paul*—The second Pianoforte Concerto—Mendelssohn introduces Bach's music to Birmingham—Mendelssohn's new home in Leipzig—The Gewandhaus Concerts—Lower Rhine Festival, 1838—Compositions, 1838-39—Festivals at Düsseldorf and Brunswick, 1839—Projects—The Leipzig orchestra—Bach monument—Visitors to Leipzig—The Gutenburg Festival—The "Hymn of Praise"—Mendelssohn in England for the sixth time—The Birmingham Festival of 1840.

ONE of the leading men in connection with the Birmingham Musical Festival at this period was Mr. Joseph Moore. It is said he visited Germany for the purpose of arranging with Mendelssohn for the performance of *St. Paul* at the festival of 1837, under the composer's personal direction. Meanwhile the oratorio had been given by the Sacred Harmonic Society, in Exeter Hall, on March 7th. The composer's summer holiday was cut short by the necessity of his being in England to superintend the rehearsals of his oratorio; accordingly, for the fifth time, Mendelssohn found himself in London, arriving on August 27th. He did

"St. Paul" in London

not like leaving home, "all, too, for the sake of a musical festival," as he wrote to his sister Fanny. He played on the organ at St. Paul's Cathedral on Sunday, September 10th, and it was then that the "gentlemen who walk about in bombazeen gowns" seduced the blower from his post, as they could not otherwise get rid of the crowd of listeners.[1] On Tuesday, the 12th, Mendelssohn played on the organ at Christ Church, Newgate Street, and had among his auditors "the father of English organists," Samuel Wesley. "At the expressed desire of M. Mendelssohn, who wished that he could hereafter say he had heard Wesley play, the veteran took his seat at the instrument and extemporized with a purity and originality of thought for which he has rendered his name ever illustrious."[2] On the evening of that day *St. Paul* was performed for the second time by the Sacred Harmonic Society, the composer occupying a seat in the gallery, in Exeter Hall. At the close of the first part he was recognized by the audience and performers, and saluted with cheers, the waving of hats, and by the performers with waving of their "music papers."

Visits Birmingham

The next day Mendelssohn left London for Birmingham. He was busily engaged with rehearsals up to the opening day of the festival, which was Tuesday, September 19th. At the evening concert, in the first part, Felix gave a grand

[1] *Musical World*, vol. vii. p. 9.

[2] *Ibid.*, p. 10. Wesley died on the 11th of October following.

extemporaneous performance on the organ in the Town Hall, and excited the greatest admiration by his marvellous pedal-playing. He also conducted the performance of his "Midsummer Night's Dream" overture, which opened the second part of the programme. On the Wednesday morning his oratorio *St. Paul* was performed under his direction, and he had a reception of the most enthusiastic description. According to the notice in the *Musical World*,[1] three or four of the later movements were omitted, although the performance was over very early. Still there was the inevitable selection at the close, in order that the public might hear the Italian *prime donne!*

Second Pianoforte Concerto

On the Thursday evening Mendelssohn played his new Concerto, in D minor, composed expressly for this festival, and was again the recipient of the most enthusiastic demonstrations of delight. A determined attempt was made to encore the last movement, but the composer was too much agitated and exhausted to go through such an ordeal again, and at last he was allowed to retire, overwhelmed with applause and congratulations. It was arranged that Mendelssohn should give another performance on the organ at the opening of the second part of the Friday morning's programme; but as it was necessary that he should leave Birmingham by the morning mail coach, in order to reach Leipzig by a given time, he played at the beginning of the concert,

[1] *Musical World*, vol. vii. p. 26.

and left Birmingham at half-past eleven. He gave Bach's Prelude and Fugue in E flat (St. Anne's), and again created a *furore*. That was, in all probability, the first composition by the Leipzig Cantor that had ever been heard in Birmingham; but Mendelssohn did not stop at Bach's organ music, and it was through his influence that a selection from *The Passion according to St. Matthew* was included in this same programme. The selection was very short, including only the duet, "'Tis done! the Holy One is taken" (sung by Miss Clara Novello and Mrs. A. Shaw); the semi-chorus, "Loose him! bind him not;" and the chorus, "Ye lightnings! ye thunders!" Still, it deserves to be placed on record that Birmingham was the first festival centre to present the music so dear to the heart of Felix Mendelssohn.[1]

Bach's "Matthew" Passion

This festival was an important event in the life of Mendelssohn, and his references to it show that he appreciated it. He says that he never had such brilliant success, and that the offers made to him from all sides were of a very different tenor from what they ever were before. On the other hand, he created a most favourable impression in Birmingham, and made many a friendship that lasted through life.

It was nearly midnight on the Friday when Felix reached London. With his friend Klingemann he met

[1] The first performance in England of any of Sebastian Bach's vocal music, was at Dr. Gauntlett's lectures at the London Institution, in March, 1837. See *Musical World*, vol. v. p. 29.

the committee of the Sacred Harmonic Society, and was presented with a large silver snuff-box with an inscription. Then by half-past twelve he was off by mail to Dover, and travelling without stoppage, he arrived at Frankfort on the 27th. There he joined his wife, and the two journeyed on to Leipzig, reaching that place at two in the afternoon of October 1st, in time to conduct the concert which began at six.

The house to which Felix took his bride was in Lurgenstein's Garden, by the Promenade. His letters to Hiller and others tell how happy he was in his home and in his work; though he chafes at times against the routine of conducting, and thinks no official post would be the best of all.[1]

Mendelssohn's new home

His sister Fanny visited Leipzig in the autumn, and saw the "beautiful eyes" of which the family had heard so much. She considers Felix most fortunate in his choice, and that Cécile, by the equanimity with which she treats Felix when in capricious moods, will most likely cure his fits of irritability altogether.[2]

The Gewandhaus Concerts went on flourishing. There were four historical concerts; Beethoven's cantata *Glorreiche Augenblick* was produced; and on November 11th, Clara Novello sang in Leipzig for the first time, and the public became wild about her. Mendelssohn contributed to the programmes his own

[1] Hiller, p. 104.
[2] "Mendelssohn Family," vol. ii. p. 37.

setting of the 42nd Psalm; his Serenade and Allegro giojoso, and string Quartet in E flat.

On February 7, 1838, the first child, a son, was born, who received the names of Carl Wolfgang Paul. Cécile had a dangerous illness afterwards, and the spring was an anxious time for Felix. But he conducted the Lower Rhine Festival, held this year at Cologne, in June. There he brought out Bach's cantata, *Gott fähret auf*, and a selection from Handel's *Joshua*. The summer was spent in Berlin, and was marked by the number of compositions then completed. These included *Psalm* 95, "Come, let us worship," the Sonata in B flat for pianoforte and violoncello, the string Quartet in D, and the *Andante and Presto agitato* for pianoforte. In a letter dated July 30th, he mentions a violin concerto that runs in his head, and the new oratorio, *Elijah*, is throwing its shadow before. During his stay in London, in 1837, he stayed with his friend Klingemann, and the two spent some time in planning a book on the subject.[1] But the work was not to be accomplished yet. Cécile was, this summer, introduced for the first time to the Mendelssohn family, and they were happy days passed in the Leipziger Strasse. An epidemic of measles broke out in September, and frightened Felix away. He was not to escape, however, and his second attack came on just as the performance of *St. Paul* was due. His friend David had to conduct in his stead.

Compositions of 1838

[1] "History of *Elijah*," pp. 3–6.

The winter of 1838–39 was busy, but in the spring Felix found time to write the *Ruy Blas* overture, for the Theatrical Pension Fund, though he condemned the play in no measured terms. Other compositions of 1839 were—the pianoforte Trio in D minor, the eight-part setting of *Psalm* 114, an organ piece, and songs and part-songs. In May Felix conducted the Lower Rhine Festival, held at Düsseldorf; in September he officiated in a like capacity at Brunswick, when his *St. Paul* was performed. It was at this festival that the late H. F. Chorley first met Mendelssohn.[1] The third day of this festival was a "Mendelssohn" concert, when Felix played his D minor Concerto, and the Serenade and Allegro giojoso.

Festivals at Düsseldorf and Brunswick

The year 1840 was of great importance, artistically, and the life of Felix became busier than ever. One of the things he had set his heart upon was the establishing at Leipzig of "a solid music Academy." To effect this he wrote a long letter to his friend von Falkenstein, of Dresden, asking if it would be possible to induce the King of Saxony to devote to that purpose a sum, bequeathed by a Herr Blümner for an institution dedicated to art and science.[2] The project was not yet to be carried out, however. Another undertaking he entered upon with the utmost zeal was the erection of a monument to his idol, Sebastian Bach. In August

[1] "Modern German Music," vol. i. p. 7, *et seq*.

[2] "Mendelssohn's Letters from 1833 to 1847," p. 188.

he gave an organ concert in the Thomas Church, and cleared three hundred dollars. For this he practised so hard that he could scarcely stand upright, "and walked nothing but pedal passages in the street."[1] But there was a matter of a more pressing nature for settlement, compared to which the claims even of Bach were of secondary importance. The Gewandhaus orchestra was poorly paid. Felix wrote to his friend Moscheles: "My present hobby is our poor orchestra and its improvement." He tells how he has scraped together five hundred thalers, but he wants twice that sum. If the town gives it, then it can proceed to the Bach monument. "But first of all, the extra pay."[2] Three years later Felix personally addressed the Corporation of Leipzig on the same subject.

His care for his orchestra

The concert season was brilliant. On January 9th Mendelssohn gave Beethoven's four *Leonora* and *Fidelio* overtures. Schubert's Symphony in C was played four times within twelve months.[3] In March, Liszt was at Leipzig, but did not seem to get on very well with the public. Felix arranged a *soirée* at the Gewandhaus in Liszt's honour. There were three hundred and fifty guests, and the performances included the *Meeresstille* overture, a Psalm, Bach's Triple Concerto (Liszt, Hiller,

[1] "Mendelssohn's Letters from 1833 to 1847," p. 192.

[2] Ibid., p. 177.

[3] It was first performed, in MS., March 21, 1839; the repeats were—December 12, 1839; March 3, 26; October 29, 1840.

and Felix),[1] and solos for Liszt. The "mulled wine and cakes" were appreciated as much as the music, a letter from Felix seems to imply.

On the 2nd of April, Hiller's oratorio "The Destruction of Jerusalem" was produced at the Gewandhaus Concerts, the composer conducting. Felix pressed this work on the directors, though it was only finished during Hiller's visit to Leipzig at this time. Concerts, visits, and affairs of all kinds notwithstanding, Felix never relaxed in his work of composition. For the festival in commemoration of the Invention of Printing held at Leipzig in June, he composed the *Festgesang*, for men's voices and brass band, and the *Lobgesang* ("Hymn of Praise"), a Symphony-Cantata, Op. 52. The first was performed in the open market-place, Leipzig, on Wednesday, June 24th, and the *Lobgesang* in the Church of St. Thomas, on Thursday, June 25th.

Lobgesang

In July Felix conducted a festival at Mecklenburg-Schwerin, when *St. Paul*, the *Creation*, and other works were performed. Chorley quotes this festival as a signal illustration of the extent to which Music brought "gentle and simple" together in Germany; and adds that the Duke placed all his officers and attendants at the service of the committee.[2]

[1] The Concerto in D minor, apparently, as that seemed the only one known at the time, and Mendelssohn took part in two performances of it at the Gewandhaus Concerts, in 1835 and 1843.

[2] "Modern German Music" (Chorley), vol. i. p. 54.

The work and excitement of the last few months told upon Mendelssohn's health, and his physician wished to send him to some watering-place for rest; but the energetic Mr. Moore had been after him again, and already in July he had accepted the invitation to produce the "Hymn of Praise" at the Birmingham Festival in the following September. Felix had a few days' pleasant rest in Berlin after leaving Schwerin, but he was soon back in Leipzig, arranging for his visit to England.

In his correspondence with Mr. Moore, Mendelssohn is very precise in his stipulations as to the works to be performed, and goes on to say, "I am not sure whether I shall complete my concerto[1] in time for your Festival; I hope so, but if not I will perform something else on the pianoforte."[2] He also recommends a preliminary rehearsal in London of the "Hymn of Praise," which duly took place in the Hanover Square Rooms, Moscheles sitting by the organist to advise as to the *tempi*.

On September 8th Felix arrived in London for the sixth time. He stayed with his friend Klingemann, and was soon enjoying the society of the Moscheleses, Horsleys, and other of his old acquaintances. On the 20th he left for Birmingham, where he stayed with Mr. Moore. In the festival he had a large share of the work. On the Tuesday morning, September 22nd, he played the Bach Prelude and Fugue in A minor on

Birmingham Festival of 1840

[1] This must have reference to the Violin Concerto.

[2] Polko, p. 233.

the organ, midway in the selection from *Israel in Egypt*, a proceeding which would hardly commend itself to present-day festival audiences. On Wednesday morning the "Hymn of Praise" formed the second half of the programme. Miss Charlotte Ann Birch sang the solo "Praise the Lord," and Mrs. Knyvett took the second part in the duet, "I waited for the Lord," with Madame Caradori-Allan. Mr. Braham was the tenor. Both text and music were altered later, as will be shown in another place. In the evening Mendelssohn played his pianoforte Concerto in G minor, described in the "word-book" as "A New Grand Concerto, composed by him expressly for this Festival"—a pardonable (?) lapse of memory on the part of the committee, or perhaps the programme might have been printed when the concerto was the subject of correspondence between Mendelssohn and Mr. Moore. This performance took place on the stage of the Theatre Royal, in the interval between the representation of Rossini's *La Gazza Ladra* and Gnecco's *La Prova d'un Opera Seria*, each compressed into one act. On the Thursday evening he conducted a performance of his overture, *A Midsummer Night's Dream*, and on the Friday morning he gave an extemporaneous performance on the organ in the Town Hall. This was immediately after a selection from Handel's *Jephtha*, and Mendelssohn took his subjects from that work. He also played the organ on the Wednesday morning to a few friends after the audience had left; and this performance was, from all accounts, the happiest of all. The second part of the Friday morning's programme opened with Mendelssohn's eight-part setting of Psalm 114, "When Israel out of Egypt came," which was performed for the first time in England. Moscheles says that the audience rose involuntarily from their seats during the performance of the *Choral* in the "Hymn of Praise," so powerfully did the music affect them.[1] The final chorus was repeated by the President's command. Mendelssohn was the hero of the festival. On his return to London he gave what Chorley termed an appendix to its finest feature, in the form of an organ recital at Christ Church, Newgate Street, September 29th.[2] Then, with Chorley and Moscheles, Mendelssohn returned to Leipzig.

Production of Ps. 114

[1] "Life of Moscheles," vol. ii. p. 70.

[2] *Athenæum*, 1840, p. 781. Grove and Rockstro mention a performance at St. Peter's, Cornhill, on the 30th.

CHAPTER XI

Musical life at Leipzig, 1840-41—Proposed Academy of Arts, Berlin—An offer to Mendelssohn from the King of Prussia—Negotiations—Once more at Berlin—A busy life—Compositions, 1841—The "Scotch" Symphony—Music to *Antigone*—In London, 1842, with his wife—Popularity of Mendelssohn—Visits to Buckingham Palace—Music in Frankfort—Kindly intercourse between musicians—Tiresome business at Berlin—Appointed Director of Church Music at the Cathedral—Leipzig Conservatorium becoming a realized fact—The Bach monument—The shadow of death—Loses his mother.

THE concerts had already begun when Mendelssohn reached Leipzig, but he was in time for the second. His friend Chorley fell lame, so Felix had a piano sent to his hotel, and, with Moscheles, gave him an evening's music. Then he arranged a *soirée* at the Gewandhaus (October 19th), when his 42nd Psalm was performed; Moscheles played his own Concerto in G minor, and joined Madame Schumann and Mendelssohn in Bach's Triple Concerto.

By command of the King of Saxony, an extra subscription concert took place in October, when the "Hymn of Praise" was the great attraction. Between the parts the King sent for Mendelssohn; after the second part, which consisted of the "Hymn," the King went straight to the conductor's desk, and thanked all for the pleasure the performance had given him. "Perhaps the King will now," wrote Felix to his mother, "bestow the 20,000 thalers which I long ago petitioned might be given towards the music here. In that case, I could with truth say that I had done good service to the music of Leipzig."[1] Before very long he *was* able to say it.

But now a change was impending which caused Felix much anxiety and unhappiness. Frederick William III., of Prussia, had died, and was succeeded on the throne by Frederick William IV., June 7, 1840. This sovereign desired to fix Mendelssohn, with other distinguished men, at Berlin. To that end he proposed to establish an Academy of Arts, to consist of four divisions—Painting, Sculpture, Architecture, and Music. Each department was to have its Director, who should in turn take the superintendence of the whole Academy. Paul Mendelssohn, instructed by Privy Councillor Herr von Massow, went to Leipzig to negotiate with Felix. Much correspondence ensued, for Felix desired to make everything clear and precise, and was unwilling to give up his position at Leipzig for one less favourable to his own freedom of action. At Leipzig he had a vacation of half the year, and, though there was a Board of Directors, he had the virtual control of the Gewandhaus Concerts. He had brought the orchestra

[1] "Mendelssohn's Letters from 1833 to 1847," p. 197.

to a perfection until then unheard of; and in Berlin he wanted, as he said himself, "despotic" power over the musicians, and to have such a position as should command their respect, and make him independent of everybody.[1] It was not a question of money, though the salary offered—3000 thalers (£450)—was much higher than any he had yet received. He foresaw difficulties in carrying out the duties. On the other hand, there was the alluring prospect of being united once more with the family life at the "Garden House" in the Leipziger Strasse. His mother and sister urged him to accept the flattering offer of the King, and in May, 1841, with his wife and family, he was again in the old home.

Removal to Berlin

The concert season at Leipzig, 1840–41, had been unusually brilliant and busy, and Felix had almost worn himself out. His correspondence, too, at this time was enormous, and he was constantly on the move. The negotiations for the new Academy were protracted, and though Mendelssohn drew up a plan for the Music Academy, the scheme came to nothing. However, he had pledged himself to remain in Berlin for a year, and had taken a house opposite to the family abode. This period was not favourable for composition, but Mendelssohn, never for a moment idle, contrived to write at odd times the "Serious" Variations, the Variations in E flat and B flat, and the *Allegro brillant*

Compositions of 1841

[1] "Mendelssohn Family," vol. ii. p. 161.

in A for duet. But the most important work of the year 1841 was the music to Sophocles' *Antigone*, the outcome of the "many thousand schemes of the King,"[1] and one with which Mendelssohn was fully in accord. But even in this there were hindrances, and had not Felix "got hold of old Tieck, and said 'Now or never!'" the thing would not have been done. It was here that Felix realized the advantage of his classical education. With Tieck and Böckh he went through the play, and adopted the translation of Donner. The music was composed in September and October, 1841, and the first performance took place on October 28th in the King's private theatre at Potsdam, the piece being repeated on November 6th.

Music to "Antigone."

As nothing had been definitely settled about the Berlin appointment, Felix did not resign the conductorship of the Leipzig Gewandhaus Concerts. An arrangement was made for Ferdinand David to conduct during the season 1841–42, but Mendelssohn went over for a short time, and, according to Rockstro, played at one concert Beethoven's Concerto, No. 1, in C, "then quite unknown in Leipzig."[2]

By command of the King, Mendelssohn began a

[1] "Mendelssohn Family," vol. ii. p. 164.

[2] "Mendelssohn" (Rockstro), p. 80. This would hardly be a first performance of the concerto there, as the statistics of the concerts, published by Breitkopf and Härtel, mention performances of pianoforte concertos by Beethoven in 1802 and 1803, which must refer to Nos. 1 and 2.

series of concerts in Berlin. The first took place January 10, 1842, when *St. Paul* was performed in the concert-room of the theatre, and the choruses were sung by a company of amateurs. According to Devrient, Felix did not get on very well with the members of the orchestra, and it was not a very happy time for him. Meanwhile, composition was going on, and already, on January 20th, he had written *Finis* to the score of the Symphony in A minor, known as the "Scotch" Symphony. The first performance was given at Leipzig, March 3rd, and a week later it was performed at Berlin. His last official concert of the season was on April 25th, when the "Hymn of Praise" was performed. *Antigone* was produced for the first time in public at the *Schauspielhaus*, Berlin, on April 13th, and within three weeks six more representations were given. This was the most gratifying feature of the season, for otherwise neither Felix nor his music seemed to have been very cordially received. Things were far otherwise at the "Garden House." The Sunday music under Fanny Hensel flourished exceedingly, and the visitors included many celebrities. In the society of Cornelius, Bunsen, Thorwaldsen, Pasta, Ernst, Madame Unger-Sabatier, her husband, Lepsius, Böckh, Mrs. Austin, the great pianist Liszt, who created a *furore* at Berlin this season—in such society Felix could forget or smile at the coldness of the Berlin public.

"Scotch" Symphony

In May he went to Düsseldorf, where he conducted

the festival on the 15th and 16th. Before that time, however, he had arranged to visit London for the purpose of producing his new symphony. Early in March the *Musical World* referred to his coming, and in April he was in correspondence with Sterndale Bennett concerning the arrangements for the concerts, and also mentioning certain alterations he had made in his symphony. This time Felix was accompanied by his wife, whose gentle charm was felt by all. The pair arrived towards the end of May, and made their stay in London with the Beneckes. There was a private trial of the symphony on May 26th, which must have been immediately after his arrival in London. It was produced at the seventh Philharmonic Concert, June 13th, when Felix conducted the whole programme, and Thalberg played fantasias on themes from operas. The symphony made a great impression. The Prince Consort left her Majesty, at the French play, to listen to the performance, and G. A. Macfarren wrote a special article on the work the following day.[1] At the last concert of the season, Felix played his Concerto in D minor, and conducted a performance of his "Hebrides" overture, now called *The Isles of Fingal*. He writes to his mother: "The people make such a fuss with me that I feel really quite abashed." At Exeter Hall he received quite an ovation on being recognized

Seventh visit to England

Mendelssohn's popularity in London

[1] *Musical World*, 1842, p. 185.

at a concert. Sir Robert Peel and Lord Wharncliffe were near him when the outburst of applause took place, a circumstance of which he was "immensely proud." He played the organ at Christ Church, Newgate Street, when he was nearly suffocated by the thronging admirers, and at Exeter Hall he played "before three thousand people, who shouted hurrahs and waved their handkerchiefs, and stamped with their feet till the hall resounded with the uproar.[1] Then he writes of Mrs. Butler (Fanny Kemble), how splendidly she recited Shakespeare's *Antony and Cleopatra* at Chorley's. Chorley was then living at Victoria Square, and among his visitors were Mendelssohn, Liszt, Madame Viardot-Garcia, Miss Mitford, Lady Blessington, Bryan Procter, Browning, Kenyon, and others.

Felix with his wife paid a brief visit to Manchester to see their cousins, but were back in time for the crowning incident of the visit. On the evening of June 20th Felix was sent for by the Queen, and the visit to Buckingham Palace was repeated on the 9th of July; but more of this in another place.

Visits the Queen

On the 10th of July Felix and his wife left London, and spent the summer holiday chiefly in Switzerland. In September, a fortnight was spent at Frankfort. Ferdinand Hiller, with his wife, had returned from Italy, and Charles Hallé was there in the course of a concert tour. Hallé refers to it thus: "At Frankfort I

[1] "Mendelssohn's Letters from 1833 to 1847," p. 259.

had the happiness to meet Mendelssohn, and to spend a few weeks closely associated with him and rich in musical delight. At the concert I gave, he and Hiller played with me Bach's triple concerto in D minor, and at Hiller's house, where we usually met, I became acquainted with the Scotch Symphony, then unpublished, of which he had just finished the admirable arrangement as a pianoforte duet, which we played over and over again from the manuscript."[1] It was through Hiller's good offices that Felix took part in the concert, which brought Hallé both profit and honour. Felix, for his part, did a good turn for his friend Hiller, by negotiating with Simrock for the publication of some of his works—a generous deed kept secret until the letter was made public in 1863.[2]

On the 25th of September Mendelssohn went to Leipzig, and conducted the first Gewandhaus Concert, October 2nd, and then went on to Berlin. Things were not progressing at all satisfactorily there. A sort of compromise was arrived at. The Academy of Arts scheme was abandoned, and Felix asked to accept office as Director of the Cathedral Choir, which, with a small picked orchestra, was to be available for church festivals, and to form the nucleus of an organization for special grand concerts. Meanwhile, Felix was free to reside where he chose until he

A new office

[1] "Life of Hallé," p. 71.

[2] Hiller, p. 188; "Mendelssohn's Letters from 1833 to 1847," p. 271.

was actually wanted, and so November found him and his family again settled in Leipzig. The new appointment involved the resignation of the office of Kapellmeister to the King of Saxony which had recently been offered him. Mendelssohn had an interview with the King on the subject, and again pressed the matter of the music school in Leipzig. He had the gratification of being able to tell his friend Klingemann, in November, that the King had granted his request, and that the Conservatorium was to be organized that very winter.[1]

The stipend Mendelssohn was now to receive from the King of Prussia was 1500 thalers per annum, and for this sum he was to compose the music for the concerts. The works already commissioned were *The Midsummer Night's Dream*, *The Tempest*, *Œdipus Coloneus*, and *Athalie*. There were the arrangements for the new Conservatorium, the proofs of *Antigone*, and the "Scotch" Symphony, the "frightful heap of letters," the practical rewriting of the *Walpurgisnacht*, visitors without number, and yet amid all these distractions he could find time to interest himself in the affairs of his humble friend Michael, of the Krone Inn, Meiringen, who wanted his Swiss hostelry to be named in "Murray."

But another dark shadow was soon to cross his life-path. On December 4th he received from the King his official nomination as General Music Director, and he fixed on the 17th for the journey to Berlin to settle in

1 "Mendelssohn's Letters from 1833 to 1847," p. 285.

person with Masson. On the 11th he wrote to his mother a joyous letter. The music school was to make a beginning the next February; the Bach monument had now "become very beautiful," and was almost ready for unveiling; these two desires of his heart were now realized. He concludes with: "This is a hallowed day for us all" (it was his father's birthday), "with its delightful and memorable recollections; think of me too on this anniversary, as I do of you and him, so long as life endures."[1] The letter never reached his mother, for on the 12th the Angel of Death lightly touched her, and her spirit fled. The end came swiftly and painlessly, as it came to her husband seven years before. Henceforward Mendelssohn had another anniversary to keep sacred.

Death of his mother

[1] "Mendelssohn's Letters from 1833 to 1847," p. 294.

CHAPTER XII

The Conservatorium, Leipzig—Its first professors—The Bach monument—The freedom of the city of Leipzig conferred upon Mendelssohn—The centenary of the Gewandhaus Concerts—Compositions of 1843—*St. Paul* performed at Dresden—Wagner present—Work and worry—Joachim, the wonderful boy-violinist, at Leipzig—Mendelssohn's work at Berlin—Ferdinand Hiller to carry on the Leipzig Concerts—The "Midsummer Night's Dream" music—Production at Potsdam and Berlin—More compositions, 1843-44—Sterndale Bennett and the Edinburgh Professorship of Music—Music in Berlin—Mendelssohn engaged as conductor of the Philharmonic Concerts, London—Eighth visit to England.

It was at the Garden House that the Christmas Eve gatherings took place, but there were no festivities this year. The house became the property of Felix, but he hesitated to put forward any claim, fearing possible unpleasant feeling on the part of his sisters. But he had too much work on hand at this time to indulge his personal feelings, though his bereavement was a heavy affliction. In January, 1843, the prospectus of the new music school was published. The professors for composition and pianoforte were Mendelssohn and Schumann; for harmony and counterpoint, Moritz Hauptmann; for violin and orchestral ensemble, Ferdinand David; for organ,

Leipzig Conservatorium

Carl Ferdinand Becker; and for singing, Christian August Pohlenz. This was a brilliant galaxy of talent, but before the school was opened, Pohlenz was called away by death. A portion of the Gewandhaus was set apart for the new school, and on the 3rd of April it was formally opened. Mendelssohn wrote to Hiller: "I shall have to go to the Gewandhaus three or four times a week and talk about 6-4 chords in the small hall there. I am quite willing to do this for the love of the cause, because I believe it to be a good cause."[1]

Bach monument

On the 23rd of April, the monument to the great Leipzig Cantor, Sebastian Bach, was unveiled, when Felix conducted a concert consisting of Bach's music. The presence at the ceremony of Bach's last surviving grandson, Wilhelm Friedrich Ernst Bach, was not the least interesting incident. Thus Felix witnessed the fulfilment of the two wishes dearest to his heart. The city of Leipzig now conferred on Mendelssohn the freedom of the city, the letters-patent being presented in a beautiful silver-gilt box. The *Athenæum*, commenting on the proceeding, said: "We wish that our English corporations would testify a like respect for those who instruct, or improve, or delight mankind, by conferring like inexpensive honours on such of their townsmen as have become distinguished in literature, in art, or in science." Others may wish the same.

[1] Hiller, p. 201.

DAS ALTE GEBÄUDE DES K. CONSERVATORIUMS DER MUSIK
ZU LEIPZIG

This must have been a happy time for Felix, despite the burden of sorrow he yet had to bear. The concert season at Leipzig had many interesting features. On February 2nd the revised *Walpurgisnacht* was performed, when the overture and several numbers were "encored over and over again; and the whole performance was received with enthusiasm approaching delirium."[1] Then, two days later, February 4th, an "extra" concert was devoted to the works of Berlioz, who was on a visit to Leipzig. His overture "King Lear," among the pieces then given, was repeated at the concert for the poor, February 23rd. A symphony by Niels Gade had been taken in hand in January, and was produced on March 2nd. This symphony, No. 1, in C minor, Op. 5, was the first work by Gade that had been heard at the Gewandhaus, and it made a favourable impression. Mendelssohn's friendly expressions in more than one letter must have gladdened the heart of the young composer.

Gewandhaus Concerts

The centenary of the Gewandhaus Concerts was celebrated on March 9th. Mendelssohn chose the programme from the works of former cantors or directors, and included Sebastian Bach's Suite for flute and strings; the motet, *Ein' feste Burg*, by Johann Friedrich Doles; and compositions by J. A. Hiller and Schicht. Moritz Hauptmann conducted a performance of a *Kyrie* and *Gloria* of his own, and Mendelssohn conducted his 114th

[1] *Musical World*, 1843, p. 104.

Psalm. This period, too, was rich in compositions. The music to "The Midsummer Night's Dream" was finished, the choruses for Racine's *Athalie*, the Sonata for pianoforte and violoncello, in D, Op. 58, Psalm 98, anthems, songs, and various other pieces, all were completed during this year. Mendelssohn did not leave Leipzig during the summer. He was invited to conduct a performance of *St. Paul* at Dresden in April. This took place on Palm Sunday, and Wagner, who was present, wrote a most appreciative note on the work. This paper was only discovered in the year 1898, in the Royal Library, Berlin.[1] Wagner had, only two months before, been appointed *Kapellmeister* to the Court of Saxony. In July, Herr von Masson sent Felix a commission to arrange for chorus and orchestra the chorale *Herr Gott, dich loben wir*, for the celebration of the thousandth anniversary of the empire, and this necessitated a visit to Berlin. He went to the capital on August 1st, and the performance took place in the cathedral on Sunday, August 6th. All this time he was worried with correspondence relating to his official position, and the newly founded *Conservatorium* caused him some anxious moments. Even in the month of the opening, April, he wrote to Moscheles that the Direction wanted to build, and all the scholars wanted to compose and theorise, whereas he, Felix, thought for

Compositions of 1843

[1] "Wagner's Prose Works" (Ellis), vol. viii. p. 279.

the first ten years the two rooms they had, and vigorous practical work, were quite sufficient.[1]

Joseph Joachim, then a boy of twelve, came to Leipzig from Vienna, where he had been a pupil of Joseph Böhm. He played at a concert given at the Gewandhaus by Madame Viardot on August 19th. Mendelssohn had by this time returned from Berlin, and at the concert accompanied young Joachim's solo (a rondo by De Beriot) on the pianoforte, and also took part with Madame Schumann in a performance of her husband's Andante and variations for two pianos, the work then being in manuscript. Joachim stayed at Leipzig for six years, and Mendelssohn, as long as he lived, was in closest friendship with the young artist.

Joachim

Felix had not been in Leipzig many days before he received a communication from Berlin, with particulars of the concerts the King desired to have in September. *Antigone*, *The Midsummer Night's Dream*, and *Athalie* were to be performed. This threw an immense amount of work upon Felix, as the scores were not ready. But the performances were postponed. As Mendelssohn seemed likely to be in Berlin all the winter, it was arranged that Ferdinand Hiller should be appointed conductor of the Gewandhaus Concerts for the ensuing season. He arrived in Leipzig in good time, and Felix remained for the first concert, October 1st, when he played his Concerto in G minor,

Hiller

[1] "Mendelssohn's Letters from 1833 to 1847," p. 308.

which David allowed Hiller to conduct—a great compliment, as it was David's function to conduct all solos with orchestral accompaniment. Hiller says there was a slight constraint at their first meeting, and Felix confessed to Cécile and David "that he felt rather a pang at seeing the person who was to fill the place he so loved and so unwillingly gave up."[1] But that did not disturb the friendship existing between them.

Production of "The Midsummer Night's Dream"

After all the changes in the arrangements, *Antigone* was performed on September 19th, Mendelssohn conducting. "The Midsummer Night's Dream" was produced at the New Palace, Potsdam, on October 14th, Hiller, David, Gade, and the "young prodigy," Joachim, going from Leipzig on purpose to witness the performance. Hiller said it enchanted him. Fanny Hensel wrote to her sister Rebecka, then in Rome: "Never did I hear an orchestra play so *pianissimo*. The dead-march for Thisbe and Pyramus is really stupendous; I could scarcely believe up to the last that Felix would have the impudence to bring it before the public, for it is exactly like the mock preludes he plays when you cannot get him to be serious."[2] The play was given at the King's Theatre, Berlin, on October 18th, and three nights following. The music was universally admired, but the play puzzled the audience. Some folk voted it vulgar. But the Mendelssohn family understood it. To use Fanny's own words: "They

[1] Hiller, p. 211. [2] "Mendelssohn Family," vol. ii. p. 217.

were really brought up on the 'Midsummer Night's Dream,' and Felix especially had made it his own."

These performances over, Mendelssohn was once more back in Leipzig. On October 26th, Gade conducted a second performance of his Symphony in C minor, and G. A. Macfarren's overture to "Chevy Chase" was produced. On the 30th, at the Pension-Fund Concert, Felix joined Madame Schumann and Ferdinand Hiller in yet another performance of Bach's Triple Concerto in D minor; and there was a special farewell concert on November 18th, when Mendelssohn played, with Robert Wittmann, his new Sonata for pianoforte and violoncello, and took the first viola part, Gade being second, in his Octet. A week later, Felix was settled, with his family, in the old home at Berlin.

Macfarren

The winter of 1843–44 gave Felix full occupation. He conducted, alternately with Taubert, the weekly symphony concerts; composed several Psalms for the grand services at the cathedral, among them Psalms 43, 22, and 2; and in January, 1844, finished, for his friend Mr. W. Bartholomew, the soprano solo and chorus, "Hear my Prayer."[1] About October, 1843, Fanny Hensel resumed her musical *matinées*, and there was much social gaiety during the season. Mendelssohn forgot his official worries in the society of his friends, and entered with zest into

"Hear my Prayer"

[1] First performed at Miss Mounsey's Sacred Concert, Crosby Hall, January 8, 1845.

all the amusements of the hour. His correspondence was a great tax upon his time, and the amount of letter-writing he got through was extraordinary. Before he left Leipzig he wrote a long letter to the Town Council, asking for an increase of pay for the orchestra, and suggesting various reforms in the regulations. In December, 1843, hearing that his friend Sterndale Bennett was a candidate for the Professorship of Music in the University of Edinburgh, Mendelssohn wrote a strong letter of recommendation.[1] This testimonial Mendelssohn supported by other letters; but, as is well known, the Professorship was conferred upon Henry Hugo Pierson. In December, too, Felix was in correspondence with the Directors of the London Philharmonic Society, who desired to engage him as conductor for the season of 1844. Writing to Sterndale Bennett in January, 1844, Mendelssohn states that he cannot leave Berlin until after Easter. He had to conduct the music at the great festivals of the Church. His Psalm 98 was sung in the cathedral on New Year's Day, 1844; and Psalm 22 on Good Friday. In February, Miss Birch, "an English singer, who sings just like Clara Novello,"[2] appeared with success at one of the weekly

Sterndale Bennett testimonial

[1] This letter was published in the *Musical World* of February 15, 1844; it is also given in full in Grove's "Dictionary of Music and Musicians," vol. ii. p. 283.

[2] Letter from Fanny to Rebecka. "Mendelssohn Family," vol. ii. p. 260.

soirées, and Beethoven's Choral Symphony was performed at the last concert, March 27th. On Palm Sunday, *Israel in Egypt* was given in the garrison church, with about 450 performers. The preparation of these works almost prostrated Felix, and as if this was not enough, he had another vexatious episode with the officials at the Court. The King wished Mendelssohn to compose music to the *Eumenides* of Æschylus, and when Mendelssohn pointed out to Councillor Tieck that it was an almost impracticable problem, yet he would attempt it, this was construed into a refusal, and some unpleasant correspondence followed. Directly after Easter, however, Felix and his family removed to Frankfort, and negotiations being completed with the Philharmonic Society, he set off early in May, and once more found himself in that "smoky nest," London, and was received by his old friend, Karl Klingemann, at 4, Hobart Place. This was his eighth visit to England.

Eighth visit to London

CHAPTER XIII

Mendelssohn and the Philharmonic Concerts, 1844—Joachim in London—*Début* of Piatti—Production of the music to "A Midsummer Night's Dream"—The Walpurgis Night—A busy time for Felix—Rest after worry—The violin concerto finished—An impromptu concert at Soden—Gade—Jenny Lind—Felix leaves Berlin—Compositions, 1844–45—Invitation to conduct the Birmingham Festival, 1846—Production of *Œdipus in Colonus—Antigone* in London—Moscheles accepts invitation to Leipzig—Mendelssohn a teacher in the Conservatorium—Festivals at Aix-la-Chapelle, Liége, and Cologne—Festivities and serenades—Spohr and Wagner at Leipzig—Oratorio, *Elijah*, completed—Mendelssohn in London—Rehearsals — Mendelssohn arrives in Birmingham — A curious coincidence.

Philharmonic Concerts, 1844

OWING to his inability to leave Berlin earlier, Mendelssohn's engagement with the Philharmonic Society was limited to the direction of the last five concerts. He had previously written to his friend Bennett to let him have at any rate "some fine Symphonies and Overtures" to conduct for his *début*,[1] so the programme of the first concert, May 13th, contained Mozart's Symphony in E flat, and Mendelssohn's "Scotch" Symphony. At this concert Bennett played his own Concerto in C

[1] Hogarth, p. 128.

minor. The new work was Beethoven's *Leonora* overture, No. 1, never before heard in London. Mendelssohn's young friend Joachim, strongly recommended, had already made his mark in London,[1] and at the fifth concert, May 27th, made quite a sensation as the soloist in Beethoven's violin concerto. The whole of the music to "A Midsummer Night's Dream" was given at this concert, and it made such an impression that it was repeated at the next concert, June 10th, when Her Majesty, Prince Albert, and the King of Saxony were present. At the concert of June 24th Felix played Beethoven's Concerto in G, and at the last concert, July 8th, the *Walpurgisnacht* was produced. The Philharmonic season was most brilliant, and was signalized not only by the production of Mendelssohn's compositions, but by the introduction of works by Bach—orchestral Suite in D; Beethoven—the overture *Leonora*, and a selection from "The Ruins of Athens." Then, at the concert of June 24th, Alfredo Piatti made his first appearance, though his actual *début* took place at Mrs. Anderson's concert, on May 31st, given in the concert-room of Her Majesty's Theatre.

"Walpurgisnacht" produced in London

Début of Piatti

Mendelssohn's reception in London was more cordial than ever. As conductor of the Philharmonic Concerts, he won the warm regard of directors and orchestra, though his discipline was very strict. The *Athenæum*

[1] He played at the concert of the *Societa Armonica*, April 22nd, and at the Melodists' Club on the 25th.

regarded his appointment as virtually amounting to a reconstruction of the Society. It was hoped that he would be engaged for the next season; but he was destined to conduct only one more Philharmonic Concert, in 1847, a few months before his death. Social functions were pressed upon Mendelssohn to such a degree that he never had an hour to himself. In addition to conducting the Philharmonic Concerts, he was constantly assisting at the concerts of his brother artists. On the very day of his arrival (May 8th), he played over with Moscheles his Variations in B flat, for four hands, and during the same month went through a good deal of music in private. With Moscheles and Thalberg he took part in Bach's Triple Concerto in D minor, on June 1st, and played in the same at Ernst's concert, July 5th, his colleagues being Moscheles and Döhler. He gave an extemporaneous performance at Crosby Hall on June 3rd, and again on the 15th at an invitation concert of the Society of British Musicians. On the 14th he assisted at Benedict's annual concert, when the programme contained thirty-eight items; acted as accompanist at Sterndale Bennett's concert on the 25th—the band being detained at an opera rehearsal—and conducted afterwards; accompanied Miss Dolby in Schubert's *Erlkönig* at François Cramer's benefit on the 27th; and conducted *St. Paul* at Exeter Hall on the 28th, with a repetition on July 5th. But this does not exhaust the list of his engagements. He found time, moreover, for a visit to Manchester, and amid all his distractions was not altogether idle with his pen. He wrote a *scena* for Henry Phillips, undertook the editing of *Israel in Egypt* for the London Handel Society, and being informed from Berlin that his *Athalie* was to be produced almost immediately, set to work to write the overture, which he completed on June 13th. This turned out to be another capricious arrangement, as the performance was postponed for a year. There was a farewell *soirée* at the house of Klingemann on July 9th, when Felix played his *Variations Sérieuses*, and with Moscheles the jointly produced variations in *Preciosa*.

Well-earned holiday

The next day he left London, and on the 13th was with his wife and family at Soden, near Frankfort. There he spent a few months in happy repose. But he was, even then, far from being idle. He had promised to conduct the Bavarian Palatinate Festival at Zweibrücken, and that occupied him on July 31st and following day. In September he finished his violin concerto, which he had begun to think of in 1838. His friend Moscheles, being at Frankfort, finds his way to Soden, and Felix insists on getting up a concert—"though there is a regular congress of pianists here."[1] This takes place on September 25th, and the two play the *Hommage à Handel* to a crowded audience.

Conducts festival at Zweibrücken

The direction of the Gewandhaus Concerts, 1844-45, was confided to Niels W. Gade, and Felix intended

[1] "Life of Moscheles," vol. ii. p. 121.

passing the winter at Frankfort. To do this he had to obtain permission from Berlin. At the end of September he returned thither, and begged the King to release him from all official duties, and allow him simply to undertake such commissions as His Majesty might command. The King assented, and Mendelssohn's stipend—he wished to resign that—was fixed at 1000 thalers, and he was free to reside where he pleased.

He stayed with the Hensels while in Berlin, and was a frequent visitor to the house of Professor Wichmann, the sculptor. There he met Magnus, the painter, Taubert, Werder, Count Redern, and many of his old friends. At a *soirée* given by Madame Wichmann on October 21st, Mendelssohn first saw Jenny Lind. In a letter the great singer thus alludes to the event: "Last night I was invited to a very pleasant and elegantly furnished house, where I saw and spoke to Mendelssohn Bartholdy, and he was incredibly friendly and polite, and spoke of my 'great talent.'"[1]

Jenny Lind

Felix conducted a few of the symphony *soirées*, and, by request of the King, a performance of *St. Paul* at the *Sing-Akademie*, on November 28th. After the general rehearsal, his friends gave him a pretty serenade, and there was a crowded attendance at the performance, "the whole music-loving population of Berlin being present, and everybody in a state of distress at Mendelssohn's going away, though they had all, or nearly all,

[1] "Jenny Lind" (Holland and Rockstro), vol. i. p. 201.

contributed to make him go."[1] Felix left Berlin on November 30th, his departure being hastened by the illness of his youngest boy, Felix. The child recovered, but the long attack of measles nearly proved fatal. At this time there was an epidemic of sickness in the Mendelssohn family. Rebecka was ill, in Rome, and her husband had a violent attack of Roman fever. Then Paul's little daughter was taken dangerously ill in October, and in the spring of 1845 Hensel was seriously ill.

During the autumn of 1844, and the winter and spring following, Felix got through a great amount of work. His letters to the London publishers, Coventry and Hollier, from August, 1844, are full of details concerning a series of Bach's organ works, which Felix was editing, and by April, 1845, it is evident that he had finished the six organ sonatas. Many songs, and "Songs without Words," belong to this time. In March, 1845, Felix writes to his sisters: "A symphony and a trio are begun, and I have an idea for a new oratorio." This probably refers to the fragment *Christus*, for *Elijah* was already far advanced, at least as to the plan of the work.

Compositions, 1844-45

Moscheles was at Leipzig in December, 1844, and was approached by Schleinitz with a view to accept a post in the *Conservatorium*, but nothing then came of the matter. In March, 1845, further communications passed between Minister Eichhorn and Councillor Müller of Berlin and Felix relative to the musical section

[1] "Mendelssohn Family," vol. ii. p. 302.

of the Academy, and the proposed setting of the choruses of *Agamemnon*, the *Choëphoræ*, and the *Eumenides*, Felix declaring the task beyond the power of any living musician to fulfil conscientiously. He had, however, already completed the scores of *Œdipus Coloneus*, and *Athalie*, and these he offered at any time for performance. The matter seems to have ended here, and though the King may have been disappointed, His Majesty graciously accepted the situation.

On March 13th Mendelssohn's violin concerto was played for the first time at the Gewandhaus Concerts, by Ferdinand David, but the composer did not leave Frankfort for the occasion. In June the committee of the Birmingham Festival passed a resolution inviting Mendelssohn to conduct the festival of 1846, and to provide a new oratorio, or other music, at the celebration. In June, too, Felix received an intimation that the King of Saxony desired him to resume his position at Leipzig. According to Devrient there was some intention of securing Mendelssohn for Dresden, and even of transferring the *Conservatorium* to that city.[1] But nothing came of either project. By September, 1845, Felix was once more in Leipzig, residing this time at Königstrasse, No. 3, his last earthly home. He conducted the first Gewandhaus Concert, October 5th, and was received with a flourish of trumpets from the orchestra, and a storm of applause

Invitation to the Birmingham Festival of 1846

Again at Leipzig

[1] Devrient, p. 264, *et seq.*

from the audience. Madame Schumann played at this concert. Miss Dolby appeared at the concert of October 23rd, and Jenny Lind made her *dèbut* on December 4th. After the first concert Felix left for Berlin for the production of his *Œdipus Coloneus.* It was first performed at Potsdam, November 1st, and *Athalie* at Charlottenburg on the 30th of the month.[1] Both works were subsequently given in Berlin. It is curious that about this time it was stated that the house of Moses Mendelssohn had been purchased by the Jewish communion, for conversion into a free school for the children of poor Jews.[2]

Œdipus Coloneus

In October Mendelssohn wrote to Mr. Moore saying he was uncertain of having his oratorio finished in time for the festival of the next year; but in December, when he was back at Leipzig, he wrote: "I have now made up my mind to come to Birmingham in August; but I wish to conduct only my own music, as in former years, and have nothing to do with the other parts of the programme."[3] That his other friends in England had not forgotten him was evident from the production of *Antigone* at Covent Garden, on January 2nd, with Miss Vandenhoff as the heroine. In March Felix was applied to for his *Œdipus.* "I have referred them to the King of Prussia."[4] His violin concertc was performed on December 23rd,

"*Antigone*" *in London*

[1] *Musical World*, 1845, p. 608. [2] *Athenæum*, 1845, p. 1223.
[3] "Recollections of Felix Mendelssohn" (Polko), p. 238.
[4] Letter to his sisters. "Mendelssohn Family," vol. ii. p. 317.

at one of Mr. Henry Lincoln's lectures at the Western Library Institution. A Herr Kreutzer was the violinist, but there was only a pianoforte accompaniment.[1] Its introduction, with orchestra, was at the Philharmonic Concert of June 29, 1846, Camille Sivori being the soloist. Moscheles, towards the end of December, received an important letter from Felix, wishing to know if any result was to be looked for after their frequent discussions on the Leipzig appointment. On January 2, 1846, Moscheles receives a formal offer, and later another letter from Felix; and on the 25th his reply is a letter of acceptance. "When you do come," Felix wrote, "I'll have some houses painted rose-colour, but your arrival alone will give a rose-coloured tinge to the old place."[2]

Mendelssohn a teacher

In January, 1846, Mendelssohn himself undertook two classes for pianoforte, and one for composition; and he threw himself with enthusiasm into his self-imposed task. All this while, too, he was hard at work upon his oratorio, *Elijah*, and even as late as May 23rd was corresponding with Schubring in relation to the text. The first part was quite finished by this time. At the beginning of the year he had accepted a commission to compose a *Lauda Sion* for a festival at Liége, and this he finished in February; for a festival at Cologne, he composed a setting of Schiller's *An die Künstler*. The concert season

"Lauda Sion" and "Festgesang"

[1] *Musical World*, 1845, p. 618; *Athenæum*, 1845, p. 1250.

[2] "Life of Moscheles," vol. ii. pp. 149–153.

at Leipzig was exceptionally brilliant, and kept Felix incessantly employed. Indeed, this seems to have been the most active period of his busy life; but it could not last, for already the sword was wearing out the scabbard. At the concert of April 12th, Jenny Lind sang, and Felix played her accompaniment, and also Beethoven's Sonata in C sharp minor. This is generally supposed to have been his last appearance in public as a pianist; but he played once more at the Gewandhaus, July 19th, when he took part, with Ferdinand David, in a performance of Beethoven's *Kreutzer* Sonata.[1]

Last performance at Leipzig

The Lower Rhine Festival was held at Aix-la-Chapelle, May 31st, and June 1st and 2nd. Jenny Lind sang in the *Creation* and *Alexander's Feast*, and, at the Artists' concert, the last day, Mendelssohn's *Auf Flügeln des Gesanges* and *Frühlingslied*. Her singing produced such an effect that the meeting was afterwards known as the *Jenny-Lind-Fest*. Mendelssohn conducted the festival, and came in for his share of the honours. Then he went to Düsseldorf, where he was serenaded twice, as the two *Liedertafeln* there hated each other so much that they would not combine. He found much to sadden him there. His friend Rietz was so badly treated by the musicians of the place that he had made up his mind to leave.[2]

1 "Life of Jenny Lind," vol. i. p. 377, note; also the Statistics of the Gewandhaus Concerts.

2 In 1847, Rietz was appointed conductor at the theatre, Leipzig.

The *Fête-Dieu* was held in the Church of St. Martin, Liége, on June 11th. Felix only arrived just before the rehearsal of his *Lauda Sion*. He did not conduct the performance, which was very bad, owing to the inadequate means at disposal. The clerical authorities would not permit women to sing, and the boys were persistently out of tune. Chorley was present, and sent home a long account of the festival.[1] From Chorley's notice it appears that the commission came to Mendelssohn from an enthusiastic amateur of Liége, M. Mathis-Gheysens, and out of delicacy to him the management was left in his hands. Felix must have gone on immediately to Cologne, for the first rehearsal of the combined choirs took place on the 13th. The first festival of the German-Flemish Vocal Associations began on the 14th. There were over two thousand singers, a band of ninety, and the meetings were held in the Gürzenich Hall. The gentlemen had to stand, to economize space. At the first concert Felix conducted his cantata, and the "Hymn to Bacchus" from *Antigone*. No bad prelude to the drinking-bouts which were to come after the concert, as Chorley remarked. On the night of the 15th the societies gave Mendelssohn a serenade with a torch-light procession, and presented him with a gold medal, and an exquisitely emblazoned

Production of "Lauda Sion"

Production of "An die Künstler"

[1] *Athenæum*, 1846, p. 634. See also "Modern German Music," vol. ii. p. 320.

address. Felix made a speech—the ceremony took place in front of the house where he was staying—and Chorley wrote: "I doubt if his life of many successes ever yielded him a moment which pleased and touched him more."[1] The whole period was one round of excitement, and Felix's friends were literally killing him with kindness.

Presentations and processions

He was hardly back again at Leipzig before he was visited by Spohr, who had arranged to meet Wagner in that city. He left on the 26th, and Mendelssohn refers to the fatigue his visit caused at that time, though he was always glad to have him as a guest. There was an extra Gewandhaus Concert expressly arranged for Spohr, and of his music exclusively. The genially egotistic "Autobiography" of the great violinist—for such assuredly he was—ended in 1838, but the record was continued by his family. The account of an evening with the Mendelssohns in this June of 1846 makes mention of the performance of two of Spohr's quartets, among them the newest—"on which occasion Mendelssohn and Wagner read from the score with countenances expressive of their delight."[2] Happy Spohr!

Spohr and Wagner

Toward the end of May, Felix sent the whole of the first part of *Elijah* to Moscheles, and by him it was played over, at his house, to a select party on Sunday, June 14th.

[1] "Modern German Music," vol. ii. p. 349.
[2] Spohr's "Autobiography," vol. ii. pp. 277, 278.

This was the first rehearsal of any of the music. The *Birmingham Herald* at the end of June announced the completion and arrival of the whole work, but that could only have referred to the chorus parts. The choral rehearsals were conducted by Mr. James Stimpson, and when "Thanks be to God" was first tried, the dissonances at "But the Lord was above them, and Almighty," puzzled the chorus-master, and a close scrutiny of the separate parts was made before the startling harmonies were accepted. All through July and the early part of August, letters were passing between Mendelssohn and Bartholomew respecting the English text.[1] On Monday evening, August 17th, Felix was, for the ninth time, in London, and, on Wednesday the 19th, there was a private rehearsal at Moscheles' house. This was followed by band rehearsals at the Hanover Square Rooms on the Thursday and Friday. On Sunday the 23rd Mendelssohn and Moscheles arrived in Birmingham. Was it by accident or design that a long review of Handel's *Israel in Egypt*, as edited by Mendelssohn for the London Handel Society, appeared in the *Athenæum* of August 22nd?

First rehearsal of "Elijah"

Back to England

[1] "History of *Elijah*," pp. 52, *et seq.*

CHAPTER XIV

Birmingham Musical Festival of 1846—Production of *Elijah*—Vagaries of festival committees—Mendelssohn to the rescue—Publication of *St. Paul* in French—Moscheles at Leipzig—Mendelssohn engaged on an opera, and a new oratorio—The Conservatorium and its work—Tenth visit of Felix to England—Performance of *Elijah* as revised and rewritten—Mendelssohn's last visit to Birmingham—An amusing sequel—Jenny Lind in London—Mendelssohn's last public appearance—Death of Fanny Hensel—Days of gloom and broken health—Latest compositions—Felix touches the organ for the last time—At home once more—Brief visit to Berlin—Last labours—The beginning of the end—Death of Mendelssohn—Funeral ceremonies—The last journey—Tributes of loving homage.

"*Elijah year*"

THE Birmingham Musical Festivals have given to the world more than one masterpiece, but the year 1846 is still looked upon as the epoch of its greatest glory. It is difficult at this time to realize the impression the production of *Elijah* created in the world of music. Locally, "*Elijah* year" is still a beacon-mark on the shores of time.

Monday morning, August 24th, was devoted to a full rehearsal of the oratorio, the composer being most enthusiastically received. Moscheles, who had been appointed conductor-in-chief of the festival, became so ill on Monday that Mendelssohn undertook the evening rehearsal for him. On Tuesday the festival opened with Haydn's *Creation*, the performance of which Moscheles was sufficiently recovered to conduct. The Tuesday evening concert was given up in order to secure an extra full rehearsal of *Elijah*. The promoters of the provincial festivals have been charged with placing charity first and art second in consideration; the Birmingham Committee of 1846 deserve praise, therefore, for sacrificing the pecuniary to the artistic result on this occasion—an instance never known before, nor since!

Production of "Elijah"

On Wednesday morning, August 26th, the anxiously-looked-for event came off, and the new oratorio was introduced to the world. There was a scene of extraordinary enthusiasm, and the sun's rays brilliantly illumined the beautiful hall as the composer stepped upon the platform.[1] The principal vocalists were Madame Caradori-Allan, Miss M. B. Hawes, Mr. Charles Lockey, and Herr Staudigl. The Misses Anne and Martha Williams, Miss Bassano, and Messrs. J. W. Hobbs, Henry Phillips, and William Machin sang in the double quartet and other concerted numbers, the sisters singing the duet (as it then was) "Lift thine eyes." Dr. Gauntlett was specially engaged for the organ in *Elijah*, Mr. Stimpson, chorus-master, giving up his official post, and turning over the leaves for the doctor. The band numbered 125 (93 strings), of whom 85 only went from London,

[1] Benedict, p. 52.

FACSIMILE OF PAGE OF "ELIJAH."

Birmingham and the district providing the remainder. The chorus consisted of 79 sopranos, 60 altos (the contralto was then unknown in the chorus), 60 tenors, and 72 basses. This was the last Birmingham Festival at which the chorus was placed in front of the band.[1] Of the soloists Herr Staudigl gave by far the finest performance. The work of the chorus and orchestra was good throughout. Mendelssohn was delighted with the rendering of his work, and in his letters to his brother Paul, and to Frau Doctorin Frege, he said no work of his ever went so admirably at a first performance, and he doubted whether he should ever hear one so good again.[2] His reference to the young English tenor (Mr. Lockey) was generous. No fewer than eight numbers were encored, and the composer evidently enjoyed this part of his triumph as much as did the audience. But there was "the fly in the ointment." Felix was greatly annoyed when, in 1837, his *St. Paul* was followed by a miscellaneous selection. In a letter to Moscheles, dated July 28, 1846, he wrote: "To be sure, it must rest with the committee whether they will give one or two pieces before; but, however that may be, don't let us have a ragout afterwards."[3]

Supplement to "Elijah"

[1] The change to the present arrangement was made in 1849, when the late Sir Michael (then Mr.) Costa first appeared as conductor.

[2] "Mendelssohn's Letters from 1833 to 1847," pp. 373-376.

[3] "Mendelssohn's Letters to I. and C. Moscheles," p. 277.

The committee's response was this:

PART THIRD.

Aria, Signor Mario, "A te fra tanti affani," *Davide Penitente*, Mozart; Recitative and Aria, Madame Grisi, "Ah parlate," *Il sacrificio d'Abramo*, Cimarosa; *Coronation Anthem*, "The King shall rejoice," Handel.

So was the graceful act of the Tuesday evening neutralized. Let this record stand as an example of the dark and devious ways of festival managers in the past; the moral it points is, happily, not needed in the present, nor will be in the future.

On the Thursday evening of the festival Felix took part, with Moscheles, in the latter's duo for two pianofortes, *Hommage à Handel*, and conducted a performance —unhappily a very indifferent one—of his "Midsummer Night's Dream" music. On the Friday morning, the final chorus from Handel's *Zadok the Priest* was the concluding piece. The programme was well advanced when it was discovered that there was no music for the recitative preceding the chorus, the words of which were printed in the books in the hands of the audience. Mendelssohn, who was a listener in the great gallery, was approached with a view to the solution of the difficulty. He at once proceeded to the retiring-room, and wrote the recitative for tenor, with accompaniment of strings and two trumpets; the parts were quickly copied, and Mr. Lockey and the instrumentalists gave the music

An impromptu composition

with complete satisfaction to the audience, who maybe thought it was Handel's.[1]

An interesting, though brief, record of the festival appeared in a French paper, in which Mendelssohn is credited with being the author of the German text of the oratorio, as well as of the music.[2] By another curious coincidence, immediately under this notice is the announcement of the publication of *St. Paul*, with a French text; and the previous number of the *Revue*, dated August 30th, opens with a study of the work from the pen of M. Maurice Bourges.

"St. Paul" in Paris

Mendelssohn left Birmingham, with Mr. and Mrs. Moscheles, for London, where his only "important business" was a fish dinner at Lovegrove's at Blackwall. Then he stayed with the Beneckes four days at Ramsgate, and on Sunday, September 6th, with Staudigl, crossed the Channel from Dover; rested a day at Ostend because he felt sleepy; another day at Cologne because he was too tired to go on; four days at Horchheim, where his uncle walked him about in the broiling sun, and he felt ashamed to acknowledge his fatigue; then another day at Frankfort because he was weary; and finally arriving at Leipzig, where he did nothing but rest. All this he told in a letter to his sister Fanny

[1] For further details of the production of *Elijah*, the reader is referred to the admirable book by Mr. F. G. Edwards, already quoted.

[2] *Revue Musicale*, 1846, p. 287.

on September 29th [1]—a letter no one can read without feeling that the writer, whether he knew it or not, was broken and worn, at thirty-seven. The pity of it!

Revising "Elijah"

But his rest was of short duration. He soon began the work of revision and improvement in connection with *Elijah.* This he mentions in a letter to his brother, dated October 31st, and in one to Klingemann, of December 6th. In this he writes: "Unluckily I never find out this kind of thing till *post festum.*" [2] Some composers never seem to "find out this kind of thing" at all. Mendelssohn had at this time to compose for the King the whole of the German Liturgy afresh. This was for two four-part choirs. Then he appears to have undertaken the travelling arrangements for his friend Moscheles, who, giving up his splendid position in London, arrived at Leipzig on October 21st, to take up a post in the *Conservatorium.* With such a friend at hand to help and advise, Felix felt himself relieved of much anxiety as well as work. The Gewandhaus Concerts he once more gave up to Gade, only occasionally undertaking the direction himself. His good servant Johann Krebs fell ill, and died in November, distressing Mendelssohn greatly; and he was further worried with correspondence, this time with Lumley, on the everlasting subject of opera, which came to nothing. For some time he had been occupied with a subject provided by Geibel, the

[1] "Mendelssohn Family," vol. ii. p. 333.

[2] "Mendelssohn's Letters from 1833 to 1847," pp. 380–384.

legend of *Loreley*. Chorley surmises that Mendelssohn had Jenny Lind in view when he wrote the principal portion of that work—the *finale* to the first act.[1] But this opera remained a fragment. The compositions of the autumn and winter were chiefly for the cathedral at Berlin, including the Liturgy already mentioned, and one or more motets. He was also preparing a new oratorio, *Christus*. The *Conservatorium* was not neglected. Felix assisted at the examination of candidates for admission at the end of October, and in January, 1847, he drew up an elaborate memorandum on the work of the students, with criticisms and recommendations.[2]

Loreley

Compositions, 1846–47

Christus

The last birthday Mendelssohn was destined to attain was celebrated by his friends in Gerhard's Garden, where Moscheles lived. Later in the month of February—the 27th—he was once more in Dresden, at a Court concert, in his official capacity as Kapellmeister to the King of Saxony. On Good Friday, April 2nd, he conducted a performance of *St. Paul*, at the Church of St. Paul, Leipzig; and on Tuesday, April 13th, with Joachim, he arrived, for the tenth time, in London,[3] and found again a home in the house of his attached friend, Klingemann.

The object of this—unhappily, his last!—visit was to

[1] "Modern German Music," vol. ii. p. 368, note.

[2] "Dictionary of Music and Musicians" (Grove), vol. ii. p. 290.

[3] *Musical World*, 1847, p. 257.

fulfil an engagement with the Sacred Harmonic Society, that body desiring to be the first to perform the revised and improved oratorio, *Elijah*. The first performance took place in Exeter Hall on Friday, April 16th, so there was very little time for the composer to give the finishing touches to the work of preparation. According to Benedict the chorus of the Society was then "most unruly and inefficient."[1] The performance on the part of chorus and band was bad; "such as entirely to confuse outline, form, texture, light and shade, throughout the greater part of the work."[2] Miss Birch, Miss Dolby, and Mr. Henry Phillips replaced the former principals, but Mr. Lockey again took the tenor part. The scathing criticism of the *Athenæum* drew a letter from a chorister of the Sacred Harmonic Society, pointing out the cause of some of the deficiencies of the performance. The first complaint was the meagre supply of copies of the choral parts; two, and in many cases, three singers had to look over one copy! Another complaint was lodged against the method of conducting the rehearsals.[3] Mendelssohn found much to try him in the few days he had for rehearsal.

Sacred Harmonic Society

What he now undertook was enough to tax the powers of the strongest man; the effect upon his enfeebled frame was evident full soon. On Monday, April 19th, he conducted a full rehearsal of *Elijah* in

[1] Benedict, p. 53. [2] *Athenæum*, 1847, p. 441.
[3] *Ibid.*, pp. 473, 474.

the Free Trade Hall, Manchester; another, and the performance—a good one—on the Tuesday, receiving a magnificent ovation. Then back to London for the second performance at Exeter Hall—a great improvement, Chorley admits, upon the first. This was on the 23rd. Three days later, the 26th, Mendelssohn conducted his Symphony in A minor and "Midsummer Night's Dream" music at the Philharmonic Concert, and played Beethoven's Concerto in G. The Queen and Prince Consort were present. Next morning he was off to Birmingham, arriving there at half-past one in the afternoon, just in time for the rehearsal, and conducted *Elijah* in the evening, the concert being for Mr. Stimpson's benefit. He left the next day, the 28th, at half-past nine in the morning, but found time for a chat with his friend Mr. Moore.[1] Arriving in London, he conducted a third performance of *Elijah* that same evening, and a fourth on Friday, the 30th. Six performances of *Elijah* in a fortnight, and all conducted by the composer! Is there such a record in the career of that typical oratorio writer, Handel?[2]

The visit to Birmingham was Mendelssohn's last appearance in the provinces. He refused to take any fee, or accept travelling expenses, giving his services as an

[1] "Reminiscences of Felix Mendelssohn" (Polko), p. 244.

[2] Handel's *Samson* was given eight times during the oratorio season of 1743; *Judas Maccabæus* six times in 1747, and again in 1748, but these alternated with performances of other works. See Rockstro's "Handel," pp. 269–289.

expression of his gratitude for Mr. Stimpson's work in the preparation of *Elijah* for the festival of 1846. This performance was good on the part of all but the band, which was inefficient, and caused Mendelssohn pain and trouble in keeping it together.[1] There was a comical sequel to this Birmingham performance, one that would have made Mendelssohn laugh, as he did at the woodcut in *Punch* "taking off" the performance of *Antigone* in 1845.[2] It may relieve the sadness of the remaining narrative to relate the incident. Big posters were stuck on the walls in many places advertising the performance of *Elijah*. A little after, other posters, relating to a Whitsun trip, were pasted over them, but not covering the lower part. The combination read thus: "The *Odd Fellows* of Birmingham will make an extraordinary trip to Worcester, Gloucester, and Bristol, returning next day. Leader: Mr. Willy. Conductor: Dr. Mendelssohn."[3]

A ludicrous "poster"

On the 1st of May Mendelssohn lunched at the Prussian Embassy, and played; then went to Buckingham Palace, and played for two hours to the Queen and Prince Consort. On Tuesday, the 4th, he accepted the invitation of the Beethoven Quartet Society to hear

[1] *Dramatic and Musical Review*, 1847, p. 224.

[2] "Mendelssohn Family," vol. ii. p. 317. The woodcut is reproduced in "Dictionary of Music and Musicians" (Grove), vol. ii. p. 287.

[3] *Musical World*, 1847, p. 351.

some of his own compositions at their rooms in Harley Street. He took part in the performance of his Trio in C minor, played Beethoven's Thirty-two Variations in the same key, and extemporized. In the evening, at Her Majesty's Theatre, he witnessed the *début* of Jenny Lind, who appeared as Alice, in Meyerbeer's *Robert le Diable*. On the 5th, at the Concert of Ancient Music, director Prince Albert, Mendelssohn played, on the wretched, out-of-tune organ, Bach's Fugue on the name of Bach, a performance characterized by Chorley as "among the marvels of the season."[1] The next day he played to the Bunsens and a large party at the Prussian Embassy, and on the 8th was again summoned to Buckingham Palace, when he took leave of Her Majesty and the Prince Consort. The same evening he left London with the Klingemanns, crossed over to Ostend on the 9th, was detained at Herbesthal, on the Prussian frontier, by a police official who took him for a political offender—a blunder that caused infinite pain and annoyance—and finally arrived at Frankfort, weary and ill.

Jenny Lind's London début

Last public appearance

Pressed to stay a little longer in London, his reply was, "Ah! I wish I may not already have stayed too long here! One more week of this unremitting fatigue, and I should be killed outright!"[2] In his state of complete prostration it needed but little to bring about the worst.

Gloomy forecast

[1] *Athenæum*, 1847, p. 498. [2] Benedict, p. 55.

The blow soon fell. Scarcely had he arrived at Frankfort, than—all too abruptly—he received the news of his sister Fanny's death. With a shriek, he fell senseless to the ground. His own death was directly caused by this sad event, for his physician stated that there was a rupture of a blood-vessel in the head at the moment of this sudden shock.[1]

Death of Fanny Hensel

Fanny Hensel died on Friday, May 14th, while conducting a rehearsal by her little choir of the music for the next Sunday. She was seated at the pianoforte, when suddenly her hands fell powerless by her side. Medical aid was at hand, but death—painless as sudden—occurred at eleven o'clock at night.[2] The blow was terrible to Mendelssohn, for his sister had, artistically, been his second self. The two had been inseparable, had shared each other's confidences, artistic aims, and ambitions. "This will be a changed world for us all now," he wrote to his brother-in-law. And so it proved.

Early in June Felix with his family removed to Baden-Baden, where he was joined by his brother Paul and his brother-in-law Hensel. Later they stayed for some time in various parts of Switzerland, principally at Interlachen. Then, ever thoughtful of others, he wrote a birthday letter to his nephew, Sebastian Hensel: "I must send

A dreary summer

1 "Life of Mendelssohn" (Lampadius), p. 133.

2 "Mendelssohn Family," vol. ii. p. 334.

you my good wishes on your birthday, the most mournful you have yet known."[1] During the summer Felix sought relief in work. Many of the greatest creations in musical art have been wrung from the heart in times of keenest suffering; so Mendelssohn's Quartet in F minor, Op. 80, written at Interlachen, has a depth of expression, a sad passion, not found in his earlier works of the same class. Other compositions, begun or finished during the stay in Switzerland, were the three Motets, Op. 69, the Andante and Scherzo for strings, Op. 81, and some songs. Commissions were pouring in from all sides. The Philharmonic Society of London wanted a new symphony; Liverpool asked for a cantata with which to inaugurate the new concert hall of the Philharmonic Society;[2] and there were projects in connection with Frankfort, Cologne, and other places. None of these, however, came to anything. He did some sketching, and had an occasional bright day; but the atmosphere was one of gloom. His sad forebodings extended beyond his own self to his country, and he fancied dense misty fogs and thunderclouds in the beloved Fatherland.

Relief in work

Final compositions

Hensel and Paul Mendelssohn left in July, but Felix

[1] "Mendelssohn's Letters from 1833 to 1847," p. 392.

[2] In Grove's "Dictionary of Music and Musicians," vol. ii. p. 291, it is stated that the work was desired for the opening of St. George's Hall, but that was a mistake. See *Musical World*, 1848, p. 27. The Philharmonic Hall was opened August 27, 1849.

had other visitors during the summer. Mr. Grote, "whom I am always very glad to see, and listen to,"[1] came early in August, and the last three days of that month Chorley spent in the composer's company. On one of those days the two went to the little village of Ringgenberg on the lake of Brienz, and entered the church. There Felix sat down to the organ for the last time. Chorley wrote: "I feel, when I think of this organ-playing, as if I had taken leave of the greatest music for ever."[2] The next day the friends parted, he much depressed and worn, walking heavily.

Mendelssohn plays the organ for the last time

The family returned to Leipzig in September, reaching home on the 17th. Felix found a new grand pianoforte had been sent to him by Broadwoods, and this gave him great pleasure to play upon. Moscheles found his friend the same as ever in mind, but physically altered, aged, and weakened.[3] Soon after his return to Leipzig, Felix paid a week's visit to Berlin, where the sight of Fanny's rooms—left untouched since her death—upset him, and undid all the good of the holiday in Switzerland. The concert season began on October 3rd, but Felix took no part in the direction, leaving that to his friend Julius Rietz. He seemed to dread publicity, declared that the air of Leipzig—his once beloved city

Home again

Last visit to Berlin

[1] "Mendelssohn's Letters from 1833 to 1847," p. 399.
[2] "Modern German Music," vol. ii. p. 396.
[3] "Life of Moscheles," vol. ii. p. 177.

—stifled him, and talked only of retirement. However, on October 8th, at the Conservatorium examination, he wrote on a slate a thorough-bass exercise to test the pupils; and "whilst they worked it out, he made some charming pen-and-ink sketches. What a sleepless genius!"[1]

Last lesson at the Conservatorium

On the 9th he took a walk with the Moscheleses in the Rosenthal, becoming more cheerful as the morning wore on; and in the evening called upon Madame Frege to consult her about the order of a book of songs he was about to publish—his Op. 71. One of these, the *Nachtlied*, written for the birthday of Conrad Schleinitz, October 1st, was Mendelssohn's last composition. The songs were sung over by Madame Frege, and then Felix wished to hear something from *Elijah*. Madame Frege went for lights, and returning found Felix in a shivering fit, with cold hands, and head aching violently. He went home, but the attack continued, and he was put to bed. By the 12th he had somewhat recovered, and saw Benedict, then in Leipzig; talked to him of the promised performance of *Elijah* at Berlin, begging Benedict to apologize to the authorities for its non-fulfilment. The next day Benedict saw him again—for the last time.[2]

His last composition

On the 25th Felix wrote to his brother: "God be praised, I am now daily getting better,"[3] though he

[1] "Life of Moscheles," vol. ii. p. 179.
[2] Benedict, p. 59.
[3] "Mendelssohn's Letters from 1833 to 1847," p. 402.

thought the visit to Vienna, that day week, was out of the question. *Elijah* was to be produced there, with Jenny Lind as the principal soprano. By the 28th Felix felt so much stronger that he took a walk with his wife, dining heartily afterwards. He wished to go out again, but Cécile persuaded him to abandon the intention. Soon after he had a serious relapse, and on the 30th his brother Paul was summoned from Berlin. An attack on November 3rd robbed him of all consciousness, and in this state he remained till the evening of Thursday, November 4th, when, at twenty-four minutes past nine, the earthly struggle was over, and the spirit returned to God who gave it. Round the death-bed were the wife, brother, David, Moscheles, and Schleinitz. Upon this scene of grief let the curtain be drawn; it is too sacred for description or comment.

Death

The whole population of Leipzig showed the greatest sympathy during his illness, and on the two days after his death "hundreds of mourners pressed into the house to have one last look at the familiar features,"[1] the family offering no hindrance. On Sunday afternoon, the 7th, the body was borne to the Pauliner-kirche, preceded by the *Stadt-Musiker-Corps* playing the "Song without Words," in E minor (Book v. No. 3), specially scored by Moscheles. The pall-bearers were Moscheles, David, Hauptmann, and Gade. The senior student of the *Conservatorium*, M. de Sentis, preceded the bier, bearing

Funeral obsequies

[1] "Life of Mendelssohn" (Lampadius), p. 137.

on a cushion a silver crown, the offering of Mendelssohn's pupils, and his "Ordre pour le mérite." Then followed the professors and pupils of the *Conservatorium*, the members of the Gewandhaus orchestra, the choir of the Thomas-Schule, and the members of the choral societies of the city. Paul Mendelssohn, the chief mourner, with other relatives of the deceased, the functionaries of the Corporation and the University, and various Guilds and Societies, followed the coffin.

After the funeral oration by Pastor Howard, an organ prelude was played, and the chorale "To Thee, O Lord," and the chorus "Happy and blest," from *St. Paul*, were sung, the service concluding with the final chorus from Bach's *Passion according to St. Matthew*. At ten at night the coffin was conveyed to the railway station, followed by a torchlight procession of more than a thousand persons, and a special train bore its sad burden to Berlin. During the night, the train stopped at different places for sorrowing homage to be paid to the departed. At Cöthen, the local choir, directed by Eduard Thiele, sang a chorale, and at Dessau, Friedrich Schneider brought his choir to the station to sing an *Abschiedlied* he had composed for the mournful occasion. Berlin was reached at seven in the morning of November 8th, when the funeral rites were resumed. The cathedral choir received the procession with the chorale "Jesu, meine Freude," and the body was finally placed in the

The last home

Tributes of respect and mourning

family vault in the churchyard of Holy Trinity, just without the Halle gate.

Solemn services and memorial performances were held throughout Germany. At Leipzig the Gewandhaus Concert, which would have taken place in the ordinary course on the 4th, was abandoned, but on the 11th the programme consisted of Mendelssohn's compositions, including his last song, sung by Madame Frege, and ending with Beethoven's *Eroica* Symphony.

In England, where Mendelssohn was revered perhaps more than anywhere else, the grief was universal. In London the Sacred Harmonic Society performed *Elijah* on November 17th. The orchestra was hung with black, and performers and audience wore deep mourning. The "Dead March" in *Saul* preceded the oratorio. Similar tokens of respect were paid by the Festival Choral Society at Birmingham later, and a performance of *Elijah* was given at Manchester in December. Dublin also produced the oratorio, and the press throughout the United Kingdom teemed with sympathetic obituary notices.

CHAPTER XV

Mendelssohn the man—Born on a lucky day—A happy name—Character moulded in childhood—A fascinating young man—Personal appearance—Manner and bearing—Education—Mendelssohn not an enigma—Reveals himself in his correspondence—Family relationships and affection—Attitude to strangers—Kindness to young musicians—A letter of introduction—His love of fun and joking—Independence of character in matters professional—Sensitiveness to slights, but without vindictiveness—Felix and criticism—Weak points—Manly bearing in the company of Royalty—The Queen's compliment to Felix—Inspection of the Royal nursery—Felix and literature and art—Portraits—The family of Felix and Cécile—The Mendelssohns a short-lived family.

GOETHE wrote of Mendelssohn that he was born upon a lucky day. The name Felix was a felicitous definition of his bright, sunny nature and disposition. But was it conferred upon him in his baptism? Natalia (Lady) Macfarren, in a note to the preface of her translation of Devrient's "Recollections," gives the inscription on Mendelssohn's tombstone, as read by Gruneisen in 1868, and in which the name of Felix does not appear, and adds: "Whence the name by which he is endeared to the world, and which so fitly describes him, 'Felix,' has not been told."[1] Be that as it may, the name of

[1] Devrient, Preface, p. vii.

Felix will always be associated with the composer of *Elijah.*

Of his childhood much has already been said. He was brought up and educated at home, and freely mixed with his elders in the social gatherings at his father's house. As a child he was remarkable for personal beauty, and that, with his wonderful talents, would attract the notice of all who came in contact with him. Devrient writes of his "pretty brown curls," but Lobe describes Felix as a beautiful boy, with decidedly Jewish features, slender and supple, with long wavy black locks flowing down his back.[1] Schubring considered that if Felix had had to rough it at a public school, his disposition would have been hardened to a certain extent, and he might not have been so easily offended and out of sorts as happened at times.[2] It is certain that as a boy he was very decided in his opinion and in his expression of it. Whether he was treated with undue deference on account of his social position, or whatever the cause, he was a caustic critic on art and artists. "Over-ripe and almost dogmatic" were his utterances, according to Hiller,[3] though he grew out of much of that in after-life.

As a young man Felix was on the best of terms with himself. The world and he were very good friends, and his social position secured for him advantages denied

[1] Lobe, *Choir,* vol. xiv. p. 385.
[2] Schubring, *Musical World,* 1866, p. 301.
[3] Mendelssohn (Hiller), p. 6.

to most young musicians at the outset of their career. He had, too, the pride of the artist, and once related to Chorley how, on a visit to Goethe at Weimar, he was summoned to play before the Grand Duchess and the Court circle. On his arrival at the Belvidere, with Madame Goethe, he was asked his name by an official, and while the lady passed on, Felix was shown into a small waiting-room where cloaks and wrappings were deposited. There he was told to wait until summoned to the Court presence. He chafed and fumed for half an hour, then seized his hat and rushed out. The servants tried to stop him; he must not go—there will be much displeasure—and so forth. But the youth was off, straight across the fields, to Goethe's house, and the assembly had to go without their pianist. This was very rude, no doubt, but it did a good turn for Hummel. He had hitherto submitted to this menial treatment; henceforth he was shown becoming respect.[1]

When he first visited London, in 1829, Felix was received into society, and made much of in every direction; and the young man of twenty possessed qualities of person and mind that were calculated to attract and fascinate. It was at this age that he was described by Eduard Devrient. "Of middle height, slender frame, and of uncommon muscular power, a capital gymnast, swimmer, walker, rider, and dancer, the leading feature of his outward and inner nature was an extraordinary

Personal appearance and manners

[1] Memoirs of H. F. Chorley, vol. i. pp. 321, 322.

sensitiveness. Excitement stimulated him to the verge of frenzy, from which he was restored by his sound, death-like sleep. His brain had from childhood been taxed excessively, by the university course, study of modern languages, drawing, and much else, and to these were added the study of music in its profoundest sense. . . . His manners were most pleasing. His features, of the Oriental type, were handsome; a high, thoughtful forehead, much depressed at the temples; large, expressive dark eyes, with drooping lids, and a peculiar veiled glance through the lashes; this, however, sometimes flashed distrust or anger, sometimes happy dreaming and expectancy. His nose was arched and of delicate form, still more so the mouth, with its short upper and full under lip, which was slightly protruded and hid his teeth, when with a slight lisp, he pronounced the hissing consonants. An extreme mobility about his mouth betrayed every emotion that passed within."[1]

Education

So, young, handsome, wealthy, it was small wonder that he found the world at his feet. He enjoyed society, and was not insensible to the charms of the gentler sex. He was always falling in love, as his letters show, but no breath of scandal bedimmed the shining brightness of his character, and he was one to be loved. He had his faults, though the glamour of his personality hid them from his friends. Again Devrient must bear witness. "To his friends he was frankly devoted; it

[1] "Recollections" (Devrient), p. 64.

was indeed felicity to be beloved by Felix. At the same time it must be confessed that his affection was exclusive to the utmost; he loved only in the measure as he was loved. This was the solitary dark speck in his sunny disposition. He was the spoilt child of fortune, unused to hardship or opposition; it remains a marvel that egotism did not prevail more than it did over his inborn nobleness and straightforwardness. The atmosphere of love and appreciation in which he had been nurtured was a condition of life to him."[1]

In his later years, the abundant, wavy black hair thinned, and with partial baldness came traces of grey. His sensitiveness brought back much of the old irritability, and he became agitated by the most trifling circumstances. Perhaps no man revealed himself so much as Felix did in his correspondence. He might be said literally to wear his heart upon his sleeve. His varying moods, his petulant outbursts, his playful and tender expressions, are so many indications of his character. He was no philosopher, pondering on the deep, or the obscure, but a bright, healthy participator in the practical things of life. In his domestic relations his character was seen at its best. He was a good son, an affectionate brother, a loving husband and father. As far as biography should be allowed to go, the domestic life of Mendelssohn has been laid bare to the world; but there are sacred recesses into which the public have no

Character

Family life

1 "Recollections" (Devrient), p. 67.

right to peer, and some passages in his letters have been published which ought to have been kept from the vulgar gaze. The relation between father and son may be summed up in one quotation—from a letter written to Schubring, December 6, 1835: "I do not know whether you are aware that, especially for some years past, my father was so good to me, so thoroughly my friend, that I was devoted to him with my whole soul, and during my long absences scarcely ever passed an hour without thinking of him."[1]

His last letter to his mother has already been quoted, and passages have been given showing the affection existing between Felix and his brother and sisters. But a further reference may be permitted with regard to the peculiar relations between Felix and Fanny Hensel, for the two were bound by the ties of art as well as blood. Writing to General von Webern, after Fanny's death, Felix says: "It is indeed true that no one who ever knew my sister can ever forget her through life; but what have not we, her brothers and sister, lost! and I more especially, to whom she was every moment present in her goodness and love; her sympathy being my first thought in every joy; whom she ever so spoiled, and made so proud, by all the riches of her sisterly love, which made me feel all was sure to go well, for she was ever ready to take a full and loving share in everything that concerned me."[2]

[1] "Mendelssohn Family," vol. i. p. 338.
[2] "Mendelssohn's Letters from 1833 to 1847," p. 391.

Happiness

That Mendelssohn was happy in his married life was evident to all who knew him. Cécile, beautiful, gentle, yet with a subtle influence—that of love—exercised a charm over the home circle. The letters of Felix abound with touches that picture the bright domestic scenes, and Cécile is always the central figure. Now she comes upon him with amazement, when, in teaching the little Marie the scale of C, he makes her pass the thumb under the wrong finger.[1] Again, on his last birthday she actually takes part, with her sister, Mrs. Schunck, in a comic dialogue between two lady's-maids, becoming a drawing-room actress for the festive occasion.[2] Then the children are an endless source of interest. At one time he is called from his work to examine a great tower they have built, and on the flat roof of which they have ranged all their slices of bread and jam! "A good idea for an architect," Felix remarks.[3] Then he tells of the four-year-old Paul making bargains with the woman who sells cherries; and at Soden the children are as brown as Moors playing in the garden all day long; and Felix with sketch-book gives himself up to unalloyed enjoyment, and even Cécile indulges in vignettes wherewith to head the letters.[4]

But Mendelssohn, though so genial in disposition,

[1] "Mendelssohn Family," vol. ii. p. 312.
[2] "Mendelssohn's Letters to I. and C. Moscheles," p. 284.
[3] "Mendelssohn Family," vol. ii. p. 317.
[4] Ibid., p. 291.

could adopt a very stand-off attitude with strangers, and was not easily to be approached at all times. Of this his sometime pupil, Charles Edward Horsley, gives an amusing instance. Felix, when in London, frequently visited the Horsley family, and the boy's musical disposition attracted his attention. By his advice, young Horsley was sent to Cassel, to study with Moritz Hauptmann. In 1841, Horsley finished his residence in Germany with a visit to Leipzig, calling first upon Ferdinand David. While at his house, "Herr Doctor" Mendelssohn arrived, and Horsley sprang forward to greet him, only to be received with frigid coldness. "Sir, I have not the honour of your acquaintance," said Mendelssohn, in German; and it was not until the identity of the young man was established—he had altered considerably since Felix had last seen him—that the coldness gave way to cordial warmth.[1]

Many anecdotes could be told of his kindness to young musicians, and of his courtesy to brother artists. It has already been seen that he took a warm interest in Sterndale Bennett while he was yet a pupil of the Royal Academy of Music. When in Birmingham, at the rehearsal for *Elijah*, in 1846, the composer came across a boy-chorister named Humphreys, who was playing over his part on the pianoforte in the committee-room. As Mendelssohn passed, he tapped the boy on the shoulder, saying, "That's not the way to play, my boy; let me

Mendelssohn and young musicians

[1] Horsley, *Choir*, vol. xv. p. 53.

show you," and sat down and played the whole number over to him. During the same visit, he heard a clever young pianist, Miss Jeannie Stevens, daughter of a member of the festival committee, and presented her with a copy of Chopin's Studies, on which he wrote his name. Dr. W. H. Cummings, when a chorister at the Temple Church, sang at the first performance of the revised oratorio, *Elijah*, at Exeter Hall, April 16, 1847, being placed in the front row of the altos. "His enthusiastic singing attracted the notice of Mendelssohn, who asked the Temple chorister his name, which he wrote on one of his (Mendelssohn's) visiting cards, and gave to the youthful singer."[1]

To the young artist he was ever willing to lend a helping hand. In 1844 he wrote to the King of Prussia on behalf of a young composer, who wished to pursue his studies in Berlin, but lacked the means. The King graciously made the grant asked for by Mendelssohn. Another request is here made public for the first time, by the insertion of a letter hitherto unpublished. It is, from internal evidence, addressed to Johannes Verhulst, Kapellmeister at that time at the Hague. Verhulst had spent a few years in Leipzig, and Mendelssohn mentions him in a letter to his sister Fanny, in 1839. "But do you know Verhulst? You will be glad to make his acquaintance when you come."[2] This is a free translation :—

[1] "History of *Elijah*," p. 123.

[2] "Mendelssohn Family," vol. ii. p. 57.

Frankfort, February 11, 1845.

Dear Mr. Kapellmeister,

Permit me to recall myself again to your memory by a request. The bearer of these lines, a young and very able Belgian violinist and composer, whose quartets and other instrumental music—which seem to me to display very much talent—I have learnt to know, and who is moreover distinguished by earnestness and modesty, intends to visit Holland, and desired an introduction to you. This I should now like herewith to give Mr. Tingry, and to recommend him very heartily to your friendly notice. By anything you can do for him, and for the object of his stay there, you will awaken the most lively gratitude in, and oblige him as also myself. Do not be angry with me on account of the liberty which I have taken in this matter; accept my hearty greetings. Kindly recall me to the recollection of your brother, and think sometimes of ever yours sincerely,

Felix Mendelssohn Bartholdy.

Then he was all kindness to those of his friends who happened to be disabled in any way. Just before his last visit to England, he spent a day by the bedside of Madame Frege's son, and beguiled the time by playing the pianoforte to him, and this because the youth had been too ill to attend the performance of *St. Paul* on the Good Friday. When Chorley returned with Felix to Leipzig, after the Birmingham Festival of 1840, a

Frankfurt d. 11 Febr
1845

Lieber Herr Kapellmeister

Erlauben Sie mir mich heut mit einer Bitte Ihrem Gedächtniß zurückzurufen. Der Ueberbringer dieser Zeilen, ein junger sehr tüchtiger belgischer Violinspieler und Componist, von dem ich Quartetten, und andere Instrumentalmusik kenne, welche mir sehr viel Talent zu verrathen scheinen, der sich außerdem auch durch Kraft und Geschicklichkeit auszeichnet, will Holland besuchen, und wünschte eine Einführung bei Ihnen. Diese möchte ich ihm hierdurch [illegible] geben, und ihn Ihrer freundlichen Aufnahme recht dringend empfehlen. Was Sie für ihn und die [illegible] seines dortigen Aufenthaltes thun können, [illegible] werden Sie ich sein mich aufs lebhafteste [illegible] verbinden. Zürnen Sie mir nicht wegen der Freiheit die ich mir hierdurch genommen habe, sein Sie herzlich gegrüßt, [illegible] Sie auch [illegible] Ihres [illegible] freundlich zurück, erinnern Sie sich zuweilen Ihres stets ergebenen

Felix Mendelssohn Bartholdy

FACSIMILE OF LETTER OF FELIX MENDELSSOHN BARTHOLDY.

painful attack of lameness confined him for a time to his hotel, and prevented his enjoying some of the musical treats prepared for him. Chorley was lying down in all the fulness of wretchedness, when a concert pianoforte was brought to his room, and Mendelssohn and Moscheles made music for him the whole evening. On one occasion Chorley was at the house of Mendelssohn, when a note was handed in. It read thus: "The Directors of the Leipzig Concerts beg leave to present to Mr. *Shurely* a ticket to the concert of to-morrow." Whereupon Felix enacted the most atrocious, not to say profane, pun possible, by going to the pianoforte and playing the opening of the chorus, "*Surely* He hath borne," etc.[1] This was as much an outbreak of "mad spirits" as that related by Hiller, who tells a story of himself and Felix when in Paris in 1831–32. One night they were going home across the deserted boulevard at a late hour, when Mendelssohn suddenly stopped, and interrupted the earnest conversation with, "We *must* do some of our jumps in Paris! our jumps, I tell you! Now for it! One!—two!—three!"—and they jumped.[2]

A pun

But to return to more serious topics. Mendelssohn was most punctilious in his demeanour to performers. On the production of his *Antigone* in Paris, in 1844, it was suggested that Felix might make a present to the leading performers. He wrote: "This would be

[1] "Memoirs of H. F. Chorley," vol. i. p. 324.
[2] "Mendelssohn" (Hiller), p. 26.

contrary to the fixed principles which I adopted at the beginning of my musical career—never in any way to mix up my personal position with my musical one, or ever to improve the latter by the influence of the former, or in any manner to bribe public or private opinion with regard to me, or even to attempt to strengthen it."[1]

When in London it is said Mendelssohn always touched his hat when he mounted the platform to conduct a rehearsal. He was a bit of a martinet when at the desk, but he won the good will of the players, because they saw that he understood his business. There was one unpleasant incident during the Philharmonic season of 1844. Mendelssohn was detained at a meeting of the committee of the Handel Society, and so was a few minutes late at rehearsal. One or two members of the orchestra expressed their displeasure in some objectionable manner, and Felix complained to the directors, with the result that one performer at least was dismissed. Then about the same time there was unpleasant tension between Felix and the band of the Sacred Harmonic Society. The musical journals of the time give very highly coloured versions, from different standpoints.[2] It is probable that Mendelssohn, sensitive to any slight, showed his fiery temper; but that he bore no malice is evident from the letter he wrote to Moscheles, in

As conductor

1 "Mendelssohn's Letters from 1833 to 1847," p. 334.

2 See *Musical World*, 1844, pp. 233, 245, 259; *Dramatic and Musical Review*, vol. iii. pp. 359, 387.

which reference is made to the Philharmonic affair. The letter is in connection with the band arrangements for the Birmingham Festival of 1846, and is dated from Leipzig, June 26th. "The occasion of these lines is a passage in Mr. Moore's letter, in which he says: 'Nearly the whole of the Philharmonic band are engaged; a few only are left out, who made themselves unpleasant when you were there.' Now I strongly object to this restriction; and as I fancy you can exercise your authority in the matter, I address my protest to you, and beg you to communicate it to Mr. Moore. There is nothing I hate more than the reviving of bygone disputes. . . . This one is, as far as I am concerned, dead and buried, and must on no account have any influence on the selection made for the Birmingham Festival. Any further disturbance on the part of these gentlemen, I am sure, is not to be feared."[1]

The same delicate sense of honour dictated his attitude towards the press, and critics generally. When Professor Dehn, in 1841, offered to write, or cause to be written, something in his musical paper, *Cæcilia*, about *Antigone*, just then produced, Mendelssohn replied: "Although I entirely agree with you that my choruses to *Antigone* will furnish an opportunity for a number of unfair and malignant attacks, still I cannot meet these unpleasant probabilities by the means which you are so good as to

Criticism

[1] "Mendelssohn's Letters to I. and C. Moscheles," p. 274.

propose to me. I have always made it an inviolable rule, never to write myself in newspapers on any subject connected with music, nor either directly or indirectly to prompt any article to be written on my own compositions; and although I am well aware how often this must be both a temporary and sensible disadvantage, still I cannot deviate from a resolution which I have strictly followed out under all circumstances."[1] This letter throws a curious side-light on journalistic practices of that time—perhaps not entirely unknown in the present day—and also seems to recall Mendelssohn's awkward experience in London, in 1829, when his confidential remarks to Fétis got into the papers. According to his mother, Felix, as a boy, was rather indifferent to praise;[2] yet later, as Dorn remarked, he was by no means insensible to praise, though not at all blind as to whether it were discriminative or the reverse.[3]

He was morbidly sensitive to criticism, and whether he liked praise or no, he looked upon any one as an enemy who received his music coldly. The criticism of his early opera, "The Wedding of Camacho," hurt him exceedingly, and he confessed to Devrient that "the most brilliant praise of the best journal has not so much power to gratify, as the contemptible abuse of the most obscure paper has to vex."[4] Hiller records

[1] "Mendelssohn's Letters from 1833 to 1847," p. 255.

[2] "Goethe and Mendelssohn," p. 35.

[3] Dorn, *Choir*, vol. xiii. p. 115.

[4] "Recollections" (Devrient), p. 30.

that it was some time before Mendelssohn got over the effects of the first criticism he saw of his oratorio *St. Paul*.[1] Both these notices seemed to have contained some element of spite, but had he been less thin-skinned he would not have been pierced by their shafts; for criticism is a discipline and ordeal all public men must make up their mind to go through. He was very touchy, too, if even a friend suggested an improvement in any of his compositions. Hiller relates an instance, when he ventured a hint as to some old-fashioned passages in the Pianoforte Trio in D minor. "Do you think that that would make the thing any better?" Mendelssohn replied. "The piece would be just the same, and so it may remain as it is." But he altered it all the same.[2] It is curious to note that towards the close of his life he cooled in his friendship toward Hiller, and poor Dorn had to lament that something in the arrangements for the Singers' Festival at Cologne (1846) must have offended Mendelssohn, for the business caused a breach between the two.

But there are spots on the sun, though rarely visible to the naked eye; and the blemishes in the character of Mendelssohn were but superficial: they did not touch the deeper nature of the man. Not that he was a man of deep, contemplative nature; he lived too much in a world of excitement for that; but if he was not the "miracle of humanity" Benedict termed him, he was

[1] "Mendelssohn" (Hiller), p. 53.

[2] Ibid., p. 154.

one of nature's truest gentlemen. He had need, indeed, to say, "Save me from my friends." He himself was no sycophant. In all his dealings with the great ones of the earth, he exhibits the finer qualities of the courtier with the manliness of the free-born. Perhaps there is nothing more delightful to remember than his demeanour on the occasions of his visits to Buckingham Palace. Ere the heavy hand of sorrow had been laid on our late Queen, she was a bright, happy, healthy-minded woman, as true a woman as a Queen; and she received the young composer in a manner as gratifying to him as a man as it was generous to him as an artist. Mendelssohn described Buckingham Palace as the one really pleasant English house where one felt at one's ease. Prince Albert played the organ, and sang to him; the Queen sang one of his own songs, as Her Majesty thought, but one of his sister Fanny's, as Felix had the grace to own—"which I found very hard, but pride must have a fall;" then Mendelssohn in turn played to his Royal hosts. This was in 1842, and a full account of the visit will be found in a letter from Felix to his mother.[1] Then, in 1847, the last time Mendelssohn was in England, he was again at Buckingham Palace. After "making music" for some time, he was about to leave, when the Queen asked if there was nothing she could do to give "Dr. Mendelssohn" pleasure. Of course the artist had already been amply

[1] "Goethe and Mendelssohn," p. 143. The song by Fanny Mendelssohn, "Italien," was published as No. 3 of Felix's Op. 8.

rewarded by the interest taken by the gracious monarch in his music; but the man had a decided wish for something, and that nothing less than a visit to, and inspection of, the Royal nursery! Delighted beyond everything, the Queen led the way, and the two were soon deep in the mysteries of children's clothing, dietary, ailments, and all that appertains to the duties of the heads of a family. Perchance he inspected the juvenile wardrobe of the future Empress of his own Germany.[1]

Accomplishments

Something has been said of Mendelssohn's accomplishments, and it may here be added that he played chess and billiards with ardour and skill. He was a fine draughtsman, and his sketches and water-colour paintings were far above the usual amateur level. Seventy years ago it was a very uncommon thing for a musician of distinction to be remarkable for scholarship, but now the case is different; still Mendelssohn's literary attainments were more than respectable, and he could turn a verse with the best. His letters form an enduring monument to his literary power, and may be compared with those left by William Cowper, Charles Lamb, or Edward Fitzgerald—to name only easily accessible English writers.

Portraits

Numerous portraits of Mendelssohn exist, though he was never anxious to pose to any one, but rather avoided the process when possible. Most of these portraits have been reproduced in one or other of the numerous works on Mendelssohn. The

[1] "Fragments of an Autobiography" (Felix Moscheles), p. 107.

Felix Mendelssohn Bartholdy

best is said to be that painted by Magnus, in 1844. The drawing by Hensel, taken after death, is also said to be a faithful likeness. It is engraved as the frontispiece to the volume of "Letters, 1833 to 1847." A bust, modelled from life by Professor Rietschel, and a medallion by Knauer, are good; both are reproduced in the volume of "Letters to Moscheles." A very charming pencil-drawing of Mendelssohn at the age of twenty-six, by Mücke, is published in the "History of *Elijah*," so often mentioned. Chorley said Mendelssohn's face was one of the most beautiful that had ever been seen, and that no portrait extant did it justice.

To Felix and Cécile Mendelssohn were born five children: Carl, February 7, 1838; Marie, October 3, 1839; Paul, January 18, 1841; Felix, May 1, 1843; and Lilli, September 19, 1845. All, save one, have now passed away. Felix, the youngest boy, always delicate, died soon after his father, and was buried by his side. The next to be taken was the second son, Paul, who died at Berlin, in January, 1880. Carl, the eldest, lived until 1897—a year that proved fatal to the elder daughter, Marie Benecke.

The gentle, loving wife, Cécile, survived her husband less than six years. After the death of Mendelssohn the life of Cécile drooped and faded; and consumption worked its fell ravages on her delicate frame, death occurring at Frankfort-on-the-Main, September 25, 1853, her span of life extending only to thirty-five years. Thus, the Mendelssohns were a short-lived family. Rebecka, the younger sister of Felix, died December 1, 1858, suddenly, like her sister, from apoplexy. Paul, the brother, died in June, 1874, the only one denied the family inheritance of a speedy and painless death, for he suffered long and severely before entering into his rest.[1]

[1] "Mendelssohn Family," vol. ii. p. 346.

CHAPTER XVI

Mendelssohn the musician—His continued popularity—His position —A many-sided genius—The spirit in which he wrote—High ideals—His detractors—The proper standpoint from which he should be judged—His oratorios, cantatas, and other vocal compositions—Attempts at opera—As an orchestral writer—His instrumentation—Novel effects and combinations —Symphonies, overtures, concertos, chamber music—Compositions for pianoforte and organ—Posthumous works, unwisdom of publishing so many—As an executant—Improvisation—As a conductor and a teacher—Musical memory—The critics and Mendelssohn—Justification of conservative views—A correct prophecy—A Royal testimonial—Memorials and Scholarships.

Mendelssohn met with very little hostile criticism during his lifetime. His principal works were produced under his own direction, and the charm of his personality added to the effect of his music. A sort of hero-worship was set up, and extended from the man to his art. Nowhere did the "Mendelssohn fever" inflame the public with more intensity than in England. Here the composer was looked upon as the direct successor of Handel and Beethoven—Bach was only known to a select few—and quite their equal. Then came the reaction. The voice of detraction was heard in Leipzig almost from the moment of Mendelssohn's death; other idols were worshipped, and the influence of the composer of *Elijah* began to wane. The English remained truer to the man they so long had idolized; but here, also, in time were found those who disparaged him; and so, as the adulation was overdone in former years, now the depreciation was equally unjust. After the lapse of fifty years it is possible to form a truer estimate of his genius. Even now his music is to be found in every home; his oratorios and cantatas form part of every festival scheme; and if his symphonies are not so often heard, it is not from want of merit in those works, but because the public palate at the present time has become jaded if not vitiated by the pungent harmonies and gorgeous glitter of the latest orchestral school. His overtures stand among the first of their order, and upon them age has not yet placed its withering hand. Then the violin concerto has no rival in popular favour save that by Beethoven. Mendelssohn was, indeed, a great composer, and if he did not reach the altitude of those giants of art, Bach, Handel, Beethoven, and Mozart, he came very near them in some respects.

Few artists were so many-sided in the manifestation of their genius as Mendelssohn. Perhaps it was his versatility that prevented his reaching the highest pinnacle of art. Then it has to be considered that all he achieved was in the space of thirty-eight years, his life, moreover, being one of constant action and excitement. Great as a composer, he was distinguished as an organist, a pianist, and conductor. As a teacher, he was scarcely in his element, but those of his pupils who have recorded their experience, speak of him with affectionate regard, and even enthusiasm.

Brought up by good, conservative Zelter, in the strict contrapuntal school, Mendelssohn was faithful to the traditions of the past. He was no innovator, no epoch-maker, no man with a mission to regenerate the world; but an artist, to make music, and to make it on the lines of the great masters. He accepted their works as models, but he was no slavish imitator. Everything he produced was characterized by a beauty of form, a grace and finish that belonged to himself alone. His mastery of form was complete, and the clearness of his design left no doubt as to his poetic intention—hence his music is less difficult to interpret than that of many composers. He did not theorise about art, but applied himself to the practice of it. When Fétis was in London, in 1829, delivering his lectures on music, the proceeding was distasteful to Mendelssohn, who was also on his first visit there. "What is the good of talking so much about it?" he said; "it is better to write well—that is the chief matter."[1]

Not much is known regarding his method of composing. His ideas were mostly thought out before being committed to paper, and he left no sketch-books after the manner of Beethoven. Schubring relates of the Overture in C that he saw Mendelssohn scoring it bar by bar, from top to bottom of the page; and

[1] "Life of Moscheles," vol. i. p. 226.

Devrient says the same thing of the first movement of the "Reformation Symphony"—this, however, Mendelssohn declared to have been so great an effort that he would never attempt such a thing again. Of greater importance than the method was the spirit which animated the composer in his work. Felix himself affords a glimpse here and there on this point. Writing to Spohr in 1835 respecting the Vienna Prize Symphony Competition—which Spohr apparently desired him to enter—he says: "The intelligence from Vienna was most interesting to me; I had heard nothing of it. It strongly revived my feeling as to the utter impossibility of my ever composing anything with a view to competing for a prize. I should never be able to make even a beginning. . . . The thoughts of a prize, or an award, would distract my thoughts."[1] Farther on, in the same letter, he states that he was then engaged in writing an oratorio (*St. Paul*), during which he enjoyed the most intense delight. Years later (1843) he wrote thus to Devrient, the subject of his letter being opera: "Ever since I began to compose, I have remained true to my starting principle: not to write a page because no matter what public, or what pretty girl wanted it to be thus or thus; but to write solely as I myself thought best, and as it gave me pleasure."[2] Then, as to his care and thoroughness, his statement to Hiller that the

Spirit in which Mendelssohn composed

[1] "Mendelssohn's Letters from 1833 to 1847," p. 67.

[2] "Recollections" (Devrient), p. 241.

"Midsummer Night's Dream" overture was the result of long and arduous work; that in his spare time between the lectures at the Berlin University he extemporized upon it for a whole year—this was one of many proofs that could be adduced.

Mendelssohn's works have been so long before the world, and the "fierce light" of criticism has penetrated into every bar that he wrote; he has been praised for what he has done, and blamed for what he has *not* done—so much so, that at this time there seems nothing further that can possibly be said on the subject of his compositions. And yet, he has been judged in part from a wrong standpoint. He has been compared with those with whom he had nothing in common. This has been the case more particularly in this country. Of the great art-revolution which began to shake the musical heavens in his day, only faint reverberations reached these shores; and it was not until some years after the death of Mendelssohn that any important productions of the new school were heard in England. In 1844, Mendelssohn brought Schubert's great Symphony in C to the notice of the Philharmonic Society, but it was so badly received that he declined to have his own "Ruy Blas" overture produced. The overture to *Fierabras*, by Schubert, was, indeed, performed on June 10th, and dismissed by the *Musical World* as beneath criticism. Schubert, of course, is not to be classed with the new school. Berlioz was introduced to London by the New Philharmonic Society in 1852, and Wagner in 1854, his

Tannhäuser overture finding a place in the programme of April 26, and being described as "such queer stuff that criticism would be thrown away upon it."[1] In the intervening year (1853) Schumann was represented for the first time by an orchestral work at the Philharmonic Concert of April 4th. The piece was the *Allegro*, *Scherzo*, and *Finale*, Op. 52, and its reception was of the kind accorded to the others. Liszt was well known as a pianist, and his compositions for pianoforte were not altogether strange; but it was left to his faithful henchman, the late Walter Bache, to make the London public acquainted with his orchestral writings. The legitimate successor, but not imitator, of Mendelssohn, Johannes Brahms, was only a boy when the former died.

The new school was bound to make its way in time, and even to flutter the dovecotes of conservative England. There was strength and purpose in it; but was it necessary to exalt it at the expense of Mendelssohn? The stage holds the mirror up to nature; music mirrors the man who creates it. The rugged, lofty-souled Beethoven portrays himself in his music. The boundless imagination, the princely splendour of thought and habit of Wagner, are reflected in his vast designs, and the prodigal display of means in his scores. The cultivated, refined, precise, and orderly disposition of Mendelssohn found expression in music, polished, beautifully balanced in harmony and phrase, and worked out with consummate

[1] *Musical World*, 1854, p. 304.

skill and address. Nothing vague, no redundant bars, but everything in correct form, symmetry being as it were a law of his nature. If his themes were trivial, as they were occasionally, so deftly were they handled that the defect escaped observation. Mendelssohn could not have belonged to the new school, because he was Mendelssohn, and none other; moreover, his work was done before that new school had obtained a firm footing, or even anything like general recognition.

There was one direction in which Mendelssohn's declining influence was an unmixed gain—that exerted over composers, his later contemporaries, and the generation that came after. "Style is the man," and Mendelssohn's style was as attractive as the man himself. It so fascinated young composers, and, unfortunately, it could be imitated, though imperfectly, that the world was inundated with diluted Mendelssohn. Happily that state of things has almost entirely passed away, and in this country something like a national school of composition is gradually taking its place. The genuine Mendelssohn claimed respect: the imitation could not long be tolerated; so now the shelves of musical libraries groan beneath the weight of things that had a borrowed life, and are now as dead as the proverbial door-nail.

Mendelssohn belonged, then, to the classical school, and can only be rightly estimated as a composer, from the standpoint of his own time. In his first oratorio, *St. Paul*, he took Bach for his model. The whole work is in the severe style of the contrapuntal school. The chorale is the foundation, and is worked into the overture, treated in chorus quite after the manner of Bach in "O Thou, the true and only Light!" and "But our God." The *aria* is subordinated to the recitative, and the composer never swerves from his high purpose in order to conciliate popular taste. There is dramatic power in the scene where Stephen is before the Sanhedrim, and the composer's own individuality in the beautiful choruses, "How lovely are the Messengers," and "O be gracious, ye Immortals," each with such fine characterization. But it is in the orchestration that Mendelssohn's genius shines forth at its brightest. Bach and Handel afforded him no precedent here. The orchestra of their day was obsolete. The lines of the modern orchestra, progressing through Haydn and Mozart, were firmly laid by Beethoven and Weber. But Mendelssohn did not leave the orchestra as he found it, as will presently be shown. In *St. Paul* the writing for strings is masterly; the violoncello is introduced as a solo instrument in the accompaniment to "Be thou faithful." Three drums are employed in places, and the brass is used with great reserve. Mendelssohn wrote an organ part, introducing that instrument with fine judgment where its effect would be greatest, therein differing from the practice of both Handel and Bach.

Oratorios

Marked by an interval of ten years, *Elijah* shows a great advance upon *St. Paul*, not in scholarship, but in the development of the composer's individuality. The forms are more free; the chorale virtually disappears, the spirit of the composition is modern, dramatic, and fugal writing is nowhere obtrusive, though the counterpoint is rich and varied. The beginning with a recitative recalls Handel's *Israel in Egypt*, but following that with an overture was quite a new thing. As every one knows, the overture was an afterthought—Mendelssohn's happiest. As if to compensate for the absence of fugue in the choral writing, Mendelssohn here indulges in the full development of that form, with subject also inverted, and rich detail, all working up to the agonized cry, "Help, Lord!" Truly magnificent is this part of the oratorio. In the overture, note the effect of the soft horn tones as the subject is propounded by the string basses; how clarinet and bassoon colour the answer from violas; observe the art with which the composer brings in the full orchestra, and listen to the coarse tone of the ophicleide as the plaint grows fiercer; and then, with the voices, comes in the organ. All this written nearly sixty years ago! That is a point that needs to be remembered. Then in *Elijah* Mendelssohn employs representative themes, of which the "curse motive" is the chief. Further, according to Emil Naumann, the great air "Hear ye, Israel," is probably derived from a Hebraic melody sung at the Dresden synagogue.[1] There is one curious parallel in this oratorio, between Bach and Mendelssohn, that

[1] "History of Music" (Naumann), p. 82.

must be pointed out. In Bach's "St. John" *Passion* there is an air for contralto, "It is finished," with an obbligato part for the *viola da gamba*. This in form Mendelssohn has closely followed in "It is enough," with its violoncello part. The initial motive, key apart, is almost identical in both. With Mendelssohn,

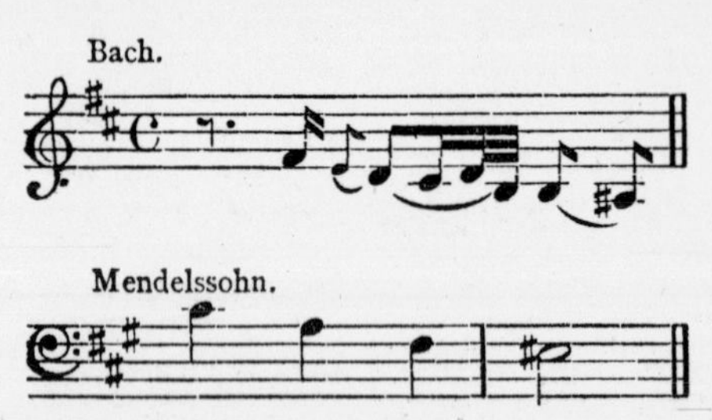

however, the pathos is more human, and the violoncello becomes, as it were, a second sympathetic voice. The viola, a favourite instrument with Mendelssohn, plays a remarkable part in the accompaniment to the air "Lord God of Abraham," dominating the string quartet throughout. But the points of interest in the score of *Elijah* are too numerous for individual mention. The chief episodes in the history of the Prophet of Mount Carmel are delineated with dramatic power and dignity. The Baal scene, the outburst of the angry Jezebel, and the fierce response of the people, these are full of force, yet with nothing meretricious or stagey. Then the grandeur of the chorus, "Behold, God the Lord passed by," the beauty of "He, watching over Israel," the fusion of science and grace in "He that shall endure to the end," where Bach is equalled in his wonderful treatment of a single theme. The whole work is great, greater in the choral numbers than in the solos. Mendelssohn's self-criticism and immense pains in revising his compositions before publication, were never more fully illustrated than in the case of his oratorios. *St. Paul*, after its production at Düsseldorf, was subjected to rigid scrutiny, and no fewer than fourteen numbers excised, some being replaced by new movements.[1]

The alterations in *Elijah*, though not of so drastic a nature as in *St. Paul*, were very numerous. Changes of one kind or other were made in all but nine numbers. Some numbers were left out, and new pieces inserted in their stead. The original book of words, reprinted as Appendix E, will enable any one to see the differences between the two texts; the last chorus, it will be noticed, is set to entirely new words.[2]

The oratorio *Christus* was left in too fragmentary a condition for judgment to be passed upon it. Whether it would have surpassed *Elijah* may be doubted. The latter was Mendelssohn's crowning effort, and the strain

[1] For a full account of the alterations in *St. Paul*, see a paper written by (Sir) George Grove, for the performance at the Crystal Palace, November 30, 1872, when the composer's own organ part was said to have been played for the first time in this country. The paper was published in the *Choir*, 1872, p. 399.

[2] For the changes in the musical settings, see Mr. Joseph Bennett's articles in the *Musical Times*, 1882, pp. 525, *et seq.*; 1883, pp. 6, *et seq.*

it put upon his powers, with the disturbing influences subsequent to its production and revision, left the composer weak and broken.

Cantatas

The *Lobgesang*, or "Hymn of Praise," was a new form of composition at that time. It differs from Beethoven's "Choral Symphony" in the unity of its design. It has a "motto" theme, given out by trombones at the commencement, forming an important episode in the *Allegro* of the symphony, employed as a leading theme in the chorus, "All that has life and breath," and appearing finally in the *Coda* of the last chorus. This, though handled with consummate skill throughout, is, it must be confessed, a sad perversion of a noble ancient Church mode:

It is related of Carl Queisser, the trombone player, that he introduced a turn at the commencement of the second bar, when the work was rehearsed for the first time. Mendelssohn thanked the performer, but requested him to play just what was written. Was he himself conscious of having converted the grave Church melody into a jaunty tune?

Of a work so well known, it should be superfluous to say anything now. What a resource it is to framers of festival schemes in these days of half-programme works!

Audiences never tire of listening to the lovely duet and chorus, "I waited for the Lord," the magnificent scene of the watchman, "The sorrows of death"—again an afterthought, suggested to the composer during a sleepless night!—and the jubilant chorus, "The Night is departing." One or two points in the score it may be permissible to refer to. In the *Allegretto* of the Symphony, the clarinets have *staccato* accompanying notes when the melody is given out in octaves by violins and 'cellos, but are silent when the theme passes to the oboes and bassoon. Mendelssohn never mixes clarinet and oboe tone save in massive passages. In the same movement, when the brass—trombones and horns—bassoons, clarinets, and flutes have the chorale, the reedy oboe penetrates the liquid tone-mass with the motto theme, while the strings have interstitial phrases from the principal subject. This part is rarely well performed, as conductors do not subdue the background, and the oboe tone is forced and coarse. Richter, not generally supposed to be in keenest sympathy with Mendelssohn, is the only conductor the present writer ever heard give the true rendering of this section. The solo voice in "Praise thou the Lord, O my spirit," is accompanied by horns, bassoon, clarinets, and flutes, with rapid repeated chords—an entirely new effect at that time—the strings entering as the chorus take up the words. Here one oboe is employed to double the voice part. Other interesting details might be named.

Of Mendelssohn's other sacred compositions, his

settings of the Psalms are the most important. The eight-part Psalms, especially the 114th, reach the loftiest attainments of his oratorios. In the 42nd Psalm, the solo "For my soul thirsteth for God," has an oboe accompaniment, which, delicately played, perfectly illustrates what Berlioz terms the instrument's timidity of character.

Other sacred compositions

What Mendelssohn would have done in opera is doubtful. He had been trying for some twenty years to find a suitable *libretto*, but always failed. He was fastidious, not to say finical, on the subject. Soon after the production of his juvenile effort, "The Wedding of Camacho," his friend Devrient wrote for him the *libretto* of *Hans Heiling*, but Mendelssohn could do nothing with it.[1] In January, 1838, J. R. Planché was invited by the Messrs. Chappell to write an opera for Mendelssohn. Terms were arranged, and the agreement duly signed. Much correspondence with the composer ensued, running into October, 1839, the ultimate issue being nothing! Planché seems to have had good reason to complain of the treatment he and his book received from Mendelssohn.[2] In February, 1847, Mendelssohn received from Geibel the poem of *Loreley*. He showed it to Devrient, in Dresden, saying: "There it is; look at it; and do not again call me obstinate and contrary when I

Attempts at opera

[1] *Hans Heiling* was afterwards set by Heinrich Marschner, and produced at Hanover in 1833.

[2] "Recollections" (Planché), vol. i. pp. 279, *et seq.*

tell you that, as it is, I cannot set it to music."[1] Devrient remarks, later: "There is a Hamlet-like tragedy about Mendelssohn's operatic destiny. During eighteen years he could not make up his mind firmly to adopt any subject and work it out, because he wanted perfection; and when at last he overcame his scruples and determined upon a poem, though far from what it should have been, he sank with his fragment into the grave." As Mendelssohn was a man of distinct literary ability, well read, and capable of turning sonnets of Boccaccio, Dante, and others into German verse, it should not have been a difficult thing for him to have written his own *libretto*. He had not the stage knowledge of Weber or Wagner, nor their experience. Mendelssohn sought his inspiration from without; Wagner was driven by his inmost nature to express himself through the medium of the word-tone drama.

Mendelssohn's juvenile operas have been equalled by the productions of other young composers; his fragment, *Loreley*, especially as regards the *finale* to the first act, is very fine, but quite as suited to the concert-room as to the stage. What he might have done in opera may perhaps be gathered from his "Midsummer Night's Dream" music, *Athalie*, *Antigone*, and the *Walpurgisnacht*.

As a song-writer Mendelssohn's work is characterized by grace and charm. There is an exquisite finish in many of his songs, and the expression is pure and

[1] "Recollections" (Devrient), p. 290.

unforced ; but the deeper note is lacking, and they have not the distinctive character of the *Lieder* of Schubert, Schumann, or Brahms. The part-songs opened a new source of delight to choral singers in England. They are indeed charming compositions, of never-fading freshness.

Songs and part-songs

As an orchestral writer, Mendelssohn ranks with the highest ; he had the technique of the art at his finger-ends. He came into the rich heritage left by Beethoven and Weber, a heritage he handed on still richer to his successors. Some of the instruments he wrote for are now obsolete. Thus in the overture to *St. Paul*, and in the *Meeresstille* overture, the serpent has a place in the score ; while the ophicleide is provided for in the "Midsummer Night's Dream" overture—and with good effect—in *Elijah*, as already stated, and in the "War March of the Priests" in *Athalie*. Players upon the serpent are not now to be found, and the same may be said of ophicleide players. Mendelssohn had an early experience in writing for strings, his unpublished symphonies, twelve in number, having been completed before he had attained his fifteenth year. Then in 1824 followed the Symphony in C minor, now known as No. 1, but really the thirteenth. To this succeeded the Octet for strings. This may reasonably be considered in connection with the composer's orchestral music. Spohr wrote his first double quartet in 1823, but it is not likely that the young Felix saw that work when engaged on his Octet,

Orchestral compositions

so he may be credited as an inventor in this case. The Octet differs in disposition of parts from the double quartet, and Mendelssohn's laying out of his score is really masterly. After this came the work that gave him undying fame, the "Midsummer Night's Dream" overture, which, to quote the happy remark of Sir George Grove, "brought the fairies into the orchestra and fixed them there." Strange, that Mendelssohn and Schubert, unknown to each other, were working in the same direction—adding grace and lightness to the orchestra, giving fuller scope to the wood-wind, inventing enchanting combinations, and—in Schubert's case—showing what the trombones could do in softest passages. It is tolerably certain that Schubert never saw or heard any of Mendelssohn's music; and it was not until 1838 that Schumann recovered the great Symphony in C of Schubert, which Mendelssohn produced at the Gewandhaus Concerts in March, 1839, long after he had formed his own style in orchestral scoring. Both composers loved to give melodies to the violoncello, but Schubert combined clarinet and oboe in plaintive strains, whereas Mendelssohn kept those instruments apart in such instances. In Mendelssohn's *Ruy Blas* overture a great effect—one of mystery—is produced at the entry of the second subject, where the strings play *pianissimo*, *staccato*, but bowed, and then in unison the clarinets, bassoons, and 'cellos give out the theme. Taken altogether Mendelssohn has put finer ideas in his overtures than in the symphonies. In the "Trumpet

Overture" he employs three drums, a very early instance, as the piece was written in 1826. In the "Wedding March" three trumpets are required, anticipating by a year or so Wagner's *Tannhäuser* march, scored for the same number. But it was in dividing the string parts that Mendelssohn opened the way for the wonderful effects of Liszt, Wagner, and others. The commencement of the "Midsummer Night's Dream" was absolutely new, with its long-drawn chords for wind, followed by the fairy motive for violins in four parts. After the first clause of the second subject the violas are for a time divided. Altogether, a wonderful composition, and one to which an American writer of repute has recently drawn the attention of students in words that carry weight.[1] Wagner's remark that it must be taken into consideration that Mendelssohn wrote the overture at seventeen was purely gratuitous: the work needs no apology. Not one of the giants of music did anything like it at the same age. His averment that Mendelssohn was a landscape-painter of the first order, and that the "Hebrides" overture was his masterpiece, is more just. That work is a true tone-poem. Mendelssohn gave the original score of the "Hebrides" overture to Moscheles, and some fifty years later it was perused by Gounod, who placed a "D" for the double-basses in the third bar, making a note to the effect that Mendelssohn must have forgotten

[1] "The Orchestra and Orchestral Music" (W. J. Henderson).

it.[1] As Mendelssohn was not in the habit of neglecting the slightest detail, it may be questioned whether he did not intentionally give that note to the violoncellos instead.

The symphonies are as much in the nature of descriptive pieces as are most of the overtures. The "Italian" Symphony, written in 1833, though only scored for the "Haydn orchestra," glows with all the warmth of the sunny South. The opening, with wind accompaniment to the violin melody, was novel; and the combination of oboes, bassoons, and violas, in the so-called Pilgrim's March, was an individual trait. The final *Saltarello* detracts from the dignity of the work as a symphony. The "Scotch" Symphony, though published as No. 3, was composed some eight years later than the "Italian," No. 4. It is a much finer work. The score is the same, with two more horns added. The Introduction and *Coda* to the *Finale* are full of dignity, the one that of pathos, the other of triumph.

Whether, from the titles of so many of his orchestral works, Mendelssohn could be classed with the writers of "programme music," is not quite clear. When Schubring told him that a certain passage in the *Meeresstille* overture suggested the tones of love entranced at approaching nearer the goal of its desires, Mendelssohn replied that his idea was quite different; he pictured some good-natured old man sitting in the stern of the vessel, and blowing vigorously into the sails, so as to

[1] "Mendelssohn's Letters to I. and C. Moscheles," pp. 76-83.

contribute his part to the prosperous voyage. Of course that was said as a joke, and to stop inquiry; for Mendelssohn hated to "explain" his music.

In his concertos Mendelssohn dispensed with the usual orchestral exordium. The solo instrument is set to work at once. Like the "Scotch" Symphony, the concertos are intended to be played through without break. Here it may be remarked that audiences are constantly defeating the composer's intention by their ill-timed applause, and these works are scarcely ever heard as they should be. That the discipline of Bayreuth could be enforced in our concert-rooms! The violin concerto may have owed much to Ferdinand David; it is as perfect as can be. The scoring for wood-wind causes the solo part always to stand out in relief. This work bears the charm of eternal youth.

Violin and pianoforte concertos

Mendelssohn enriched the stores of chamber music, without creating any epoch-making work in that branch of art. His string quartets are very fine, but in some, particularly that in D, Op. 41, No. 1, the writing is purely orchestral in character. His *Scherzi* are the most remarkable features of his chamber music. From the Octet onward, he penned a series of movements that belonged to himself alone. He brought the fairies with him everywhere. The compositions for pianoforte and strings are masterly in form, the pianoforte having its full share, sometimes even more, in the exposition of

Chamber music

the ideas. Lenz says: "The Trios of Mendelssohn are even in so far as regards the piano a degree better than the Trios of Beethoven," but one hardly knows how to reconcile this with the statement a little further on that "Mendelssohn is a mannerist (*un genre*); he has created ideas, which he expresses in the language of Beethoven."[1]

Of the compositions for pianoforte solo, the finest are the Six Preludes and Fugues, Op. 35, the first among the greatest of its kind, and the *Variations sérieuses*, Op. 54. The "Songs without Words" brought new ideas and a love for the beautiful into hundreds of homes in this country, in many possibly for the first time. But the composer's reputation was not enhanced by these smaller works, and musicians have at times lamented their excessive popularity, considering that public taste has been diverted from the larger and more important forms of composition, and that these "songs" were followed by a shoal of weak imitations.

Writer for the pianoforte

The organ music is of greater importance. Contemporary with Mendelssohn were many composers for the pianoforte, whose works were destined in after-times to eclipse, in some cases, his own achievements in that direction. Of those it is only necessary here to name Chopin, Schumann, Hummel, Henselt, Liszt, and our own Sterndale

Organ music

[1] An article from "Beethoven et ses trois styles," translated and published in the *Monthly Musical Record*, 1876, p. 152.

Bennett. But the organ music of that period that could in any way compare with the compositions of Mendelssohn was confined for the most part to the productions of Rinck, Adolf Hesse, Julius André, and the Englishmen Thomas Adams and Samuel Wesley. Mendelssohn's Three Preludes and Fugues, Op. 37, are masterpieces. It has only recently become known that the original German edition had the words "with reverence and gratitude" appended to the dedication to Thomas Attwood.[1] The Six Sonatas, Op. 65, are sonatas mainly by courtesy. The sonata form is not uniformly adhered to, and some of the writing is in the manner of the Fantasia. But they are noble works, and the treatment of the Chorale, "Vater unser im Himmelreich," in No. 6, is very fine. The Andante and Variations in D, and Allegro in B flat, published in 1898, might pass for the work of any fairly equipped organ writer of the present day.

Posthumous publications

A word must be added concerning the posthumous publications. The desire to know everything about great men, to look into every bit of their work, is not always commendable; is often, on the contrary, unpardonable. It is one of the childish characteristics of the present age, this vulgar curiosity. Mendelssohn's whole life has been laid bare to the world, and few artists have borne the scrutiny so well; but with his works the result has not been so good. He himself was his severest critic,

[1] *Musical Times*, 1900, p. 792.

and what he withheld from the public should have been left—as to the bulk of it—as he wished it; but many pieces have since been published that, however interesting to students, have not in any way added to the reputation of their author, but rather have had the reverse effect. Mendelssohn, as he told Devrient, had "a tremendous reverence for print,"[1] and he suffered nothing to be published until he had revised and re-polished to the satisfaction of his fastidious taste. Though he published among his own songs six that were composed by his sister Fanny, he was strongly opposed to her publishing anything on her own account. It was not until 1846 that she ventured, after some brilliant offers from Berlin houses, to send forth some books of melodies for the pianoforte, songs, and part-songs; and then Felix tardily sent her his "professional blessing on her becoming a member of the craft," adding the hope that she might "taste only the sweets and none of the bitternesses of authorship."[2] But had Mendelssohn lived longer there is little doubt that he would have published his *Lauda Sion*, *Athalie*, the "Italian" Symphony, the music to *Œdipus in Colonus*, the overture to *Ruy Blas*, and the string Quartet in F minor, though probably not altogether as they now appear. A writer in the *Musical World*, so far back as 1849, contended that even the earliest compositions should be published, as throwing a light on the progress and development of

[1] "Recollections" (Devrient), p. 72.

[2] "Mendelssohn Family," vol. ii. pp. 325, 326.

his genius;[1] but quite enough, or more than enough, has been done in that direction.

An executant

It was held by some that Mendelssohn was greater as an executant than as a composer; and the accounts of his playing indicate genius of no common order. It is, of course, a matter of difficulty to assess at their true value performances on the organ or pianoforte of sixty and seventy years ago. The instruments have undergone considerable change, and in particular, the organ of to-day, with its light touch and varied accessories, is a very different thing from any that Mendelssohn ever played upon. The first CC organ in England was erected in St. Peter's, Cornhill, under the superintendence of Dr. Gauntlett, in 1840, but Mendelssohn's organ performances began in this country in 1832. Let the reader imagine the organs of that date—no pneumatic lever then—instruments with heavy touch, and with, here and there, an octave of pedals. Before this time Samuel Wesley and Benjamin Jacob used to play Bach's fugues as duets, and later some were published—and performed—as duos for pianoforte and double-bass. When, therefore, a musician of distinction, like Mendelssohn, gave a brilliant performance of the fugues upon the organ in St. Peter's, Cornhill, it was an event difficult at this time fully to appreciate. But the improvizations of Mendelssohn were perhaps more striking than his performances of any set piece. Writing in 1837, Dr.

[1] *Musical World*, 1849, p. 406.

Gauntlett says: "His (Mendelssohn's) extempore playing is very diversified—the soft movements full of tenderness and expression, exquisitely beautiful and impassioned—and yet so regular and methodical, that they appear the productions of long thought and meditation, from the lovely and continued streams of melody which so uninterruptedly glide onwards in one calm and peaceful flow. In his loud preludes there are an endless variety of new ideas totally different from those usually in vogue; and the pedal passages so novel and independent, so solemn and impressive, so grand and dignified, as to take his auditor by surprise."[1]

As a pianist Mendelssohn was equally great. Clara Schumann, Ferdinand Hiller, Joachim, and many others have spoken most enthusiastically of his playing. W. S. Rockstro, Otto Goldschmid, and Charles Edward Horsley, his pupils, bear eloquent witness to the same. The last named, indeed, goes so far as to say that his mastery over the instrument was little short of miraculous. "His powers of execution were quite as great as those of Rubinstein and Liszt; his delicacy of touch and tone was not exceeded by Thalberg or Chopin."[2] Charles Hallé's opinion was not quite so eulogistic. He wrote: "Mendelssohn's playing was not exactly that of a 'virtuoso,' not to be compared with that of Liszt or Thalberg (he himself called it 'en gros spielen'), but it was remarkably perfect, and one felt the great musician,

[1] *Musical World*, vol. vii. p. 10.

[2] Horsley, *Choir*, vol. xv. p. 54.

the great composer, in every bar he played."[1] There was, however, the magic of the personality of the artist in his playing, and audiences were carried away by their enthusiasm at his concerts. His improvizations, again, were a source of never-ending wonder; and many are the stories relating to Mendelssohn's remarkable gift in this direction. But to rekindle enthusiasm in such things after a lapse of sixty years is no easy matter, so these stories need not be retold. One instance may be given as showing Mendelssohn's powers of thematic development, as contrasted with his skill in combining melodies. In this last respect the most striking example was his treatment of five songs sung by Malibran one evening at the house of Vincent Novello, which Mendelssohn afterwards took as themes for his improvization.[2] The occasion above referred to was Ernst's concert at the Hanover Square Rooms, June 1, 1844, and Horsley gives the account. Bach's Triple Concerto in D minor was performed by Moscheles, Thalberg, and Mendelssohn. Thalberg not being given to extempore playing, it was agreed that no cadenzas were to be introduced. When the first pause was reached in the *finale*, Moscheles, perhaps from the force of habit, started off with a brilliant *cadenza*. At the second pause it was Thalberg's turn, and though taken by surprise, he got through very well. Lastly, came Mendelssohn's effort. "It

[1] "Life and Letters" (Halle), p. 71.

[2] *Musical Times*, vol. x. p. 206; "Mendelssohn Family," vol. i. p. 302.

began very quietly, and the themes of the concerto, most scientifically varied, gradually crept up in their new garments. A crescendo then began, the themes ever newly presented, rose higher and higher; and at last a storm, nay a perfect hurricane of octaves, which must have lasted for five minutes" (Steady! Mr. Horsley), "brought to a conclusion an exhibition of mechanical skill, and the most perfect inspiration, which neither before nor since that memorable Thursday afternoon has ever been approached. The effect on the audience was electrical . . . at the end, rounds of cheers were given for the great artist, which sounded like salvos of artillery."[1] Horsley walked with Mendelssohn in Hyde Park afterwards, and offered his congratulations, when Mendelssohn replied: "I thought the people would like some octaves, so I played them." That little speech revealed the practical side of Mendelssohn's character. Horsley's version must have been highly coloured, for the *Athenæum* does not refer to the cadenza at all, and the *Musical World* only says that it brought down a storm of plaudits.

As a conductor

As a conductor Mendelssohn was among the first of his time. He brought discipline into the orchestra. There was a personal magnetism about him when at the conductor's desk that secured fine results. And yet, judged by modern standards, his conducting would leave something to be desired. It was like himself, bright and sunny;

[1] Horsley, *Choir*, vol. xv. p. 81.

but not penetrating deeply below the surface of musical expression. He once told Wagner that too slow a tempo was the devil, and for choice he would rather things were taken too fast.[1] Wagner further tells in his essay upon conducting that the Mendelssohnian traditions of the London Philharmonic Society were so strong and fixed that he, with but one rehearsal for each concert, was often obliged to let matters go on in their accustomed way. But the Leipzig Gewandhaus orchestra was brought by Mendelssohn to a state of efficiency hitherto undreamt of.

As a teacher

Mendelssohn can hardly be taken seriously as a teacher. Horsley says his instruction was not imparted in any formal manner, nor did he know of any single instance in which he received pecuniary recompense for his advice. Rockstro gives an account of Mendelssohn's pianoforte lessons at the Conservatorium. Each pupil in turn had to begin the piece selected, and there was instantaneous reproof for any shortcoming at the outset. He never gave a learner the chance of mistaking his meaning, often causing consternation by his vehemence; but though his pupils began by being desperately afraid of him, he soon won their confidence and affection—the good ones, that is to say; for the others he had little but contempt and satire. In composition his pupils never knew beforehand what form the lessons would take. In point of fact the

[1] "About Conducting" (Wagner), Prose Works, vol. iv. p. 306.

instruction was given after the manner of an informal lecture.[1] He had strong likes and dislikes, and would not always take the trouble to conceal them; and in particular seems to have been prejudiced against an unfortunate girl-student whose head was adorned with a mass of reddish hair, not amenable to the rule of the hairpin.[2] In short, Mendelssohn lacked the plodding patience and self-restraint so essential to the true teacher. He sums up the case against himself very fairly in a letter to Professor Naumann, of Bonn, who apparently wished to place his son (Emil) under Mendelssohn's care. This was in 1839. Mendelssohn wrote: "But I should unworthily respond to your confidence, did I not communicate frankly to you the many and great scruples which prevent my *immediately* accepting your proposal. In the first place I am convinced, from repeated experience, that I am totally deficient in the talent requisite for a practical teacher, and for giving regular progressive instruction; whether it be that I take too little pleasure in tuition, or have not sufficient patience for it, I cannot tell, but in short, I do not succeed in it."[3] However, in 1842, Emil Naumann became a private pupil of Mendelssohn, and afterwards joined the Conservatorium.

Mendelssohn's phenomenal musical memory must have

[1] "Mendelssohn" (Rockstro), pp. 105, *et seq.*

[2] "Fragments of an Autobiography" (Felix Moscheles), p. 98.

[3] "Mendelssohn's Letters from 1833 to 1847," p. 172.

been of immense service to him in all his varied work.

Musical memory

After the first performance in London of his "Midsummer Night's Dream" overture, his friend Attwood left the score in the hackney coach, and it was lost. "Never mind, I will make another," said Mendelssohn. He did so, and it corresponded with the parts in every way. Wonderful though this seemed to be, it would have been more wonderful if he had forgotten a single note, seeing that the work had become a part of his very being. At the Lower Rhine Festival at Düsseldorf in 1833, Beethoven's Pastoral Symphony was to be performed. At the rehearsal the score was not forthcoming, and Mendelssohn conducted from memory, not a single point escaping him. Lady Wallace relates that at a Court concert at Dresden in 1846, she was requested by the King of Saxony to propose a theme for Mendelssohn to extemporize upon. The lady chose Gluck's *Iphigenie*, which had been given at the opera the previous evening. Mendelssohn had not heard the work for seven years, nevertheless he introduced every important air in his improvization.[1] Mendelssohn knew the classics by heart, and could bring forth things new and old from the treasures stored in his memory.

Though Mendelssohn was outspoken even to rashness in his younger days, and spared no one whose work offended him, it was criticism of the irresponsible order :

[1] "Reminiscences of F. Mendelssohn-Bartholdy" (Polko), p. 73, note.

he never joined the body of composer-critics. And he was quite right; for the business of the composer is composition, not criticism.

The critics

On the whole, he was very kindly treated by the press, and the reason is not far to seek. He did not interfere with the accepted order of things. He added new beauties to forms recognized as the models for all time. Your man with new-fangled notions, your iconoclast, your setter-up of new forms, generally with some disparagement of the old,—he is the one to come in for criticism, and he deserves it. He has to justify himself, and to fight for his work and his principles. The hostile critic in these cases is not inevitably wrong; he upholds existing ideas, and rightly; for it is only when the newer ideas are shown to be better, that his—the critic's—work can be deemed obsolete. Davison and Chorley were staunch admirers of Mendelssohn; they were the champions of the old school, and opponents of the innovators, Schumann and Wagner. They have since been held up to ridicule, but not altogether justly. They wrote according to their conviction, and their work was honest, if now proved to be mistaken. Some of their remarks have been quoted to their discomfiture: let Chorley again speak for himself. Writing after the first performance in London of the revised oratorio *Elijah*, he says: "It is impossible for us to write of this oratorio, after hearing it a second time, without insisting even more strongly than on the former occasion"—the Birmingham performance in 1846—"on the admirable elevation and spirituality of tone preserved throughout, free from the slightest admixture of secular levity or sanctimonious foppery, of stage tinsel or that musty science which is all that many who are reputed as grave and discreet thinkers have to display in place of idea. *Elijah* is not only *the* sacred work of our time, we dare fearlessly assert, but it is a work 'for our children and for our children's children.'"[1] Chorley was right there!

Schumann's name rarely appears in the Mendelssohn literature, yet he and Felix were good friends. That Mendelssohn could fully appreciate Schumann as a composer was not very likely; but it does not follow that there was any hostile or jealous feeling in the matter. Art is subjectivity. Music is the universe. The creative artist sees or imagines the universe through his own individuality, and cannot view it from the standpoint of another. Hence composers of strong individuality are not the best judges of the work of their contemporaries. Musical history abounds with instances of the erroneous and unjust estimate formed by one composer of another. Witness Weber on Beethoven; Beethoven on Schubert, and so on. What one composer thinks of another is really of little artistic importance. Now, Schumann and Mendelssohn in temperament and disposition were opposites. Schumann was a recluse; Mendelssohn a society man, using the term in its best sense. Schumann was a romantic dreamer, with

[1] *Athenæum*, 1847, p. 441.

an unbounded capacity for admiration; Mendelssohn was wide awake, very practical, and seldom given to sentimental outbursts. Schumann worshipped Mendelssohn, and that for what in himself was lacking—the command of form; Mendelssohn, with his order and neatness, could not endure what was vague or diffuse. So contrasted were they that each, in a measure, was the complement of the other; and instead of instituting comparisons, the words of Spitta, concerning Handel and Bach, may be applied: "The German nation may rejoice in boasting that both were her sons.[1] There have been composers of note from Mendelssohn's day, who have faded from memory, and whose works are completely forgotten. If the productions of Mendelssohn could be completely blotted out, would there be no blank in the world of art? Assuredly there would. Take away *Elijah*, the violin concerto, and the "Hebrides" overture—to name only three typical works—and the machinery of the concert-giver would be thrown out of gear. The world has not done with these yet, nor with some others. The weaker productions—and Mendelssohn had his weak moments—are passing quietly away, but there is a vitality in his best works that ensures them a long life yet. Mendelssohn filled his proper place in the world, and when his work was done he was called home to his rest. He never swerved from his ideal; at any cost he did his duty; and he raised the tone of artistic life. It was no empty

[1] "Life of Bach" (Spitta), vol. iii. p. 64.

compliment that the Prince Consort wrote in the word-book of *Elijah* after the second performance in London in 1847; and this imperfect attempt at setting forth Mendelssohn the musician cannot better be brought to a conclusion than by repeating it, well known though it be—

"To the Noble Artist, who, surrounded by the Baal-worship of debased art, has been able, by his genius and science, to preserve faithfully, like another Elijah, the worship of true art, and once more to accustom our ear, amid the whirl of empty, frivolous sounds, to the pure tones of sympathetic feeling and legitimate harmony: to the Great Master, who makes us conscious of the unity of his conception, through the whole maze of his creation, from the soft whispering to the mighty raging of the elements.

"Inscribed in grateful remembrance by

"ALBERT.

"Buckingham Palace, April 24, 1847."

Very soon after the death of Mendelssohn, the Sacred Harmonic Society of London passed a resolution for the erection of a memorial to him. A deputation from the Society waited upon the Prince Consort on November 20th, to submit the proposal. Her Majesty and the Prince subscribed £50, the Philharmonic Society voted a like sum, and it was decided that the memorial should

Monument to Mendelssohn at Leipzig

take the form of a statue. After the lapse of some years the work was intrusted to Mr. C. Bacon, from whose model a bronze statue was cast by Messrs. Robinson and Cottam, of Pimlico, on November 22, 1859. The statue was eight feet in height, and weighed about a ton and a half. It was set up on the terrace of the Crystal Palace at Sydenham, and the inauguration was marked by a performance of *Elijah* on the scale of the Handel Festivals, the band and chorus numbering 3000. This ceremony took place on May 4, 1860.

Many years later, May 26, 1892, a statue of Mendelssohn was unveiled at Leipzig, the monument standing in front of the New Gewandhaus Concert House.

In 1848 a plan was originated at Leipzig to found a Mendelssohn Scholarship in connection with the Conservatorium. An appeal was made to the composer's English friends to help, and a committee was formed in London in July, 1848. A performance of *Elijah* was arranged to take place in Exeter Hall on December 15th, with Mademoiselle Jenny Lind as the principal soprano. "The hall was crowded by the most brilliant and aristocratic audience ever assembled within its walls."[1] A large profit was made, and with donations reached over £1000, which was invested as the nucleus of the Scholarship Fund. The amalgamation with Leipzig fell through, and the Mendelssohn Scholarship

[1] *Musical World*, 1848, p. 813.

was purely an English foundation. The first scholar was elected in 1856, and his name was Arthur Seymour Sullivan.

Germany was a long way behind in establishing its Scholarships. In 1877, the German Government, in exchange for the forty-four volumes of Mendelssohn MSS., arranged with the Mendelssohn family to found two Exhibitions, one for composition, the other for practical musicianship. The first election took place October 1, 1879. Engelberg Humperdinck obtained the Scholarship for composition, and the violinist Josef Kotek was awarded the other.[1]

Thus the memory of Mendelssohn will be kept alive in England and in Germany; may the day be far distant when he will be remembered only through a Scholarship!

[1] "Dictionary of Music and Musicians" (Grove), vol. ii. p. 294.

APPENDICES

APPENDIX A

THE Mendelssohn bibliography is extensive, and may be divided into three sections: the first contributed by himself in his own letters; the second consisting of biographies written by those who had personal knowledge of him; and the third of compilations, critical essays, and articles in musical periodicals and magazines.

I. LETTERS.

I. Reisebriefe von Felix Mendelssohn-Bartholdy aus den Jahren 1830 bis 1832, herausgegeben von Paul Mendelssohn-Bartholdy. Leipzig, 1861.

English translation by Lady Wallace. London: Longmans, 1862. Seventh Edition, 1876. Biographical Notice by H. F. Chorley.

II. Briefe aus den Jahren 1833 bis 1847, herausgegeben von Paul Mendelssohn-Bartholdy and Dr. Carl Mendelssohn-Bartholdy. Leipzig, 1863.

English translation by Lady Wallace. London: Longmans, 1863. Several editions since.

This volume contains a catalogue, compiled by Julius Rietz, of Mendelssohn's compositions, in chronological order, but not altogether trustworthy or complete.

III. **Letters** of Felix Mendelssohn to Ignaz and Charlotte Moscheles, translated from the originals in his possession, and edited by Felix Moscheles. Boston : Ticknor, 1888.

A selection from these letters appeared in *Scribner's Magazine*, 1888.

This volume is illustrated by fac-similes of drawings by Mendelssohn, various documents, and a drawing of Mendelssohn's study by Felix Moscheles, made a few days after the composer's death.

IV. Acht Briefe und ein fac-simile. Leipzig, 1871.

Published for the benefit of the "Deutschen Invaliden-Stiftung," and supposed to be addressed to Madame Voigt.

V. Musikerbriefe, herausgegeben von Ludwig Nohl. Leipzig, 1867. Translated by Lady Wallace, with the title "Letters of Distinguished Musicians." London : Longmans, 1867.

Contains thirty letters by Mendelssohn to various persons, dating from 1826 to 1847.

Reference to additional letters will be found in the works hereafter to be named.

II. BIOGRAPHY.

I. **Lampadius (W. A.).** Felix Mendelssohn-Bartholdy. Ein Denkmal fur sein Freunde. Leipzig, 1848. Edited and translated by William Leonard Gage. New York, 1866. London : William Reeves, 1876.

Included are supplementary sketches by Benedict, Chorley, Rellstab, Bayard Taylor, R. S. Willis, and J. S. Dwight, with additional notes by C. L. Gruneisen.

Appendix A

II. **Benedict** (Jules). Sketch of the Life and Works of the late Felix Mendelssohn-Bartholdy. London: Murray, 1850. Second Edition, with additions, 1853.

Written in an enthusiastic vein, but facts and dates rather mixed.

III. **Chorley** (Henry F.). Modern German Music. 2 vols. London: Smith, Elder and Co. 1854.

Contains many references to Mendelssohn, and an account of the Three Days' Festival at Brunswick, 1839: Conductor, F. Mendelssohn. A chapter in Mendelssohn's life omitted by his biographers. Also in "Music and Manners in France and Germany," 1844.

IV. **Magnien** (Victor). Étude Biographique sur Mendelssohn-Bartholdy. Beauvais, 1850.

V. **Neumann** (W.). F. Mendelssohn-Bartholdy, Eine Biographie. Cassell, 1854.

VI. **Reissmann** (August). Felix Mendelssohn-Bartholdy: sein Leben und seine Werke. Berlin, 1867.

VII. **Devrient** (Eduard). Meine Erinnerungen an Felix Mendelssohn-Bartholdy. Leipzig, 1869.

Translated into English by Natalia Macfarren, as "My Recollections of Felix Mendelssohn-Bartholdy, and his Letters to me." London: Bentley, 1869.

Full of information; generally to be relied upon as to dates; contains many letters. Richard Wagner published a pamphlet on this work, not impugning the facts, but criticizing the "too strictly commercial German" in which the book is written. See Wagner's Prose Works, translated by W. Ashton Ellis, vol. iv. p. 275.

VIII. **Polko** (Elise). Erinnerungen an F. M. B. Leipzig, 1868.
English translation by Lady Wallace. "Reminiscences of F. M. B." A Social and Artistic Biography. London : Longmans, 1869.

Entertaining to read, but worthless for purposes of reference. The Appendices contain forty-five letters to different persons. These give value to the book.

IX. **Barbadette** (H.). Felix Mendelssohn-Bartholdy : sa Vie et ses Œuvres. Paris, 1869.

X. **Mendelssohn-Bartholdy** (Dr. Carl). Goethe und Felix Mendelssohn-Bartholdy. Leipzig, 1871.

English translation by Miss M. E. von Glehn. London : Macmillan, 1872. Second Edition, with additional letters, 1874.

This volume contains thirty-seven letters.

XI. Musical Recollections of the Last Half-Century. 2 vols. London : Tinsley Brothers, 1872.

Published anonymously, but understood to be by the Rev. John Edmund Cox, D.D. Contains many references to Mendelssohn, with contemporary accounts of the production of *Elijah*, etc.

XII. **Planché** (J. R.). Recollections and Reflections of. 2 vols. London : Tinsley Brothers, 1872.

The first volume contains nine letters from Mendelssohn relating to the opera for which Planché was to provide the *libretto.*

XIII. Aus Moscheles Leben, von seiner Frau. 2 vols. Leipzig, 1872–3.

English translation by A. D. Coleridge. Life of Moscheles, with selections from his Diary and Correspondence. 2 vols. London : Hurst and Blackett, 1873.

References to Mendelssohn from 1824 to 1847. Letters from

Mendelssohn's father and mother, and several from himself. The latter reprinted in "Letters," vol. iii.

XIV. **Chorley** (Henry Fothergill). Autobiography, Memoir, and Letters. Compiled by Henry G. Hewlett. 2 vols. London: Bentley, 1873.

Notices of Mendelssohn, and six letters, 1840–47.

XV. **Hiller** (Ferdinand). Mendelssohn: Letters and Recollections. London: Macmillan, 1874. First published in *Macmillan's Magazine*, 1874.

English translation by Miss M. E. von Glehn. Includes many details which make the volume useful for reference; and contains over twenty letters previously unpublished.

XVI. **Hensel** (S.). Die Familie Mendelssohn, 1729–1847. Nach Briefen und Tagebüchern. 3 vols. Berlin, 1879. Second Edition, 1880.

Second revised Edition translated into English by Karl Klingemann, and an American collaborator, with a notice by George Grove, Esq. 2 vols. London: Sampson Low and Co., 1881.

A work of great value. The Sketch of Moses Mendelssohn is excellent, though not so complete, as regards his writings, as the memoir by M. Samuels. The Mendelssohn family occupies a large space; and, save for the letters, the account of Felix Mendelssohn is of less importance than other biographies.

XVII. **Rockstro** (W. S.). Mendelssohn. London: Sampson Low and Co., 1884.

Contains some personal reminiscences, and interesting notices of Mendelssohn's performances as organist and pianist.

XVIII. **Hadden** (James Cuthbert). Mendelssohn. London, 1888.

XIX. **Eckhardt** (Julius). Ferdinand David und die Familie Mendelssohn-Bartholdy. Leipzig, 1889.

A great deal more about Mendelssohn than David, but a most interesting book.

XX. **Holland** (H. E.) and **Rockstro** (W. S.). Memoirs of Madame Jenny Lind-Goldschmidt: her Early Art-Life and Dramatic Career, 1820–1851. 2 vols. London: John Murray, 1891.

In this work there are many references to Mendelssohn, and thirteen hitherto unpublished letters, chiefly to the great singer, but one or two addressed to Franz Hauser, baritone vocalist, later Director of the Conservatorium, Munich. There is much information relating to the performances of *Elijah* in promotion of the Mendelssohn Foundation, and a correction of the report that Mendelssohn had arranged for Jenny Lind to sing in the performance of *Elijah* in Vienna in 1847.

XXI. **Selden** (Camille). La Musique en Allemagne. Mendelssohn. Paris, 1867.

XXII. **Gumprecht** (Otto). Musikalische Charakterbilder. Leipzig, 1868.

Contains a notice of Mendelssohn.

III. DICTIONARY ARTICLES, CRITICAL ESSAYS, AND MISCELLANEOUS.

Schilling (Dr. Gustav). Encyclopädie der gesammten musikalischen Wissenschaften, oder Universal-Lexicon der Tonkunst. Stuttgart, 1835–38. 6 vols.

Vol. iv., 1837, contains a brief but appreciative article on Mendelssohn.

Appendix A

Fétis (F. J.). Biographie Universelle des Musiciens. 8 vols. Paris : Firmin-Didot. Second Edition, 1875–8.

Pougin (Arthur). Supplément et Complément. 2 vols. Paris : Firmin-Didot, 1878–80.

The Bibliography of Mendelssohn is very complete to date, and this compilation is indebted to it.

Clément (Felix). Les Musiciens Célèbres. Paris : Hachette, 1873.

Mendel-Reissmann. Musikalisches Conversations - Lexicon. 12 vols. Berlin : Heimann (vol. i.); Oppenheim (vols. ii.–xii.), 1870–83.

Riemann (Hugo). Musik-Lexicon, 1882. Several editions.

English translation by J. S. Shedlock. London : Augener. Last edition, 1896.

An excellent condensed article on Mendelssohn.

Barnard (Charles). Mozart and Mendelssohn. Boston, U.S.A., 1870.

Brown (James D.). Biographical Dictionary of Musicians. Paisley : Alex. Gardner, 1886.

Bibliographical section of considerable value.

Grove (Sir George). A Dictionary of Music and Musicians. 4 vols. With Appendix edited by J. A. Fuller-Maitland. London : Macmillan, 1879–89.

Contains the best monograph on Mendelssohn to be found in any language.

Lobe (J. C.). My First Meeting with Felix Mendelssohn-Bartholdy. Translated from the German. *The Choir*, vol. xiv. p. 385.

Dorn (Heinrich). Recollections of Felix Mendelssohn and his Friends. (*Temple Bar*, February, 1872.) Reprinted in *The Choir*, vol. xiii. pp. 82–114.

Schubring (Julius). Reminiscences of Felix Mendelssohn-Bartholdy. Magazin Daheim, Leipzig, 1866. English translation in *The Musical World*, 1866, pp. 300, 318.

Written as a memorial of his fifty-seventh birthday, February 3, 1866.

Briefwechsel zwischen F. Mendelssohn-Bartholdy und J. Schubring. 1891.

Rellstab (Heinrich F. L.). Aus meinem Leben. 2 vols. Berlin, 1861.

An account of Mendelssohn's visit to Goethe.

Marx-Adolph (Bernard). Erinnerungen aus meinem Leben. 2 vols. Berlin, 1865.

Various references to Mendelssohn.

Horsley (Charles Edward). Reminiscences of Mendelssohn, by his English Pupil. First published in Dwight's *Journal of Music*. Boston, U.S.A. *The Choir*, vol. xv. p. 20, *et seq.*

Enthusiastic, but not to be relied upon as to dates, etc.

Hogarth (George). The Philharmonic Society of London. From its Foundation, 1813, to its Fiftieth Year, 1862. London: Robert Cocks, 1862. Second Edition.

References to Mendelssohn, and three letters of his family to the society, and parts of seven to Sterndale Bennett.

Moscheles (Felix). Fragments of an Autobiography. London: Nisbet, 1899.

Contains an account of Leipzig in 1847, and of the death of Mendelssohn.

Jahn (Otto). Ueber F. M. B.'s Oratorium *Paulus*. Kiel, 1842.

Zander (Fr.). Ueber Mendelssohn's Walpurgisnachts. Konigsberg, 1862.

Edwards (F. G.). The History of Mendelssohn's Oratorio *Elijah*. London: Novello, 1896.

A most valuable work, with much new information, and a number of letters from Mendelssohn to William Bartholomew.

Parry (Sir C. H. H.). Studies of Great Composers. London: G. Routledge, 1886.

Edwards (F. G.). Musical Haunts in London. London: J. Curwen, 1895.

Interesting notes of Mendelssohn's visits to London, and to Mr. Thomas Attwood at Norwood.

Appendix A

Magazines, Musical Periodicals, Etc.

The references to Mendelssohn in periodical literature are endless, and only the most important can be noticed here. The greatest interest attaches to those written nearest to the times in which the composer lived.

The Athenæum. Frequent articles from the year 1839, when Chorley first became acquainted with Mendelssohn. Birmingham Festival, and production of *Elijah*, 1846. Obituary notice, 1847.

Edinburgh Review, vol. 115.

British Quarterly Review, vols. 24 and 36.

Frazer's Magazine, vol. 36, 37, 68, 79.

Dublin Review, vol. 54.

Contemporary Review, 1870. Mendelssohn's *Elijah.* A Study. Rev. H. R. Haweis.

Temple Bar, 1871 and 1874.

Journal of Speculative Philosophy, vol. 7.

Boston Review, vol. 5.

Rundschau, 1889. Twenty letters to Aloys Fuchs. Published for the first time.

The Musical World, vol. ii. (1836). Düsseldorf Festival. Production of *St. Paul.* Carl Klingemann. Vol. iv. Biographical Sketch of Mendelssohn, with pencil portrait by E. P. Novello.

—— 1846. Birmingham Festival, and production of *Elijah.*

—— 1847. Five articles on *Elijah.* Obituary notices.

—— 1849. Mendelssohn. A critical essay. G. A. Macfarren.

The Musical Times, vol. ii. Obituary notice. Vols. v. and vi. *St. Paul*: detailed analysis. G. A. Macfarren.

—— 1879. The Great Composers sketched by themselves: Mendelssohn. Joseph Bennett.

—— 1882–83. *Elijah*: a comparison of the original and revised scores. Joseph Bennett.

Mendelssohn

The Musical Times, 1891. "Hear my Prayer," a companion of the original MS. with the published score. F. G. Edwards.

—— 1897. Biographical Sketch. Family portraits.

Concordia. 1875. Mendelssohn's place in Modern Music. H. H. Statham.

The Monthly Musical Record. 1871. Mendelssohn's Unpublished Symphonies. "G."

—— 1875. On Mendelssohn and some of his Contemporary Critics. Fr. Niecks.

—— 1876. Translation of Lenz's article, "Mendelssohn, a chapter in 'Beethoven et ses Trois Styles.'"

—— 1880. Hans von Bülow on Mendelssohn's Pianoforte Music. (Preface to a new edition of Mendelssohn's "Rondo Capriccioso," Op. 14.)

Musical News. 1895. Mendelssohn's "Hymn of Praise." Historical notice. F. G. Edwards.

—— Organ Preludes and Fugues. F. G. Edwards.

APPENDIX B

List of Compositions

Compiled from all available sources

Op. 1. Quartet, No. 1, for pianoforte and strings C minor. 1822.

Op. 2. Quartet, No. 2, for pianoforte and strings. F minor. 1823.

Op. 3. Quartet, No. 3, for pianoforte and strings. B minor. 1824–1825.

Op. 4. Sonata, for pianoforte and violin. F minor.

Op. 5. Capriccio. Pianoforte solo. F sharp minor. 1825.

Op. 6. Sonata. Pianoforte. E major. 1826.

Op. 7. Seven Characteristic Pieces :

No. 1 ... ... E minor.
No. 2 ... ... B minor.
No. 3 ... ... D.
No. 4 ... ... A.
No. 5 ... ... A.
No. 6 ... ... E minor.
No. 7 ... ... E.

Published 1827.

Op. 8. Twelve Songs. Voice and pianoforte. Published 1830. Of these songs, No. 2, *Heimweh* ; No. 3, *Italien* ; and No. 12, a duet, *Zuleika und Hatem*, are compositions of Fanny Hensel.

Op. 9. Twelve Songs. Voice and pianoforte.
No. 7, *Sleepless*; No. 10, *Forsaken*; and No. 12, *The Dying Nun*, are compositions of Fanny Hensel. [1829.]

Op. 10. *The Wedding of Camacho.* Comic Opera in two acts. 1825.

Op. 11. Symphony No. 1. Orchestra. C minor. 1824.
Really No. 13, as 12 symphonies for strings were written earlier.

Op. 12. Quartet, No. 1. Two violins, viola, and 'cello. E flat. 1829.

Op. 13. Quartet, No. 2. Two violins, viola, and 'cello. A minor. 1827.

Op. 14. Rondo Capriccioso. Pianoforte. E minor. (Dated Oct. 26.)

Op. 15. Fantasia on *The Last Rose of Summer.* Pianoforte. E.

Op. 16. Three Fantasias. Pianoforte.
Andante and Allegro ... A minor.
Capriccio ... ... E minor.
Andante (*The Rivulet*) ... E major.
Composed in Wales 1829; published 1830 (?).

Op. 17. Variations Concertantes. Pianoforte and violoncello. D. 1829.

Op. 18. Quintet, No. 1. Two violins, two violas, and 'cello. A. 1831.

Op. 19. Six Songs without Words. Book I. Pianoforte.
No. 1. Andante con moto ... ... E.
No. 2. Andante expressivo ... ... A minor
No. 3. Molto allegro ... ... A
No. 4. Moderato ... ... A
No. 5. Agitato ... ... F sharp minor
No. 6. Andante sostenuto (In a gondola) ... G minor.
No. 6, Venice, 1830. Published 1832.

Appendix B

Op. 19*a*. Six Songs. Voice and pianoforte. No. 6, Venice, 1830.

Op. 20. Octet. Four violins, two violas, two 'cellos. E flat. 1825.

Op. 21. Overture, *A Midsummer Night's Dream.* Orchestra. E. 1826.

Op. 22. Capriccio brillant. Pianoforte and orchestra. B minor. [1832.] Published 1832.

Op. 23. Three Pieces, Church Music.
No. 1. *Aus tiefer Noth.* Voices and organ.
No. 2. *Ave Maria.* Eight voices and organ. A.
No. 3. *Mitten Wir.* Eight voices and organ.
Rome, 1830.

Op. 24. Overture. Wind instruments. C. 1824.
Afterwards arranged for a full military band.

Op. 25. Concerto, No. 1. Pianoforte and orchestra. G minor. 1831.

Op. 26. Concert-Overture, *Die Hebriden.* (*Fingal's Höhle*; The Isles of Fingal.) B minor. First form, Dec. 1830.

Op. 27. Concert-Overture, *Die Meeresstille und Glücklichefahrt.* (The Calm Sea and Prosperous Voyage.) D. 1828.

Op. 28. Fantasia (Sonate écossaise). Pianoforte. F sharp minor. Berlin, 1833.

Op. 29. Rondo brilliant. Pianoforte and orchestra. E flat. Düsseldorf, 1834.

Op. 30. Six Songs without Words. Book II. Pianoforte.
No. 7. Andante expressivo ... ... E flat.
No. 8. Allegro di molto ... ... B flat.
No. 9. Andante sostenuto ... ... E.
No. 10. Agitato e con fuoco ... B minor.
No. 11. Andante grazioso ... ... D.
No. 12. Allegretto (Venetian barcarole) F sharp minor.
[1833–1837.]

Op. 31. Psalm 115. *Non nobis Domine.* Soli, chorus, and orchestra. Various. 1830.

Op. 32. Concert-Overture, *Märchen von der schönen Melusine.* (The Story of the Lovely Melusina.) Orchestra. F. Berlin, 1833.

Op. 33. Three Capriccios. Pianoforte.
No. 1. Adagio and Presto ... A minor.
No. 2. Allegro grazioso ... E.
No. 3. Adagio and Presto ... B flat minor.
1833–1835.

Op. 34. Six Songs. Voice and pianoforte. 1834–1837.

Op. 35. Six Preludes and Fugues. Pianoforte.
No. 1 ... ... E minor.
No. 2 ... ... D.
No. 3 ... ... B minor.
No. 4 ... ... A flat.
No. 5 ... ... F minor.
No. 6 ... ... B flat.
1832–1837; published 1837.

Op. 36. Oratorio, *St. Paul.* Soli, chorus, orchestra, and organ 1834–1836.

Op. 37. Three Preludes and Fugues. Organ.
No. 1 ... ... C minor.
No. 2 ... ... G.
No. 3 ... ... D minor.
1833–1837; published 1837.

Op. 38. Six Songs without Words. Book III. Pianoforte.
No. 13. Con moto ... ... E flat.
No. 14. Allegro non troppo ... C minor.
No. 15. Presto ... ... E.
No. 16. Andante ... ... A.
No. 17. Agitato ... ... A minor.
No. 18. Duetto, Andante con moto ... A flat.

(No. 18 was composed by Mendelssohn as a love-song for his *fiancée* when the pair were engaged.) 1836–1837.

Appendix B

Op. 39. Three Motets. Female voices and organ. Rome, 1830.

Op. 40. Concerto, No. 2. Pianoforte and orchestra. D minor. 1837.

Op. 41. Six Part-Songs. Soprano, alto, tenor, and bass. (Open-air Music.) Various. [1834.]

Op. 42. Psalm 42. *As the Hart pants.* Soprano solo, quintet, chorus, and orchestra. F. 1837.

Op. 43. Serenade and Allegro giojoso. Pianoforte and orchestra. B minor. 1838.

Op. 44. Three Quartets (Nos. 3, 4, and 5). Two violins, viola, and 'cello. D, E minor, and E flat. 1837–1838.

Op. 45. Sonato (No. 1). Pianoforte and 'cello. B flat. 1838.

Op. 46. Psalm 95. *Come, let us sing.* Tenor solo, duet, two sopranos, chorus, and orchestra. E flat major, G minor. 1838.

At a performance of this Psalm at the Crystal Palace, November 26, 1876, a final chorus on the fifth, sixth, and seventh verses of the Psalm was sung for the first time. The composer had evidently written it in order that the Psalm should end in the key of E flat. However, he suppressed the number, and it was only published in 1876, by Novello and Co.

Op. 47. Six Songs. Voice and pianoforte. 1839.

Op. 48. Six Part-Songs. Soprano, alto, tenor, and bass. (Open-air Music, second set.) 1839.

Op. 49. Trio, No. 1. Pianoforte, violin, and 'cello. D minor. 1839.

Op. 50. Six Part-Songs. Tenor and bass voices. 1839–1840.

No. 2 (*Der Jäger Abschied*) has an accompaniment for four horns and bass trombone.

Op. 51. Psalm 114. *When Israel out of Egypt came.* Eight-part chorus and orchestra. G. 1839.

Op. 52. *Lobgesang* (Hymn of Praise, Symphony-Cantata). Soprano and tenor solo, chorus, orchestra, and organ. B flat. 1840.

(The Symphony is always counted as Symphony, No. 2.)

Op. 53. Six Songs without Words. Book IV. Pianoforte.

No. 19.	Andante con moto ...	A flat.
No. 20.	Allegro non troppo ...	E flat.
No. 21.	Presto agitato	G minor.
No. 22.	Adagio	F.
No. 23.	Allegro (*Volkslied*) ...	A minor.
No. 24.	Molto allegro vivace ...	A.

[1841].

Op. 54. Variations Sérieuses. Pianoforte. D minor. 1841.

Op. 55. Music to *Antigone* (Sophocles). Men's voices and orchestra. Various. 1841.

Op. 56. Symphony, No 3. *The Scotch.* Orchestra. A minor. Commenced in Rome, 1830; finished 1842; published [1843 ?].

Op. 57. Six Songs. Voice and pianoforte. Various. 1839–1842.

Op. 58. Sonata, No. 2. Pianoforte and violoncello. D. 1843.

Op. 59. Six Part-Songs. Soprano, alto, tenor, and bass. (Open-air Music, third set.) No. 1, 1837; Nos. 2–6, 1843.

Op. 60. Music to *Die Erste Walpurgis-Nacht* (Goethe). Soli, chorus, and orchestra. Commenced 1831; revised 1842; published 1843.

Op. 61. Music to *A Midsummer Night's Dream* (Shakespeare).

Scherzo.	Orchestra.	G minor.
Notturno.	„	E.
Wedding March.	„	C.

Songs, with chorus, female voices; incidental orchestral music. 1843.

Appendix B

Op. 62. Six Songs without Words. Book V. Pianoforte.
No. 25. Andante espressivo ... ... G.
No. 26. Allegro con fuoco ... ... B flat.
No. 27. Andante maestoso ... ... E minor.
No. 28. Allegro con anima ... ... G.
No. 29. Andante (Venetian barcarole) ... A minor.
No. 30. Allegretto grazioso ... ... A.

Op. 63. Six Two-part Songs. Voices and pianoforte. 1836–1844.

Op. 64. Concerto. Violin and orchestra. E minor. 1844.

Op. 65. Six Sonatas. Organ.
No. 1. ... F minor ... 1844.
No. 2. ... C minor ... 1839–1844.
No. 3. ... A ... 1844.
No. 4. ... B flat ... 1845.
No. 5. ... D ... 1844.
No. 6. ... D minor ... 1845.
Published 1845.

Op. 66. Trio, No. 2. Pianoforte, violin, and 'cello. C minor. 1845.

Op. 67. Six Songs without Words. Book VI. Pianoforte.
No. 31. Andante ... ... E flat.
No. 32. Allegro leggiero ... ... F sharp minor.
No. 33. Andante tranquillo ... ... B flat.
No. 34. Presto ... ... C.
No. 35. Moderato ... ... B minor.
No. 36. Allegro non troppo ... ... E.
1843–1845.

Op. 68. Festgesang, *An die Künstler* (Schiller). (To the sons of Art.) Men's voices and brass instruments. 1846.

Op. 69. Three Motets. Solo and chorus. 1847.

Op. 70. Oratorio, *Elijah*. Soli, chorus. Orchestra and organ. 1846; revised 1846–47; published June, 1847.

Op. 71. Six Songs. Voice and pianoforte. 1842–1847.

Op. 72. Six Children's Pieces. Pianoforte.
No. 1. Allegro non troppo ... ... G.
No. 2. Andante sostenuto ... ... E flat.
No. 3. Allegretto ... ... G.
No. 4. Andante con moto ... ... D.
No. 5. Allegro assai ... ... G minor.
No. 6. Vivace ... ... F.
Prepared for publication, December, 1846; published 1847.

POSTHUMOUS PUBLICATIONS.

Op. 73. *Lauda Sion.* Sacred Cantata. (Praise Jehovah. English Version by William Bartholomew.) Soprano solo, quartet, chorus, orchestra. Composed 1846; published 1848.

Op. 74. Music to *Athalie* (Racine). Soli, chorus, and orchestra. Choruses composed 1843. Overture, 1844–1845.

Op. 75. Four Part-Songs. Two tenors and two basses. 1839–1844.

Op. 76. Four Part-Songs. Two tenors and two basses. 1844–1846.

Op. 77. Three Two-part Songs. Voices and pianoforte. 1836–1847.

Op. 78. Psalm 2. *Why rage fiercely the Heathen?* Double chorus. 1843.
Psalm 22. *My God, my God.* Double chorus. 1844.
Psalm 43. *Judge me, O God.* Eight-part chorus. 1844.

Op. 79. Six Motets. Eight-part chorus. 1843–1846.

Op. 80. Quartet (No. 6). Two violins, viola, and 'cello. F minor. 1847.

Op. 81. Andante. Two violins, viola, and 'cello. E. 1847.
Scherzo. " " " A minor. 1847.
Capriccio. " " " E minor. 1843.
Fugue. " " " E flat. 1827.

Appendix B

Op. 82. Variations. Pianoforte. E flat. 1841.

Op. 83. Variations. Pianoforte. B flat. 1841.

Op. 83*a*. Variations. Pianoforte duet. B flat. (An arrangement of Op. 83 for four hands.)

Op. 84. Three Songs. Voice and pianoforte. 1831–1839.

Op. 85. Six Songs without Words. Book VII. Pianoforte.
No. 37. Andante espressivo ... ... F.
No. 38. Allegro agitato ... ... A minor.
No. 39. Presto ... ... E flat.
No. 40. Andante sostenuto ... ... D.
No. 41. Allegretto ... ... A.
No. 42. Allegretto con moto ... B flat.
1841–1847.

Op. 86. Six Songs. Voice and pianoforte. 1831–1847.

Op. 87. Quintet. Two violins, two violas, and 'cello. B flat. 1845.

Op. 88. Six Part-Songs. Soprano, alto, tenor, and bass. (Open-air Music, fourth set.) 1839–1844.

Op. 89. Operetta, *Heimker aus der Fremde*. (Son and Stranger.) Voices and orchestra. 1829.

Op. 90. Symphony, No. 4 (*Italian*). Orchestra. A. 1833.

Op. 91. Psalm 98. *Sing to the Lord a New-made Song*. Eight-part chorus, and orchestra. 1843.

Op. 92. Allegro brillant. Pianoforte duet. A. 1841.

Op. 93. Music to *Œdipus in Colonus* (Sophocles). Men's voices and orchestra. 1845.

Op. 94. Scena, *Infelice*. Soprano solo and orchestra. B flat. 1834; revised 1843.

Op. 95. Overture, *Ruy Blas*. Orchestra. C minor. 1839.

Op. 96. Psalm 13. Contralto solo, chorus, and orchestra. E flat. 1840–1843.

(Extension of a former work. Three sacred songs for alto voice, chorus, and organ. Published without opus number.)

Op. 97. Oratorio, *Christus* (unfinished). Recitative and choruses. 1847.

Op. 98. Opera, *Loreley* (unfinished).

(*a*) Finale to the first act. Soprano solo and chorus. E. 1847.

(*b*) *Ave Maria.* Soprano solo and female chorus. B flat.

(*c*) A vintage song. Chorus, tenors, and basses. G.

Op. 99. Six Songs. Voice and pianoforte. 1841–1845.

Op. 100. Four Part-Songs. Two tenors and two basses. 1839–1844.

SECOND SERIES OF POSTHUMOUS PUBLICATIONS

Op. 101. Overture (Trumpet). Orchestra. C. Composed 1826; published 1867.

Op. 102. Six Songs without Words. Book VIII. Pianoforte.

No. 43. Andante un poco agitato ... E minor. 1842.
No. 44. Adagio ... ... D.
No. 45. Presto ... ... C. 1844.
No. 46. Un poco agitato ... ... G minor. 1841.
No. 47. Allegro vivace ... ... A. 1845.
No. 48. Andante ... ... C. 1842.

Op. 103. Trauermarch. Military Band. A minor. 1836.
(Composed for the funeral of Norbert Burgmüller.)

Op. 104. Three Preludes. Pianoforte.

No. 1. ... B flat ... 1836.
No. 2. ... B minor ... 1836.
No. 3. ... D ... 1836.

——— Three Studies. Pianoforte.

No. 1. ... B flat minor ... 1836.
No. 2. ... F ... ... 1834.
No. 3. ... A minor ... 1838.

Appendix B

Op. 105. Sonata. Pianoforte. G minor. 1821.

Op. 106. Sonata. Pianoforte. B flat. 1827.

Op. 107. Symphony, No. 5 (*Reformation*). Orchestra. D minor. 1830–1832.

Op. 108. March. Orchestra. D. 1841.
(Composed in celebration of the visit of Cornelius, the painter, to Dresden, 1841.)

Op. 109. Song without Words. 'Cello and pianoforte. D. 1845.

Op. 110. Sextet. Pianoforte, violin, two violas, 'cello, and bass. D. 1824.

Op. 111. *Tu es Petrus.* Five-part chorus and orchestra. 1827.

Op. 112. Two Sacred Songs. Voice and pianoforte. 1835.
(No. 2. *Thou, who hast doomed man to die*, originally composed for *St. Paul.*)

Op. 113. Concertstück, No. 1. Clarinet, corno di bassetto, and pianoforte. F minor. 1833.

Op. 114. Concertstück, No. 2. Clarinet, corno di bassetto, and pianoforte. D minor. 1833.

Op. 115. Two Sacred Choruses (*Beati mortui*; *Periti autem*). Men's voices.

Op. 116. Funeral Song. Chorus, soprano, alto, tenor, and bass.

Op. 117. Albumblatt. Pianoforte. E minor. 1837.

Op. 118. Capriccio. Pianoforte. E.

Op. 119. Perpetuum mobile. Pianoforte. C.

Op. 120. Seven Part Songs. Two tenors and two basses. 1837–1847.

Op. 121. Responsorium and Hymnus. Men's chorus and organ.

PUBLISHED WITHOUT OPUS NUMBER

Hymn. *Hear my Prayer.* Soprano solo, chorus and organ. 1844. (Afterwards scored for orchestra.)

Hymn. *Grant us Thy Peace.* Chorus and orchestra. E flat. 1831.

Three Hymns. Alto solo and chorus. (See Op. 96.)

Kyrie Eleison. Double chorus.

Te Deum and *Jubilate Deo.* Voices and organ. A. 1846.

Magnificat and *Nunc dimittis.* Voices and organ. B flat and E flat.

Festgesang. Four numbers. Male voices and brass band. G. 1840.

Anthem : *Lord have mercy.* Voices only. A minor. 1833.

Glory to God in the Highest. Double chorus.

Songs :

There be none of Beauty's Daughters. Voice and pianoforte. A.
Sun of the Sleepless. Voice and pianoforte. E minor. 1834.
The Mountain-burgh. „ „ E minor. 1835.
A Bird is softly calling. „ „ B flat. 1841.
The Garland. „ „ A. 1829.
The Maiden's Lament. „ „ B minor.
Beware of the Rhine. „ „ G.
The Savoyard's Return. „ „ A minor.
The Sun is dancing on the Streams. „ Published 1836 (?).
(See *Musical World*, vol. iii. p. 189.)

(Written by Allan Cunningham, in commemoration of the introduction of trial by jury, and the abolition of domestic slavery in the Island of Ceylon. Profits to be applied to the education and provision of the children of emancipated slaves. Was this the outcome of the Commission from Ceylon, in 1829 ? See p. 65.)

Two Songs. Voice and pianoforte. 1835.

Two Songs. „ „ 1841.

Das Seemans Scheidelied „

Three Volkslieder. Two voices and pianoforte.

Quartet. Two violins, viola, and 'cello. E flat. Composed 1813 ; published 1879.

Appendix B

Variations on the March in *Preciosa* (Mendelssohn and Moscheles). Pianoforte duet (originally for two pianofortes with orchestra.) 1833.

Prelude and Fugue. Pianoforte. E minor. Prelude 1841; fugue 1827.

Andante cantabile and Presto agitato. Pianoforte. B. 1838.

Scherzo a capriccio. Pianoforte. F sharp minor.

Scherzo. Pianoforte. B minor.

Étude. Pianoforte. F minor. 1896.

Barcarolle. Pianoforte. A. 1837.

Two Musical Sketches:

No. 1. Andante cantabile. Pianoforte. B flat.

No. 2. Presto agitato " G minor.

Præludium. Organ. C minor. 1841.

(Written for Mr. Henry E. Dibdin, of Edinburgh, and published in fac-simile.)

Fugue. Organ. F minor. Published 1885.

(No. 3 of a set of three fugues, written in 1839.)

Andante and Variations. Organ. D. Composed 1844; the two were published in 1898.

Allegro. Organ. B flat. Published 1898.

(See letter to Mr. Coventry, Appendix to Polko's *Reminiscences*, p. 246.)

Additional Accompaniments to Handel's *Dettingen Te Deum.*

Additional Accompaniments to Handel's *Acis and Galatea.*

Pianoforte Accompaniment to Bach's *Chaconne.*

The forty-four volumes of manuscripts in the Royal Library at Berlin contain a large number of works not published. These include five operas, four cantatas, motets, songs, etc.; eleven symphonies for strings, and one for full orchestra; an overture; two concertos for two pianofortes; concerto for pianoforte and violin; and for pianoforte—a trio, and several sonatas for pianoforte and strings; many pieces for pianoforte; a sonata for pianoforte and clarinet, and other things too numerous for mention. Some of these compositions have been performed in England: an adagio from the twelfth symphony, at the Crystal Palace Concerts, Feb. 3, 1877; the whole work at the same, Nov. 2, 1878; a duet for harp and pianoforte, *The Evening Bell*, at the same, April 22, 1876;[1] and the sonata for pianoforte and clarinet, at Brighton, Nov. 29, 1884.

---

[1] Mr. F. G. Edwards, in *Musical Haunts in London*, gives an account of the origin of this little piece, which exhibits Mendelssohn's humour. The bell was the gate-bell of Attwood's house at Norwood. The piece was published by Messrs. Chappell, a few years ago.

APPENDIX C

PRINCIPAL INCIDENTS AND EVENTS IN THE LIFE OF MENDELSSOHN

1809. Born at Hamburg, February 3rd.
1811. Mendelssohn family remove to Berlin.
1816. Young Mendelssohn taken to Paris by his father, and placed under the tuition of Madame Bigot.
1818. He makes his first appearance in public as a pianist, at Gugel's concert, Berlin, October 24th.
1819. Entered the singing class of the Berlin Singakademie, as an alto, April 11th. Began musical composition this year.
1820. Musical composition systematically practised. From fifty to sixty movements, for various instruments, are computed to have been written this year.
1821. Weber visits Berlin. Mendelssohn meets him and his pupil Benedict. He goes to Weimar with Zelter, on a visit to Goethe.
1822. Second public appearance, at Aloys Schmitt's Concert, Berlin, March 31st. Composes a pianoforte concerto, symphony for strings, Psalm, etc.
1823. First mention of Mendelssohn in an English musical periodical: the *Quarterly Musical Magazine and Review*, vol. v. p. 406. He travels in Silesia with his father.

1824. Rehearsal of his operetta, "The Two Nephews." Zelter proclaims Felix a member of the brotherhood of musicians. Mendelssohn is confirmed. Acquaintance with Moscheles begun.

1825. Second visit to Paris. Opera *Die Hochzeit des Camacho* completed. The family remove to Leipziger Strasse, No. 3.

1826. He enters the University, Berlin. Composes the "Midsummer Night's Dream" overture.

1827. Production of *Die Hochzeit des Camacho*, Berlin, April 29th. Tour in the Harz Mountains. Meeting with Thibaut at Heidelberg. Rehearsals of Bach's *Matthew Passion* music began.

1828. Dürer Festival at Berlin, April 18th, for which Felix wrote a cantata.

1829. Revival of Bach's *Matthew Passion* music, Berlin, March 11th. Mendelssohn pays his first visit to England. His Symphony in C minor produced by the London Philharmonic Society, May 25th. Tour in Scotland and Wales. His parents' silver wedding. Performance of *Die Heimkehr aus der Fremde*, Berlin, December 26th.

1830–31. Travelling years. He goes to Weimar, Munich, Vienna, and on to Italy. Death of Pope Pius VIII., November. Installation of Pope Gregory XVI. He witnesses the ceremonies, February, 1831. Notes the Holy Week music. Returns through Munich, Düsseldorf, and again visits Paris.

1832. Second visit to London, April. *Hebrides* overture played by the Philharmonic Society, May 14th. First Book of "Songs without Words" published by Novello. Death of Goethe, March 22nd; of Zelter, May 15th.

1833. Election of a conductor for the Berlin Singakademie. Mendelssohn defeated. He receives a commission from the London Philharmonic for a symphony, an overture, and a vocal piece. Third visit to London, April.

Appendix C

"Italian" Symphony produced, May 13th. Fourth visit to London, this time with his father, June 5th. Is appointed musical director at Düsseldorf. Enters upon his duties in September.

1834. Mendelssohn elected a member of the Berlin Academy of Fine Arts. Oratorio of *St. Paul* commenced.

1835. Invitation to become conductor of the Gewandhaus Concerts, Leipzig. Conducts Lower Rhine Festival, Cologne, June. Begins work at Leipzig, October. Death of his father, November 19th.

1836. Ferdinand David settles in Leipzig as Concertmeister, April. Degree of Doctor of Philosophy conferred upon Mendelssohn. Production of oratorio, *St. Paul*, Düsseldorf, May 22nd. Sterndale Bennett in Germany. Betrothal of Felix to Cécile Jeanrenaud, September 9th. *St. Paul* performed at Liverpool Festival, October 7th.

1837. Marriage of Mendelssohn at Frankfort, March 28th. Fifth visit to England, August 27th. First visit to Birmingham, September. *St. Paul* performed at Birmingham Festival, September 19th. Production of Second Pianoforte Concerto, September 21st. He takes his bride to his new home in Leipzig.

1838. Birth of a son, February 7th.

1839. He conducts festivals at Düsseldorf and Brunswick.

1840. Initial steps for formation of a *Conservatorium* at Leipzig. Production of the *Lobgesang*, Leipzig, June 25th. Second visit to Birmingham, and sixth to England. The *Lobgesang* produced at the Birmingham Festival, September 23rd.

1841. Mendelssohn removes to Berlin, to carry out the wish of the King of Prussia to establish an Academy of Arts. Completion of the music to Sophocles' *Antigone*. First performance, Potsdam, October 28th.

1842. The "Scotch" Symphony completed; produced, Leipzig, March 3rd. *Antigone* produced, Berlin, April 13th.

Seventh visit to England, this time with his wife, May. The "Scotch" Symphony at the Philharmonic, June 13th. Visit to the Queen, at Buckingham Palace, July 9th. Appointed General Musical Director to the King of Prussia, December 4th. Death of his mother, December 12th.

1843. Opening of the *Conservatorium*, Leipzig, April 3rd. Unveiling of the Bach monument, April 23rd. Production of the music to *A Midsummer Night's Dream* at Potsdam, October 14th.

1844. Eighth visit to England. Engaged to conduct the last five Philharmonic concerts, London. Production of the *Walpurgisnacht*, July 8th. Music to *Athalie* finished. The Violin Concerto completed at Soden, September 16th. Released from official duties at Berlin. Meets Jenny Lind for the first time, Berlin, October 21st.

1845. First performance of the Violin Concerto, Gewandhaus (David), March 13th. Receives an invitation from the Birmingham Festival Committee to write an oratorio for the festival of 1846. Returns to Leipzig in September. Production of *Œdipus Coloneus*, Potsdam, November 1st; and of *Athalie* at Charlottenburg, November 30th. Moscheles joins the staff of the *Conservatorium*, Leipzig.

1846. Undertakes pianoforte and composition classes at the *Conservatorium.* Conducts the Lower Rhine Festival at Aix-la-Chapelle, May 31st–June 2nd. *Lauda Sion* produced at Liége, June 11th. Conducts first festival of German-Flemish Vocal Associations at Cologne, June 14th and 15th. *Festgesang*, "To the Sons of Art," produced, Cologne, June 14th. Oratorio, *Elijah*, finished. Ninth visit to England, August. Production of *Elijah*, Birmingham Festival, August 26th. Break-down in health.

1847. Celebration of his birthday—his last!—at Leipzig, February 3rd. Invitation from the Sacred Harmonic Society, to conduct performances of the revised oratorio, *Elijah*, in London. Tenth and last visit to England, April. Conducts six performances of *Elijah* in a fortnight, in London, Manchester, and Birmingham. His last public appearance, Ancient Concerts, May 5th. Return to the Continent, broken in health. Death of his sister Fanny, May 14th. Direful effect upon Felix. Spends the summer in Switzerland. Returns to Leipzig, September 17th. Alarming attack of illness, October 9th. Partial recovery. Apoplectic seizure, November 3rd. Mendelssohn's death, at twenty-four minutes past nine in the evening of November 4th, at the age of thirty-eight years nine months.

APPENDIX D

Mendelssohn Personalia and Memoranda

Adams (Thomas). Organist of distinction, and composer for his instrument. Born Sept. 5th, 1785; died, London, Sept. 15th, 1858.

Albert (Prince Consort). Musical amateur, and admirer of Mendelssohn. Born Aug. 26th, 1819; married Queen Victoria, Feb. 10th, 1840; died, Windsor, Dec. 14th, 1861. Composer of a number of songs, anthems, etc. His "L'Invocazione all' Armonia" was performed at the Birmingham Festival of 1849, and repeated in 1855.

Alsager (T. M.). Journalist and musical amateur. Founder of the City article in the *Times*. Held quartet parties at his house, and was the founder of the Beethoven Quartet Society. Died, by his own hand, Nov., 1846.

Anderson (Mrs.—*née* Philpot). Pianist. Born, Dec., 1790; died, London, Dec. 24th, 1878. Gave lessons to Queen Victoria.

André (Julius). Son of the founder of the publishing firm of André, Offenbach-on-the-Main. Born at Offenbach, June 4th, 1808; died at Frankfort, April 17th, 1880. Pianist, organist, and composer.

Astolfi (Abbaté). Sopranist, of the Pontifical Chapel, Rome. Had a considerable reputation as a composer. Dates of birth and death unknown.

Appendix D

Attwood (Thomas). Organist and composer. Born in London, Nov. 23rd, 1765; died there, March 24th, 1838. Was sent to Vienna by George IV. (when Prince of Wales) to study under Mozart. Organist of St. Paul's Cathedral, 1796–1838.

Auber (Daniel François Esprit). Famous French opera composer. Born, Caen, Jan. 29th, 1782; died, Paris, May 13th, 1871.

Austin (Mrs.). Wife of John Austin, author of "Lectures on Jurisprudence." Born 1793; died 1867. Gifted authoress. Her daughter, also of literary talent, became Lady Duff Gordon.

Ayrton (William). Writer on Music. Editor of the *Morning Chronicle*, the *Harmonicon*, and the *Examiner*. Born, London, Feb. 24th, 1777; died there, May 8th, 1858.

Bach (Johann Sebastian). Born, Eisenach, March 21st (O.S.), 1685; died, Leipzig, July 28th, 1750. The greatest organist of his day, and the greatest musical genius the world has seen.

—— (Wilhelm Friedrich Ernst). Organist and composer, born, Bückeburg, May 27th, 1759; died, Berlin, Dec. 25th, 1845. He was the son of "Bach of Bückeburg" (J. S. Bach's ninth son, Johann Christoph Friedrich Bach), and the last surviving grandson of the great Leipzig Cantor.

Bache (Walter). Pianist. Born, Birmingham, June 19th, 1842; died, London, March 26th, 1888. Pupil and disciple of Liszt, he devoted his life and means to the cause of his master, introducing many of his compositions for the first time in England.

Bacon (Richard Mackenzie). Writer on music, and editor of the *Quarterly Musical Magazine and Review*. Born, Norwich, 1776; died there, 1844.

Bader (Carl Adam). Tenor vocalist. Born, Bamberg, Jan. 10th, 1789; died, Berlin, April 14th, 1870. Great as an opera-singer; was the leading tenor at the Royal Opera, Berlin, for twenty years.

Baillot (Pierre Marie François de Sales). Distinguished French violinist. Born, Passy, near Paris, Oct. 1st, 1771; died, Paris, September, 1842.

Baini (Abbate Giuseppe). Celebrated singer, of the Pontifical Chapel, Rome. Born in that city, 1775; died there, 1844. Composer of a *Miserere*, produced, Rome, 1821, and author of a Life of Palestrina.

Bamberg, or Bamberger (Hermann). A Jew, of Berlin, who befriended Moses Mendelssohn when he arrived, penniless, in that city.

Bärmann (Heinrich Joseph). Celebrated clarinet-player, for whom Weber wrote three concertos, and Mendelssohn wrote the duos for clarinet and basset-horn, Op. 113. Born, Potsdam, Feb. 17th, 1784; died, Munich, June 11th, 1847.

Bartholomew (William). Scientific chemist, violin-player, and hymn-writer. Born, London, 1793; died there, Aug. 18th, 1867. Wrote the English texts of Mendelssohn's chief choral works. Married, in 1853, Miss Mounsey, composer and organist.

Bassano (Miss). Mezzo-soprano vocalist, pupil of Crivelli.

Bauer (Pastor), of Belzig, whom Mendelssohn consulted with reference to the text of *St. Paul.* Pastor Bauer was a friend of the Mendelssohn family.

Becker (Carl Ferdinand). Organist. Born, Leipzig, July 17th, 1804; died there, Oct. 26th, 1877. Known for his literary work and fine collection of music, which latter he bequeathed to the city of Leipzig.

Beethoven (Ludwig van). The greatest of the masters of instrumental music. Born, Bonn, Dec. 16th, 1770; died, Vienna, March 26th, 1827.

Bendemann (Eduard). Painter; friend of Mendelssohn. Became Professor at the Academy of Art, Dresden, and Director of the Düsseldorf Academy. Born, Berlin, 1811; died 1889.

Appendix D

Benecke. A family related to the wife of Felix Mendelssohn.

Benedict (Sir Julius). Composer and pianist. Born, Stuttgart, Nov. 27th, 1804; died, London, June 5th, 1885.

Bennett (James). Tenor vocalist, born, Salford, 1804; died, Brighton, June, 1870.

—— (Joseph). Musical journalist and lyric author. Born, Berkeley, Gloucester, Nov. 29th, 1831.

—— (Sir William Sterndale). Distinguished composer and pianist. Professor of Music, Cambridge University, 1856–75. Friend of Mendelssohn. Born, Sheffield, April 13th, 1816; died, London, Feb. 1st, 1875.

Berger (Ludwig). Pianist. Born, Berlin, April 18th, 1777; died there, Feb. 16th, 1839.

Berlioz (Hector). Remarkable French composer. Born, La Côte St. André, near Grenoble, Dec. 11th, 1803; died, Paris, March 8th, 1869.

Berner (Friedrich Wilhelm). Organist and church composer. Born, Breslau, May 16th, 1780; died there, May 9th, 1827.

Bernhard. An opulent Jew of Berlin, admitted Moses Mendelssohn into his family, and intrusted him with the education of his children.

Bigot (Marie, *née* Kiene). Pianist. Born, Colmar, Alsace, March 3rd, 1786; died, Paris, Sept. 16th, 1820. Played before Haydn and Beethoven. Married M. Bigot, librarian to Count Rasoumoffski.

Birch (Charlotte Ann). Soprano vocalist. Born, London, 1815. Sang at the Gewandhaus Concerts, Nov. 2nd, 1843, and later; also in the first performance in London of *Elijah*, April 16th, 1847. Miss Birch died, London, Jan. 26th, 1901.

Blessington (Lady Marguerite). Novelist. Born, Knockbrit, near Clonmel, Sept. 1st, 1789; died, Paris, June 4th, 1849. Famed for the literary and artistic gatherings she held at Gore House, Kensington.

Blum, or Blume (Heinrich). Singer and actor. Born, Berlin,

April 25th, 1788; died there, Nov. 2nd, 1856. Retired from the stage in 1848, and was manager at the Berlin Royal Opera, 1852–54.

Böckh (Philipp August). Antiquary, Professor of Philology, Heidelberg, 1805; Professor of Rhetoric and Ancient Literature, Berlin, 1811. Born, Karlsruhe, Nov. 24th, 1785; died, Berlin, Aug. 3rd, 1867.

Böhm (Joseph). Violinist. Born, Pesth, March 4th, 1795; died, Vienna, March 28th, 1876. Professor at Vienna Conservatorium, and member of the Imperial orchestra.

Bourges (Jean Maurice). Musical critic. Born, Bordeaux, Dec. 2nd, 1812; died, Paris, March 1881. Joint Editor of the *Revue et Gazette Musicale de Paris*. Wrote the French translation of the text of *Elijah*.

Braham (John). The greatest of English tenor vocalists. Born, London, 1774 [1772]; died there, Feb. 17th, 1856. Composer of several dramatic works, and a number of songs.

Brahms (Johannes). Composer and pianist. The latest German disciple of the classical school. Born, Hamburg, May 7th, 1833; died, Vienna, April 3rd, 1897.

Breiting (Hermann). Tenor vocalist. Sang in opera in Germany, Russia, and England. Born, Augsburg, Oct. 24th, 1804; died, Darmstadt, Dec. 5th, 1860.

Browning (Robert). One of the few poets who have written with appreciation and understanding of music. Born, London (Camberwell), May 7th, 1812; died, Venice, Dec. 12th, 1889; buried in Westminster Abbey.

Brühl (Count Carl Friedrich). Nephew of the notorious prime minister of Augustus III. of Poland and Saxony. Born, Saxony, May 18th, 1772; died, Berlin, Aug. 9th, 1837. In 1815 was appointed General Director of the Royal Drama, Berlin. It was through his good offices that the "Wedding of Camacho" was produced in 1827.

Bull (Ole Bornemann). Celebrated violinist. Born, Bergen, Norway, Feb. 5th, 1810; died there, Aug. 17th, 1880.

Appendix D

Bülow (Baron von). Prussian Ambassador at the English Court. Entertained Felix Mendelssohn when he visited London in 1829; and extended like hospitality to Felix and his father in 1833.

Bunsen (Baron Christian Carl). Was resident minister at the Papal Court when Mendelssohn was in Italy in 1830; and was appointed Ambassador to England in 1842. Scholar and Archæologist. Friend of the Mendelssohn family. Born, Korbach, Aug. 25th, 1791; died, Bonn, Nov. 28th, 1860.

Caradori-Allan (Maria Caterina Rosalbina—*née* de Munck). Soprano vocalist. Born, Casa Palatina, Milan, 1800; died, Surbiton, Oct. 15th, 1865. Made her *début* at the King's Theatre, 1822, as Cherubino in *Figaro*. Also sang, but with less success, in oratorio. Mendelssohn wrote of her performance in *Elijah*, at the Birmingham Festival, 1846, as being "so pleasing, so pretty, so elegant,—so slovenly, so devoid both of soul and head," as almost to drive him mad at the recollection of it.

Cherubini (Maria Luigi Carlo Zenobia Salvatore). One of the greatest of Italian masters. Born, Florence, Sept. 14th, 1760; died, Paris, March 15th, 1842. It was to Cherubini that Felix Mendelssohn was taken by his father in 1825, and that master's opinion of the boy's talent did much to decide the father upon his future career.

Chopin (François Frederic). Pianist and composer. Born, Zela Zowa Wola, Feb. 22nd, 1810; died, Paris, Oct. 17th, 1849. Between Chopin and Mendelssohn a warm friendship sprang up, despite the different schools to which each belonged.

Chorley (Henry Fothergill). Journalist, novelist, and musical critic. Born, Blackley Hurst, Lancashire, Dec. 15th, 1808; died, London, Feb. 16th, 1872. He was engaged as a member of the staff of the *Athenæum* towards the close of 1833, but he had contributed occasional papers before that date.

He began his work as musical critic in 1834, and held that post until the close of 1871. A man of spotless integrity, and fearless in the expression of his views, his writings command respect, however erroneous some of his opinions may seem to be at the present time.

Cornelius (Peter von). Historical painter. Born, Düsseldorf, Sept. 23rd, 1783; died, Berlin, March 6th, 1867. Director of Berlin Academy, 1841.

Cramer (François). Violinist. Born, Schwetzingen, near Mannheim, 1772; died, London, July 25th, 1848. Brother of J. B. Cramer. For many years leader of the London Philharmonic orchestra, and of the Birmingham and other provincial festivals.

Cramer (Johann Baptist). Pianist and composer. Born, Mannheim, Feb. 24th, 1771; died, London, April 16th, 1858. Occasional conductor—"at the pianoforte"—of the Philharmonic Concerts, 1813-34.

Cranach (Lucas). Famous painter. Born, Kronach (whence his name), Oct. 4th, 1472; died Weimar, Oct. 16th, 1553. His masterpiece is a "Crucifixion" in the Stadtkirche, Weimar.

Cummings (Dr. William Hayman). Tenor vocalist and composer. Born, Sidbury, Devon, Aug. 22nd, 1831. Principal of the Guildhall School of Music, London, since 1896.

Cuvillon (Jean Baptiste Philémon de). Violinist. Born, Dunkirk, 1809. Professor, Paris Conservatoire.

Czerny (Carl). Pianist, and industrious composer, pupil and friend of Beethoven. Born, Vienna, Feb. 21st, 1791; died there, July 15th, 1857.

David (Ferdinand). Violinist and composer. Born, Hamburg, Jan. 19th, 1810; died, Kloster, Switzerland, July 19th, 1873. Eminent as a composer, David was pre-eminent as a teacher. His devotion to Mendelssohn is a beautiful chapter in artistic annals.

Davison (James William). Musical critic. Born, London,

Oct. 5th, 1813; died, Margate, March 24th, 1885. In 1860 Davison married his pupil, Miss Arabella Goddard. He composed some songs and pianoforte pieces, but was better known as a journalist. He had a brilliant style, and was honest in his support of the classic school and dislike of the modern composers. Mendelssohn was his idol.

Dehn (Siegfried Wilhelm). Writer on music. Originally intended for the Law. Born, Altona, Feb. 25th, 1799; died, Berlin, April 12th, 1858. In 1842 appointed librarian of the musical department, Berlin Royal Library. Distinguished as a Bach scholar. Published a number of educational works and some vocal music.

Devrient (Eduard Philipp). Baritone vocalist and actor. Born, Berlin, Aug. 11th, 1801; died, Carlsruhe, Oct. 4th, 1877, having held for some years the post of official director of the opera in that place.

Döhler (Theodor). Pianist and composer. Born, Naples, April 20th, 1814; died, Florence, Feb. 21st, 1856. His compositions are not of great value. Schumann termed him "A ladies' man."

Dolby (Miss Charlotte Helen). Contralto vocalist. Born, London, May 17th, 1821; died there, Feb. 18th, 1885. Married, Feb. 4th, 1860, to M. Sainton, the distinguished violinist. Composer of several cantatas, songs, etc.; better known as an oratorio singer.

Donner (Professor). Translator of the *Antigone* of Sophocles, the text employed by Mendelssohn in his setting of the musical portion of the drama.

Dorn (Heinrich Ludwig Edmund). Conductor and composer. Born, Königsberg, Prussia, Nov. 14th, 1804; died, Berlin, Jan. 10th, 1892. Conductor, Royal Opera, Berlin, 1847–68. Strong anti-Wagnerite.

Drouet (Louis François Philippe). Flutist. Born, Amsterdam, 1792; died, Berne, Sept., 1873.

Dürer (Albert). Painter and designer. Born, Nuremberg, May 21st, 1471; died there, April 6th, 1528.

Dussek (Johann Ludwig). Composer and pianist. Born, Czaslau, Bohemia, Feb. 9th, 1761; died, St. Germain-en-Laye, near Paris, March 20th, 1812.

Eichhorn (Johann Albrecht Friedrich). Prussian statesman, with whom Mendelssohn had some correspondence relative to the proposed Academy of Arts, Berlin. Born, 1779; died, 1856.

Ernst (Heinrich Wilhelm). Violinist. Born, Brünn, Moravia, May 6th, 1814; died, Nice, Oct. 8th, 1865.

Ertmann (Baroness Dorothea). Friend of Beethoven, to whom he dedicated the Sonata, Op. 101. Born, Offenbach. Daughter of a wealthy merchant named Graumann. Lived many years in Vienna. Married an Austrian Captain, Baron von Ertmann, who became a Field Marshal. Baroness Ertmann died at Vienna in 1848.

Eskele. A family Mendelssohn met at Vienna in the summer of 1830, and with whom he "made music."

Falkenstein (von). Home Minister at the Court of Dresden (1840), whose good offices Mendelssohn sought in furtherance of the establishment of a Conservatorium at Leipzig.

Fetis (François Joseph). Musical historian, essayist, and composer. Born, Mons, March 25th, 1784; died, Brussels, March 26th, 1871. His best-known work is the "Biographie Universelle des Musiciens."

Franchomme (Auguste). Violoncellist. Born, Lille, April 10th, 1808; died, Paris, Jan., 1884. Friend of Chopin, in conjunction with whom he wrote a duo for pianoforte and 'cello on themes from *Robert le Diable.*

Fränkel (David). Jewish Rabbi. When at Dessau, Fränkel was Moses Mendelssohn's teacher; and when he was appointed chief Rabbi at Berlin, he continued to befriend the poor youth.

Frederick the Great, of Prussia. Born, Berlin, Jan. 24th, 1712; died, Potsdam, Aug. 17th, 1786. It was enacted during his reign that every Jew on his marriage had to purchase a certain amount of China from the newly established Royal factory at Berlin, and that at the choice of the manager, who thus got rid of unsaleable articles. Frederick the Great was an amateur flute player, and a composer.

Frederick William I., of Prussia. Born Aug. 15th, 1688; died May 31st, 1740. Among the cruel edicts of his reign was that which compelled the Jews of Berlin to purchase the wild boars killed at the Royal hunting parties.

Frederick William IV., of Prussia. Born Oct. 15th, 1795; died Jan. 2nd, 1861. A patron of the fine arts. Afflicted with insanity, in 1857, resigned the administration of the kingdom to his brother William, who became the First German Emperor.

Frederick Augustus II., King of Saxony, 1836–54, was a zealous patron of art. In 1841 he invited Mendelssohn to become his Kapellmeister, and in 1842 gave the grant for founding the Conservatorium at Leipzig.

Frege (Madame Livia—*née* Gerhard). Vocalist. Born, Gera, June 13th, 1818. Pupil of Pohlenz. Made her *début* at Clara Wieck's concert, Leipzig, July 9th, 1832. Sang in opera at Leipzig and Berlin. Married Dr. Frege, of Leipzig, 1836. Friend of Mendelssohn, and one of the best interpreters of his songs. Died, Leipzig, Aug. 22nd, 1891.

Fürst (Julius). Hebrew scholar, who helped Mendelssohn in compiling the text of the oratorio *St. Paul.*

Gade (Niels Wilhelm). Composer. Born, Copenhagen, Feb. 22nd, 1817; died there, Dec. 21st, 1890. First brought into notice by the production of his Symphony, No. 1, in C minor, at the Gewandhaus Concerts, by Mendelssohn in 1843. Gade has written music in all the branches of the art save opera.

Gans. A Professor at the University, Berlin, under whom Mendelssohn studied. Became a friend of the Mendelssohn family. He is mentioned several times in the letters of Fanny Mendelssohn, and in 1829 Hensel painted his portrait.

Gauntlett (Dr. Henry John). Born, Wellington, Salop, July 9th, 1805; died, London, Feb. 21st, 1876. Originally a solicitor, he became an organist, and was among the first to introduce the C compass to England. Wrote many hymn tunes.

Geibel (Emanuel von). Poet. Born, Lübeck, 1815; died there, April 6th, 1884. His opera, *Loreley*, was set by Max Bruch, and produced at Mannheim in 1863. Schumann composed music to many of his short poems.

Gerke (Otto). Born, Lüneburg, July 13th, 1807; died, Paderborn, 1878.

Goethe (Johann Wolfgang von). Poet. Born, Frankfort-on-Main, Aug. 28th, 1749; died, Weimar, March 22nd, 1832.

Goldschmidt (Otto). Pianist and composer. Born, Hamburg, Aug. 21st, 1829. Accompanist to Jenny Lind on her American tour in 1851; married her at Boston, Feb. 5th, 1852. Founder of the Bach Choir, London; conducted the first performance in England of Bach's Mass in B minor, St. James's Hall, April 26th, 1876.

Gounod (Charles François). Composer. Born, Paris, June 17th, 1818; died, St. Cloud, Oct. 18th, 1893. The Hensel's saw much of him in Rome in 1840, and his name is frequently mentioned in Fanny Hensel's diary and letters.

Grabau (Henriette Eleonore). Vocalist. Born, Bremen, March 29th, 1805; died, Leipzig, Nov. 28th, 1852.

Gregory XVI. (Pope). Born, 1765; died, 1846. Succeeded to the Pontificate in 1831. Mendelssohn records the election in his letter from Rome, dated Feb. 8th, 1831.

Grisi (Giulietta). Celebrated opera singer, soprano. Born, Milan, July 28th, 1811; died, Berlin, Nov. 25th, 1869.

Grote (George). Banker, historian, and Member of Parliament. Born, Clay Hill, Beckenham, Kent, Nov. 17th, 1794; died, June 18th, 1871. Principal work, "History of

Greece," 12 vols. Mrs. Grote, *née* Harriet Lewin, born, 1790; died, Dec. 29th, 1878, was an authoress of repute.

Grove (Sir George). Civil engineer, biblical scholar, and writer on music. Born, Clapham, Surrey, Aug. 13th, 1820; died, London, May 28th, 1900. Secretary to the Crystal Palace Company, 1852–73; director, Royal College of Music, 1883–94. His monumental work is the "Dictionary of Music and Musicians."

Gruneisen (Charles Lewis). Journalist. Born, London, Nov. 2nd, 1806; died there, Nov. 1st, 1879. Sometime musical critic of the *Athenæum*, *Morning Post*, and other papers. Though not a musician, technically, Gruneisen was well informed and painstaking. He was mercilessly attacked by the *Musical World*.

Gugel (Joseph and Heinrich). Brothers: celebrated virtuosi on the French horn. Born, Stuttgart. Heinrich was living at St. Petersburg in 1837.

Habeneck (François Antoine). Violinist and conductor. Born, Jan. 22nd, 1781; died, Paris, Feb. 8th, 1849. Founder of the "Société des Concerts des Conservatoire," Paris. Conductor at the opera, 1824–47. He obtained remarkable precision in chorus singing in opera, by using pedals, which, by a simple mechanism, beat time in both wings of the stage.

Halévy (Jacques François Fromental Elias). Dramatic composer. Born, Paris, May 27th, 1799; died, Nice, March 17th, 1862.

Hallé (Sir Charles). Pianist and conductor. Born, Hagen, near Elberfeldt, April 11th, 1819; died, Manchester, Oct. 25th, 1895. Settled in England in 1848; started his orchestral concerts at Manchester, Jan. 30th, 1858, the series of thirty yielding a profit of half a crown! The concerts afterwards acquired great fame.

Handel (George Frederick). The great master of oratorio. Born, Halle, Saxony, Feb. 23rd, 1685; died, London, April 14th,

1759. The *Gentleman's Magazine* for 1759, in an obituary notice, gives April 12th as the date of Handel's death.

Hanstein (August). Mendelssohn's young friend, who died in 1827. It was by Hanstein's death-bed that Mendelssohn composed the pianoforte Fugue in E minor, Op. 35, No. 1.

Hauptmann (Moritz). Theoretical writer and composer. Born, Dresden, Oct. 13th, 1792; died, Leipzig, Jan. 3rd, 1868. Cantor, St. Thomas's School, Leipzig, from 1842 to his death.

Hauser (Franz). Baritone vocalist. Born, Krasowitz, near Prague, Jan. 12th, 1794; died, Freiburg, Baden, Aug. 14th, 1870. A great favourite with Abraham Mendelssohn.

Hawes (Maria Billington, afterwards Mrs. Merest). Contralto vocalist. Daughter of William Hawes. Born, London, April, 1816; died, Ryde, I.W., April 24th, 1886. Mendelssohn addressed several letters to her.

Hawes (William). Composer. Born, London, June 21st, 1785; died there, Feb. 18th, 1846. Gentleman of the Chapel Royal. Master of the Choristers, St. Paul's Cathedral.

Hegel (Georg Wilhelm Friedrich). Philosopher. Born, Stuttgart, Aug. 17th, 1770; died, Berlin, Nov. 14th, 1831. A frequent visitor to the Garden House in the Leipziger Strasse.

Heine (Heinrich). Poet. Born, Düsseldorf, Dec. 13th, 1799; died, Paris, Feb. 18th, 1856.

Henderson (W. J.). Musical critic, of New York. Author of a number of works on music: "What is Good Music;" "How Music Developed;" "The Orchestra and Orchestral Music," etc.

Henning (Carl Wilhelm). Violinist and composer. Born, Berlin, Jan. 31st, 1784; died there, April, 1867.

Hensel (Sebastian). Son of Wilhelm and Fanny Hensel. Born, Berlin, June, 1830. Author of "Die Familie Mendelssohn." Berlin, 1879.

Appendix D

Hensel (Wilhelm). Painter. Born, Trebbin, July 6th, 1794; died, Nov. 24th, 1861, from injuries received in saving a child from being run over. Married Fanny Mendelssohn, October 3rd, 1829. Left a collection of pencil portraits filling forty-seven volumes, consisting of likenesses of the Mendelssohn family, and of the visitors who frequented their house.

Henselt (Adolph). Pianist and composer. Born, Schwabach, Bavaria, May 12th, 1814; died, Warmbrunn, Silesia, Oct. 10th, 1889. Mendelssohn in a letter to Hiller describes Henselt's untiring practice of widespread chords.

Herz (Heinrich-Henri). Pianist, composer, and pianoforte-maker. Born, Vienna, Jan. 6th, 1803; died, Paris, Jan. 5th, 1888. Schumann described Herz as "the military music in the great score of the world."

Hesse (Adolph Friedrich). Organist and composer. Born, Breslau, Aug. 30th, 1809; died there, Aug. 5th, 1863. Pupil of Berner. He composed an oratorio, symphonies, chamber and organ music.

Heydemann (Louis). A lawyer, who, with his brother, were numbered among Mendelssohn's University friends. Louis was a good pianist.

Heyse (Dr.). Tutor to Felix Mendelssohn and his brother and sisters. Father of Paul Heyse, poet and dramatist, born, Berlin, March 15th, 1830.

Hildebrand (Theodor). Historical painter. Born, Stettin, 1804; died, Düsseldorf, 1874. One of Mendelssohn's intimate friends.

Hiller (Ferdinand). Composer, pianist, and writer. Born, Frankfort-on-Main, Oct. 24th, 1811; died, Cologne, May 10th, 1885.

Hobbs (John William). Tenor vocalist. Born, Henley-on-Thames, Aug. 1st, 1799; died, Croydon, Jan. 12th, 1877.

Horn (Wilhelm). Physician. Early friend of Mendelssohn. Horn appears to have been in London during the latter part of Mendelssohn's stay there in 1829.

Horsley (Family of). Distinguished in the world of art and science. William Horsley, the father, born, London, Nov. 15th, 1774; died there, June 12th, 1858; was a glee composer and organist, and one of the founders of the Philharmonic Society. His son, John Callcott Horsley, born, London, Jan. 29th, 1817, was a painter of distinction; and the younger son, Charles Edward Horsley, born, London, Dec. 16th, 1822, distinguished himself as a musician, but without attaining full recognition or success in England. He died in New York, May 2nd, 1876.

Howard (Pastor). Minister of the Reformed Congregation, Leipzig; delivered the funeral oration at the obsequies of Mendelssohn, in the Church of St. Paul, Leipzig.

Humboldt (Alexander). Traveller and naturalist. Born, Berlin, Sept. 14th, 1769; died, May 6th, 1859.

Hummel (Johann Nepomuk). Pianist and composer. Born, Pressburg, Nov. 14th, 1778; died, Weimar, Oct. 17th, 1837.

Humperdinck (Engelbert). Born, Sieburg, on the Rhine, Sept. 1st, 1854. Came suddenly into notice through the success of his fairy opera, "Hänsel und Gretel," in 1894. He was appointed professor of composition in the Berlin Conservatorium in 1900.

Humphreys (Frederick W.). Violinist and conductor. For forty years musical director at the Theatre Royal, Birmingham. Retired, 1900.

Immermann (Carl Leberecht). Dramatist. Born, Magdeburg, 1796; died, 1840. Director, Düsseldorf Theatre, during Mendelssohn's engagement there.

Jacob (Benjamin). Organist and composer. Born, London, April, 1778; died there, Aug. 24th, 1829.

Jeanrenaud (Madame). Widow of a clergyman of the French Reformed Church, Frankfort-on-Main. Her elder daughter, Julie, married Herr Schunk, of Leipzig; Cécile, the younger, became the wife of Felix Mendelssohn.

Appendix D

Joachim (Joseph). Violinist and composer. Born, Kittsee, near Pressburg, June 28th, 1831. Composer of overtures, a violin concerto, and other pieces.

Johnston (Sir Alexander). Reorganizer of the government of Ceylon. Born, April 25th, 1775; died, London, March 9th, 1849.

Kalkbrenner (Friedrich Wilhelm Michael). Pianist and composer. Born, near Berlin, 1788; died, Enghien, near Paris, June 10th, 1849.

Kemble (Charles). Actor. Born, Brecon, Nov. 27th, 1775; died, Nov. 12th, 1854. In 1840 he was appointed Examiner of Plays.

Kemble (Frances Anne). Actress. Born, 1809; died, London, Jan., 1893. For many years gave Shakespearian readings, and published several volumes of "Recollections."

Kenyon (John). Friend of Coleridge, the Brownings, etc., and something of a poet himself. Born, Jamaica, 1784; died, Cowes, I.W., 1856.

Klingemann (Carl). Secretary to the Hanoverian Legation in Berlin, and in London, from 1828. Cultivated amateur, and lyrical poet. Born, Limmer, Hanover, Dec. 22nd, 1798; died, London, Sept. 25th, 1862.

Knauer (of Leipzig). Modelled a medallion of Mendelssohn shortly after his death. This was presented to the Directors of the Gewandhaus, and placed at the back of the orchestra in the concert-room.[1] A fac-simile is published in "Letters of F. M. B. to Ignaz and Charlotte Moscheles."

Knyvett (Deborah, *née* Travis). Soprano vocalist. Born, Shaw, near Oldham, 1796 (?); died there, Jan. 10th, 1876. Married (as his second wife) William Knyvett, alto vocalist and composer.

Kotek (Josef). Violinist and composer. Born, Kamenez-Podolsk, Russia, Oct. 25th, 1855; died, Davos, Switzerland, Jan. 4th,

---

[1] See Illustration. Interior of Gewandhaus Concert-room.

1885. Studied at the Moscow Conservatorium, and later under Joachim, who appointed him, in 1882, teacher at the Royal High School, Berlin.

Krebs (Johann). Mendelssohn's manservant. The friendly footing between Krebs and his employers was shown in many ways, and recalled the best aspect of old feudal days. In his last illness he was nursed in Mendelssohn's house, and when a dinner-party was given, he was perpetually ringing his bell, in order to be told what guests had arrived, who served them, etc. At last, Cécile had to sit by his bedside and give him a full account of everything. What a happy household!

Kreutzer, violinist, who played Mendelssohn's Violin Concerto for the first time in England, was described as Director of Music to the Grand Duke of Baden. No further particulars of him can be gleaned.

Lang (Josephine). Song composer. Born, Munich, Mar. 14th, 1815; died, Tübingen, Dec. 2nd, 1880. Married, 1842, to Karl Reinhold Köstlin, professor of æsthetics, Tübingen.

Lavater (Johann Caspar). Protestant clergyman. Born, Zurich, Nov. 15th, 1741; died there, Jan. 2nd, 1801. Lavater dedicated to Moses Mendelssohn his translation from the French of Bonnet's "Enquiry into the Evidences of the Christian Religion," hoping either to convert Mendelssohn, or induce him to refute the book. Mendelssohn's noble letter in reply to the challenge will be found in the Memoir by M. Samuels.

Leo. A musician (?) frequently mentioned in Abraham Mendelssohn's letters from Paris, 1820–30, probably a pianist, but concerning whom no information is forthcoming. He may have been the Louis Leo who gave Henry Phillips, in 1846, a MS. collection of "Jewish Chaunts," now in the possession of the present writer.

Lepsius (Karl Richard). Egyptologist. Born, Naumburg, Dec. 23rd, 1810; died, July 10th, 1884. Was among the frequenters of the "Sunday Music" at the Mendelssohns in 1841.

Lessing (Dotthold Ephraim). Famous writer, author of the "Laocoon." Friend of Moses Mendelssohn. Born, Kamenz, Saxony, Jan. 22nd, 1729; died, Brunswick, Feb. 15th, 1781.

Lichtenstein. Professor in the University, Berlin, under whom Mendelssohn studied.

Lincoln (Henry John). Lecturer and critic. Born, London, Oct. 15th, 1814. Began his lectures on music at Crosby Hall in 1843. Produced Mendelssohn's Violin Concerto there Dec. 23rd, 1845. Musical critic, *Daily News*, 1866–86. Living in retirement in London.

Lind (Jenny). Soprano vocalist. The "Swedish Nightingale," born, Stockholm, Oct. 6th, 1820; died, Malvern, Nov. 2nd, 1887. Married to Ollo Goldschmidt, Feb. 5th, 1852. The greatest singer of the nineteenth century.

Liszt (Frans). Pianoforte virtuoso, and composer. Early champion of Wagner. Born, Raiding, Hungary, Oct. 22nd, 1811; died, Bayreuth, July 31st, 1886.

Lobe (Johann Christian). Composer and writer. Born, Weimar, May 30th, 1797; died, Leipzig, July 27th, 1881.

Lockey (Charles). Tenor vocalist. Born, Newbury, Berks, 1820. Sang in oratorio from 1842, until his retirement, owing to a throat affection, in 1859. Married, 1853, Martha Williams (*q.v.*). Of Lockey, Mendelssohn wrote, after the performance of *Elijah* in 1846: "A young English tenor sang the last air ('Then shall the religious') so beautifully, that I was obliged to collect all my energies so as not to be affected, and to continue beating time steadily."

Loewe (Carl Gottfried). Composer. Born, Loebejuen, Prussian Saxony, Nov. 30th, 1796; died, Kiel, April 20th, 1869. Was an organist at Stettin for some years.

Louis I. King of Bavaria. Born, 1768; came to the Throne, 1825; provoked discontent by his extravagance, and abdicated in 1848; died, 1868.

Lumley (Benjamin—A Jew whose real name was Levy). Solicitor. Induced to become Manager of Her Majesty's Theatre, 1841, a post he held with fluctuating success until 1858, when he resumed his original profession. Author of "Reminiscences of the Opera." London, 1864.

Macfarren (Sir George Alexander). Composer. Born, London, Mar. 2nd, 1813; died there, Oct. 31st, 1887. Professor of Music, Cambridge University; Principal, R.A.M., from 1875 to time of his death. Author of didactic works.

Macfarren (Lady—*née* Natalie Andræ). Contralto vocalist. Born, Lübeck. Translator of numerous works on music, opera *libretti*, etc.

Machin (William). Bass vocalist. Born, Birmingham, 1798; died, Handsworth, Sept. 1870. Sang at the Birmingham Festival, 1834-49. Gentleman of the Chapel Royal, Vicar-choral, St. Paul's Cathedral.

Magnus (Gustav and Edward). Brothers. Friends of Mendelssohn. Edward Magnus painted what is considered the best portrait of Mendelssohn, at Berlin, in 1844.

Maimonides (Rabbi Moses ben Maimon). One of the greatest of Jewish teachers. Born, Cordova, Mar. 30th, 1135; died, Cairo, Dec. 13th, 1204.

Mainvielle-Fodor (Josephine). Soprano vocalist. Born, Paris, 1793. Sang in opera in Russia, France, England, and Italy. Retired in 1833.

Malibran (Maria Felicità). The name by which this wonderful singer will always be known, though she was a Garcia by birth, and became the wife of the violinist De Beriot. Born, Paris, Mar. 24th, 1808; died, Manchester, Sept. 23rd, 1836.

Mario (Giuseppe—Conte de Candia). The greatest operatic tenor of his day. Born, Cagliari, 1810; died, Rome, Dec. 11th, 1883.

Marx (Adolph Bernhard). Composer, theorist, and writer. Born, Halle, May 15th, 1795; died, Berlin, May 17th, 1866.

Appendix D

Massow (Privy Councillor von). Entrusted by Frederick William IV. to negotiate with Mendelssohn concerning the appointment at Berlin.

Mathis-Gheysens. A musical amateur, of Liége. He appears to have given the commission to Mendelssohn to compose the *Lauda Sion* for the Corpus Christi Festival, 1846. He had taken great interest in, and done much for music in Liége, and, as Chorley puts it, "had acquired Church influence."

Mendelssohn (Paul), to whom his brother Felix dedicated the Variations, Op. 17, was a violoncello player of considerable attainment. Died, Berlin, June 21st, 1874, at the age of 61. Edited the first collection of his brother's letters.

Merk (Joseph). Violoncellist and composer. Born, Vienna, Jan. 18th, 1795; died there, June 16th, 1852.

Meyerbeer (Giacomo). Dramatic composer. Born, Berlin, Sept. 5th, 1791; died, Paris, May 2nd, 1864.

Milder-Hauptmann (Pauline Anna). Soprano vocalist. Born, Constantinople, Dec. 13th, 1785; died, Berlin, May 29th, 1838. Beethoven wrote the part of Leonora (*Fidelio*) for her.

Mitford (Mary Russell). Novelist and dramatist. Born, Alresford, Hants, Dec. 16th, 1787; died, Swallowfield, Berks, Jan. 10th, 1855.

Montfort (Alexandre). Composer. Born, Paris, May 17th, 1804; died there, Feb. 12th, 1856.

Moore (Joseph). Die-sinker, button maker, and philanthropist. Born, Worcestershire, 1766; died, Birmingham, April 19th, 1851. Founded the Gentlemen's Private Concerts about 1799, the Oratorio Choral Society in 1808, and from 1802 was chairman of the Festival Committee until the time of his death.

Mori (Nicholas). Violinist. Born, London, Jan. 24th, 1796; died there, June 14th, 1839.

Moscheles (Ignaz). Famous pianist and composer. Born, Prague, May 30th, 1794; died Leipzig, March 10th, 1870. Friend of Beethoven and of Mendelssohn.

Moser (Karl). Violinist. Born, Berlin, Jan. 24th, 1774; died there, Jan. 27th, 1851.

Mounsey (Ann Sheppard—Mrs. W. Bartholomew). Pianist, organist, and composer. Born, London, April 17th, 1811; died there, June 24th, 1891. Her sister, Miss Elizabeth Mounsey, born, London, Oct. 8th, 1819, was organist of St. Peter's, Cornhill—where the first C organ was erected—from 1834 to 1882.

Mozart (Karl). Elder son of the great composer. Born, 1784; died, Milan, 1859. Musical amateur, and, while in the Austrian Service at Milan, used to get up performances of his father's works there.

Mozart (Wolfgang Amadeus). The most wonderful musical genius the world has seen. Born, Salzburg, Jan. 27th, 1756; died, Vienna, Dec. 5th, 1791.

Mücke. Painter, of the Düsseldorf School under Schadow.

Mühlenfels, a mercantile family, of Frankfort. Felix mentions one member as among his friends in London, in 1829.

Naumann (Emil). Writer on music, and composer. Born, Berlin, Sept. 8th, 1827; died, Dresden, June 23rd, 1888. His father, to whom Mendelssohn wrote in 1839, was a physician, settled in Bonn, in 1828.

Neukomm (Sigismund). Amateur composer. Born, Salzburg, July 10th, 1778; died, Paris, April 3rd, 1858. His oratorio *David* was produced at the first Birmingham Festival held in the Town Hall, Oct. 1834.

Nicholson (Charles). Flutist. Born, Liverpool, 1795; died, London, March 27th, 1837.

Nohl (Carl Friedrich Ludwig). Writer on music. Born, Iserlohn, Westphalia, Dec. 5th, 1831; died, Heidelberg, Dec. 16th, 1885.

Novello (Clara Anastasia). Soprano vocalist. Born, London,

June 10th, 1818; married Count Gigliucci, 1843, and retired in 1860. Celebrated as an oratorio singer.

Novello (Vincent). Father of the preceding. Composer, organist, and publisher. Born, London, Sept. 6th, 1781; died, Nice, August 9th, 1861. During his early visits to England, Mendelssohn was a frequent visitor to the house of Novello.

Onslow (George). Amateur composer. Grandson of the first Lord Onslow. Born, Clermont-Ferrand, France, July 27th, 1784; died there, Oct. 3rd, 1853.

Paganini (Nicolo). Violinist. Born, Genoa, Oct. 27th, 1782; died, Nice, May 27th, 1840.

Pasta (Giuditta). Soprano vocalist. Of a Jewish family named Negri. Born, Como, April 9th, 1798; died, Como, April 1st, 1865. Married the tenor singer, Pasta.

Peel (Sir Robert). Statesman. Born, Lancashire, Feb. 5th, 1788; died, London, July 2nd, 1850.

Phillips (Henry). Bass vocalist. Born, Bristol, Aug 13th, 1801; died, Dalston, Nov. 8th, 1876. For Phillips Mendelssohn wrote a scena, "On Lena's Gloomy Heath," bass solo and orchestra. Phillips sang this at the Philharmonic concert, Nov. 15th, 1847.

Piatti (Alfredo). Violoncellist. Born, Bergamo, Jan. 8th, 1822. Retired into private life, Aug. 1898. Died, July 19th, 1901.

Pierson (Henry Hugo). Composer, whose real name was Henry Hugh Pearson. Born, Oxford, April 13th, 1815; died, Leipzig, Jan. 28th, 1873. Resided in Germany from 1839 to the time of his death, with the exception of a short period in 1844, when he was elected to the Chair of Music in Edinburgh University. His oratorio *Jerusalem* was produced at the Norwich Festival of 1852, but he was less appreciated as a composer in this country than in Germany, his adopted home.

Pius VIII. (Pope). Filled the Pontifical Chair for little more than a year—his death, in 1830, is referred to in Mendelssohn's "Letters from Italy."

Pixis (Johann Peter). Pianist and composer. Born, Mannheim, 1788; died, Paris, Dec. 22nd, 1874.

Planché (James Robinson). "Somerset Herald," and dramatist. Born, London, Feb. 27th, 1796; died there, May 30th, 1880. Wrote the *libretto* of "Oberon" for Weber.

Pleyel (Camille). Pianist. Born, Strassburg, Dec. 18th, 1788; died, Paris, May 4th, 1855.

Pohlenz (Christian August). Born, Salgast, July 3rd, 1790; died, Leipzig, March 10th, 1843. Organist, St. Thomas's, Leipzig, cantor, 1848; conductor, Gewandhaus concerts, 1827–35.

Procter (Bryan). "Barry Cornwall." Poet. Born, London, Nov. 21st, 1787; died there, Oct. 5th, 1874.

Queisser (Carl Traugott). Trombonist. Born, Döbeln, near Leipzig, Jan. 11th, 1800; died, Leipzig, June 12th, 1846. Principal trombone, Gewandhaus orchestra; later, viola player; also played the trumpet, and serpent.

Rammler (Professor). Poet, of Berlin. Wrote an elegy on the death of Moses Mendelssohn, in alternate stanzas by the Jewish and Christian nations, represented by two mourning females, *Sulamith* and *Eusebia*.

Reck (Von der). The family to whom formerly belonged the House and Garden, Leipziger Strasse, No. 3.

Redern (Count Friedrich Wilhelm). Born, Berlin, Dec. 9th, 1802; died there, Nov. 5th, 1883. Privy councillor, General Superintendent of the Court Music, Berlin, and composer of an opera, cantatas, overtures, church music, etc.

Rellstab (Heinrich Friedrich Ludwig). Critic. Born, Berlin, April 13th, 1799; died there, Nov. 27th, 1860. His satirical and violent criticisms resulted more than once in his imprisonment.

Richter (Hans). Distinguished conductor. Born, Raab, Hungary, April 4th, 1843. Friend of Richard Wagner.

Rietschel (Ernst). Sculptor, of Dresden. Born, 1804; died, 1861.

Appendix D

Rietz (Eduard). Violinist. Born, Berlin, Oct. 17th, 1802; died there, Jan. 23rd, 1832. Mendelssohn's early friend.

—— (Julius). Composer and conductor, brother of the foregoing. Born, Berlin, Dec. 28th, 1812; died, Dresden, Sept. 12th, 1877.

Rinck (Johann Christian Heinrich). Organist and composer. Born Elgersburg, Thuringa, Feb. 18th, 1770; died, Darmstadt, Aug. 7th, 1846. The late Sir Charles Halle was one of his pupils.

Ritter (Heinrich). Professor of Philosophy, Berlin University. Born, Zerbst, 1791; died, 1869. Mendelssohn studied under him.

Robert (Ludwig). Poet, friend of the Mendelssohns, and, with his wife Frederike, a frequenter at their house.

Rockstro (William Smyth). Organist, composer, and writer. Born, North Cheam, Surrey, Jan. 5th, 1823; died, London, July 2nd, 1895.

Rösel (Professor). Taught landscape-drawing to Felix Mendelssohn and his brother and sisters.

Rosen (Friedrich August). Sanskrit scholar. Born, Hanover, Sept. 2nd, 1805; died, London, Sept. 12th, 1837. Appointed professor of Oriental languages, University College, London, 1828. Friend of Klingemann, Moscheles, and Mendelssohn. His sister Sophie was married to Klingemann in 1845.

Rossini (Gioacchino Antonio). Opera composer. Born, Pesaro, Feb. 29th, 1792; died, Ruelle, near Paris, Nov. 13th, 1868.

Rubinstein (Anton Gregor). Pianist and composer. Born, Wechwotynetz, Podolia, Russia, Nov. 16th, 1829; died, St. Petersburg, Nov. 20th, 1894.

Rungenhagen (Carl Friedrich). Composer and conductor. Born, Berlin, Sept. 27th, 1778; died there, Dec. 21st, 1851.

Rust (Wilhelm Carl). Son of Friedrich Wilhelm Rust. Born, Dessau, April 29th, 1787; died, April 15th, 1855.

Santini (Abbate Fortunato). Born, Rome, July 5th, 1778; became a priest in 1801. Formed a valuable library of music which came into the possession of a Russian, Wladimir Stassoff. Santini retired to a monastery. The date of his death is unknown.

Schadow (Friedrich Wilhelm). Painter. Born, 1789; died, 1862. Head of the Düsseldorf Academy, 1826–59.

Schätzel (Pauline von). Soprano vocalist. Born, Berlin, 1812; died, Sept. 9th, 1882. Sang in opera and oratorio, and was a song composer. Married Herr Decker, Court Printer.

Schauroth (Delphine von). Pianist and composer. Born, Magdeburg, 1814. Married an Englishman, Mr. Hill Handley. Appeared as a pianist in London, in 1823. Mendelssohn dedicated his Concerto in G minor to her. She was still living in 1881.

Schelble (Johann Nepomuk). Born, Höffingen, Black Forest, May 16th, 1789; died, Frankfort, Aug. 7th, 1837.

Schirmer. Painter, friend of Mendelssohn at Düsseldorf.

Schlegel (August Wilhelm von). Professor of Literature, Bonn. Shakespearian scholar. Born, Hanover, Sept. 8th, 1767; died, May 12th, 1845.

Schleinitz (Dr. Conrad). Born, Zechanitz, Saxony, Oct. 1st, 1805; died, Leipzig, May 12th, 1881. Musical amateur. A director of the Gewandhaus concerts, and one of the founders of the Leipzig Conservatorium. The friendship begun in 1835, was cordially maintained until the death of Mendelssohn.

Schmitt (Aloys). Pianist. Born, Erlenbach-on-Main, Aug. 26th, 1788; died, Frankfort, July 25th, 1866. Famous as a teacher.

Schneider (Friedrich Johann Christian). Composer and organist. Born, Alt-Waltersdorf, Silesia, Jan. 3rd, 1786; died, Dessau, Nov. 23rd, 1853.

Schubert (Franz Peter). Composer. Born, Lichtenthal, near Vienna, Jan. 31st, 1797; died, Vienna, Nov. 19th, 1828.

Schubring (Pastor Julius). Born, Dessau, June 2nd, 1806; died there, Dec., 1889. Rector of St. George's Church, Dessau.

Appendix D

Schumann (Robert Alexander). Composer. Born, Zwickau, Saxony, June 8th, 1810; died, Endenich, near Bonn, July 29th, 1856.

Schunck (Madame). Cécile Mendelssohn's sister. Moscheles lived in the same house with the Schuncks at Leipzig, where many festive gatherings took place.

Schunke (Carl). Pianist. Born, Magdeburg, 1801; died, Paris, Dec. 16th, 1839; threw himself from the window of a hospital.

Seidler (Caroline—*née* Wranitzki). Soprano vocalist. Born, Vienna, 1794; died, Berlin, Sept. 4th, 1872.

Shaw (Mrs. Alfred—*née* Mary Postans). Contralto vocalist. Born, Lee, Kent, 1814; died, Hadleigh Hall, Suffolk, Sept. 9th, 1876. Married, 1835, Alfred Shaw, an artist.

Sivori (Ernesto Camillo). Violinist. Born, Genoa, Oct. 25th, 1815; died there, Feb. 18th, 1894. Nephew and pupil of Paganini.

Smart (Sir George Thomas). Composer and conductor. Born, London, May 10th, 1776; died there, Feb. 23rd, 1867.

Sohn (Carl). Painter. Another of Mendelssohn's Düsseldorf friends.

Spitta (August Philipp). Musical historian and editor. Born, Wechold, Hanover, Dec. 27th, 1841; died, Berlin, April 13th, 1894.

Spohr (Louis). Violinist and composer. Born, Brunswick, April 5th, 1784; died, Cassel, Oct. 22nd, 1859.

Spontini (Luigi Gasparo Pacifico). Opera composer. Born, Majolati, Ancona, Nov. 14th, 1774; died there, Jan. 24th, 1851. Spontini was the recipient of many orders and decorations which he was fond of displaying. A member of his orchestra once remarked how thickly Spontini's breast was covered with orders, while Mozart had not a single one. Spontini, who overheard him, said, "My dear sir, Mozart could afford to do without them."

Staudacher. One of Mendelssohn's Munich friends, 1830.

Staudigl (Joseph). Bass vocalist. Born, Wöllersdorf, April

14th, 1807; died, Vienna, March 28th, 1861. Has never been surpassed as an interpreter of the titular part in Mendelssohn's *Elijah.*

Stevens (Jeannie M.—Mrs. Wm. Hale). Pianist and vocalist. Daughter of Joseph Stevens, sometime chorus-master of the Birmingham Festival. Born, Birmingham, Sept. 11th, 1831; died, Worthing, Nov. 5th, 1898.

Stimpson (James). Organist. Born, Lincoln, Feb. 29th, 1820; died, Birmingham, Oct. 14th, 1886. Was Town Hall Organist at Birmingham for 44 years.

Stümer (Johann Daniel Heinrich). Tenor vocalist. Born, Frödenwalde, 1789; died, Berlin, Dec. 24th, 1857.

Sullivan, Knt. (Arthur Seymour). Composer. Born, London, May 13th, 1842; died there, Nov. 22nd, 1900.

Taubert (Wilhelm Carl Gottfried). Composer and conductor. Born, Berlin, March 23rd, 1811; died there, Jan. 7th, 1891. Conductor, Royal Opera, Berlin, and court concerts.

Taylor (Edward). Musician and writer. Born, Norwich, Jan. 22nd, 1784; died, Brentwood, March 12th, 1863. Revived the Norwich Musical Festivals, 1824. Gresham Professor of Music, from 1837.

Taylor (John). Mining engineer, of Mold, Flintshire. Uncle of the above. Became known to Mendelssohn through Mrs. Austin (*q.v.*). Mendelssohn visited the family in 1829, and composed the three Fantasias, Op. 16, in Wales, dedicating them to the daughters of Mr. Taylor.

Thalberg (Sigismond). Pianist and composer. Born, Geneva, Jan. 7th, 1812; died, Naples, April 26th, 1871.

Thibaut (Anton Friedrich Justus). Writer on music. Born, Hameln, Jan. 4th, 1774; died, Heidelberg, March 28th, 1840. Professor of Law, Heidelberg University. Schumann attended his lectures there.

Thiele (Eduard). Court conductor, Dessau. Born there, Nov. 21st, 1812; died Jan. 10th, 1895.

Thomson (John). Composer. Born, Sprouston, Roxburgh,

Oct. 28th, 1805; died, Edinburgh, May 6th, 1841. Made the acquaintance of Mendelssohn at Edinburgh in 1829. First Reid Professor of Music, Edinburgh University. Wrote the "Notes of a Musical Tourist," which appeared in the *Harmonicon*, vol. viii., and which contain many references to Mendelssohn and his compositions. See J. T. p. 45.

Thorwaldsen (Bertel). Sculptor. Born at sea, Nov. 19th, 1770; died, Copenhagen, March 24th, 1844.

Tieck (Johann Ludwig). Critical writer, and translator of Shakespeare. Born, Berlin, May 31st, 1773; died there, April 28th, 1853.

Tingry (properly Tingri, Jean Nicholas Célestin). Violinist and composer. Born, Verviers, Sept. 7th, 1819; died, Algar, July 1892.

Türrschmidt (Auguste—*née* Braun). Contralto vocalist. Born, Berlin, Nov. 20th, 1800; date of death unknown. Began as a soprano, developed a deep contralto; at a concert at Berlin sang a tenor solo, and on the occasion of a performance of the *Messiah*, when the bass singer was taken suddenly ill, Madame Türrschmidt took up his part.

Unger (Caroline). Celebrated opera singer. Born, near Pesth, Oct. 28th, 1805 (1800?); died, near Florence, Mar. 23rd, 1877. Married, 1840, a Florentine, M. Sabatier, and retired.

Vandenhoff (Charlotte Elizabeth). Actress. Born, Liverpool, 1815; died, Birmingham, Aug. 7, 1860. Daughter of John M. Vandenhoff, the tragedian.

Verhulst (Johannes Josephus Herman). Composer and conductor. Born, The Hague, Mar. 19th, 1816; died there, Jan. 17th, 1891.

Vernet (Emile Jean Horace). Painter. Born, Paris, 1789; died, 1863. Director, French School of Art, Rome, 1828–34.

Viardot-Garcia (Michelle Pauline). Soprano vocalist. Born, Paris, July 18th, 1821. Gifted vocalist and teacher of singing. Appeared as a pianist, Paris, Oct. 15th, 1882.

Victoria (Queen of Great Britain and Ireland, Empress of India). Born, Kensington Palace, May 24th, 1819; died, Osborne, I. W., Jan. 22nd, 1901. Musical amateur. In the early years of her reign took an active part in musical matters, singing at the private concerts given at Buckingham Palace. Some curious notices will be found in the *Revue et Gazette Musicale de Paris* for 1840 and 1841. Her Majesty is credited with having composed music to Schiller's "An Emma," and "Der Jüngling am Bache."

Voigt (Henriette—*née* Kunze). Musical amateur. Born, 1809; died, Leipzig, Oct. 15th, 1839. Her house was the centre of musical life at Leipzig, and her friends included Mendelssohn, Schumann, Ludwig Berger (whose pupil she was), and every musician of note at that time.

Wagner (Wilhelm Richard). Dramatic poet and composer. Born, Leipzig, May 22nd, 1813; died, Venice, Feb. 13th, 1883.

Wallace (Lady—*née* Grace Stein). Translator of the Letters of Mozart, Beethoven, Mendelssohn, etc. Born, Edinburgh, 1815(?); died, 1878. Married to Sir James Maxwell Wallace in 1836.

Weber (Carl Maria von). Composer. Born, Eutin, Dec. 18th, 1786; died, London, June 5, 1826, soon after the production of his opera, "Oberon." In 1844 his remains were transported to Dresden, and interred in the family vault.

Webern (General von). Soldier. Veteran of the Napoleonic War, 1813–15. Friend of the Mendelssohn family in Berlin.

Weimar (Karl August, Grand Duke of). Art patron. Invited Goethe to Weimar. Hummel was Capellmeister there for some years. The Duke died in 1828; the Duchess died in 1829.

Werder. A member of the artistic circle Mendelssohn met at the house of Professor Wichmann, Berlin.

Wesley (Samuel). Organist and composer. Born, Bristol, Feb. 24th, 1766; died, London, Oct. 11th, 1837.

Appendix D

Wharncliffe (Baron). Statesman. Born, 1776; died, London, Dec. 19th, 1845.

Wichmann (Professor Ludwig Wilhelm). Sculptor, of Berlin, at whose house were met all the artistic celebrities of the time. Madame Wichmann, *née* Feilner, was a great friend of Jenny Lind.

Wieck (Clara Josephine). Pianist. Born, Leipzig, Sept. 13th, 1819; died, Frankfort-on-Main, May 20th, 1896. Married to Robert Schumann, Sept. 12th, 1840.

Williams (Anne and Martha). Sisters, known as the Misses Williams, vocalists. Born, Bitterley, Salop, Anne, 1818, Martha, 1821. They sang the duet, "Lift thine Eyes," in the first performance of *Elijah*. Anne Williams married Mr. Price, of Gloucester, in 1850, and retired. Martha was married in 1853 to Charles Lockey (*q.v.*); and died, Hastings, Aug. 28th, 1897.

Willy (John Thomas). Violinist. Born, London, July 24th, 1812; died, Clapham, Aug. 8th, 1885.

Wittmann (Robert). Violoncellist and pianist. Born, Dresden, Dec. 6th, 1804.

Woelfl (Joseph). Pianist and composer. Born, Salzburg, 1772; died, London, May 21st, 1812.

Zelter (Carl Friedrich). Director of the Singakademie, Berlin. Born, Berlin, Dec. 11th, 1758; died there, May 15th, 1832.

APPENDIX E

ELIJAH

A SACRED ORATORIO.

The Author of this English Version of the Oratorio of ELIJAH *has endeavoured to render it as nearly in accordance with the scriptural texts as the music to which it is adapted will admit.*

PART FIRST.

PROLOGUE—(ELIJAH.)

As God the Lord of Israel liveth, before whom I stand, there shall not be dew nor rain these years, but according to my word. —1 *Kings* i. 17.

OVERTURE.

CHORUS—(THE PEOPLE.)

Help, Lord ! wilt Thou quite destroy us ?

The harvest now is over, the summer days are gone, and yet no power cometh to help us ! Will, then, the Lord be no more God in Zion ?—*Jeremiah* viii. 20.

RECITATIVE CHORUS—(THE PEOPLE.)

The deeps afford no water ; and the rivers are exhausted !

The suckling's tongue now cleaveth for thirst to its mouth ;

the infant children ask for bread, and there is no one breaketh it to feed them.—*Lamentations* iv. 4.

DUET AND CHORUS—(The People.)

People. Lord ! bow Thine ear to our prayer !

Duet. Zion spreadeth her hands for aid ; and there is neither help nor comfort.—*Lamentations* i. 17.

RECITATIVE.

Ye people, rend your hearts and not your garments for your transgressions ; even as Elijah hath sealed the heavens through the word of God.

I therefore say to ye, Forsake your Idols, return to God : for He is slow to anger, and merciful, and kind and gracious, and repenteth Him of the evil.—*Joel* ii. 12, 13.

AIR.

If with all your hearts ye truly seek me ; ye shall ever surely find me. Thus saith our God.

Oh ! that I knew where I might find Him, that I might even come before His presence !—*Deuteronomy* iv. 29.

CHORUS—(The People.)

Yet doth the Lord see it not: He mocketh at us ; His curse hath fallen down upon us ; His wrath will pursue us till He destroy us !

For He is Lord and God : He is a jealous God : and He visiteth all the fathers' sins on the children to the third and the fourth generation of them that hate Him : His mercies on thousands fall—fall on all them that love Him and keep His commandments.—*Exodus* xx. 5, 6.

RECITATIVE—(An Angel.)

Elijah! get thee hence; depart and turn thee eastward: thither hide thee by Cherith's brook. There shalt thou drink its waters; and the Lord thy God hath commanded the ravens to feed thee there: so do according unto His word.—1 *Kings* xvii. 3.

DOUBLE QUARTET—(Angels.)

For He shall give His angels charge over thee, that they shall protect thee in all the ways thou goest; that their hands shall uphold and guide thee, lest thou dash thy foot against a stone.—*Psalm* xci. 11, 12.

RECITATIVE—(An Angel.)

Elijah! now Cherith's brook is dried up, arise and depart; and get thee to Zarephath: thither abide. Behold, I have commanded a widow woman there to sustain thee; and thou shalt want nothing, nor she and her house, through the word of God.—1 *Kings* xvii. 9.

The Widow and Elijah.

The Widow. Help me, man of God! my son is sick; and his sickness is so sore that there is no breath left in him. Art thou come to call my sin to remembrance—to slay my son? Help me, man of God, help my son! for if thou willest, he still by thy power may be assisted.—1 *Kings* xvii. 17, 18.

RECITATIVE.

Elijah. Give me thy son. O Lord, my God! turn unto her; in mercy help this widow's son! Lord, my God, let the spirit of this child return, that he again may live.—*Psalm* lxxxvi. 16.

Widow. Wilt thou indeed shew wonders to the dead? Say, will the dead arise and praise Thee?—*Psalm* lxxxviii. 10.

Appendix E

ELIJAH. Lord, my God, let the spirit of this child return, that he may praise Thee.—1 *Kings* xvii. 21.

WIDOW. The Lord hath heard thy prayer! the soul of my child is returning—my son reviveth!—1 *Kings* xvii. 22.

ELIJAH. Now, behold, thy son liveth!—1 *Kings* xvii. 23.

WIDOW. Now by this I know that thou art a man of God; and that His word in thy mouth is the truth. O blessed are the men who fear Him!—1 *Kings* xvii. 24.

CHORUS.

Blessed are the men who fear Him, who delight in His commands! They ever walk in the ways of peace. Through darkness riseth light; light to the upright; they are gracious, compassionate, and ever righteous.—*Psalm* cvi. 3.

RECITATIVE—(ELIJAH, AHAB, AND CHORUS.)

ELIJAH. As God, the Lord of Sabaoth, liveth, before whom I stand, three years this day fulfilled, I will shew myself unto Ahab: and God the Lord will send rain again upon the earth.—1 *Kings* xviii. 1, 15.

AHAB. Art thou Elijah? Art thou he that troubleth Israel?

CHORUS. Thou art Elijah, he that troubleth Israel!—1 *Kings* xvii. 17.

AHAB. All accuse thee.

ELIJAH. I never troubled Israel's peace: it is thou, Ahab, and all thy father's house. Ye have forsaken God's commands; and thou hast followed Baalim.

Now send, and gather to me the whole of Israel unto mount Carmel. There summon the prophets of Baal, and also the prophets of the groves, who are feasted at Jezebel's table: then we shall see whose God is the Lord.

CHORUS. And then we shall see whose God is God the Lord!—1 *Kings* xviii. 18, 19.

ELIJAH. Rise then, ye priests of Baal: select and slay a

bullock, and put no fire under it: uplift your voices, and call the god ye worship: and I then will call on the Lord Jehovah. And the God who by fire shall answer, let Him be God!

CHORUS. Yea; and the God who by fire shall answer, let Him be God.—1 *Kings* xviii. 23, 24.

ELIJAH. Call first upon your god: your numbers are many; I, even I, only remain, one prophet of the Lord. Invoke your forest gods and mountain deities.—1 *Kings* xviii. 25.

CHORUS—(PRIESTS OF BAAL.)

Baal, we cry to thee, hear and answer us! heed the sacrifice we offer! hear us, O hear us, Baal!

Hear us, Baal! hear, mighty god! Baal, O answer us! Let thy flames fall and extirpate the foe! O hear us, Baal!—1 *Kings* xviii. 26.

RECITATIVE—(ELIJAH.)

Call him louder, for he is a god! He talketh; or he is pursuing; or he is in a journey; or peradventure, he sleepeth; so awaken him: call him louder!—1 *Kings* xviii. 27.

CHORUS—(PRIESTS OF BAAL.)

Hear our cry, O Baal! now arise! wherefore slumber?

RECITATIVE—(ELIJAH.)

Call him louder! he heareth not. With knives and lancets cut yourselves after your manner: leap upon the altar ye have made: call him and prophesy! not a voice will answer ye; none will listen, none heed ye.—1 *Kings* xviii. 28, 29.

CHORUS—(PRIESTS OF BAAL.)

Hear and answer, Baal! Mark how the scorner derideth us! Hear and answer!

Appendix E

RECITATIVE AND AIR—(ELIJAH.)

Draw near, all ye people; come to me. Lord God of Abraham, Isaac, and Israel! this day let it be known that Thou art God; and I am Thy servant! O shew to all this people that I have done these things according to Thy word! Hear me, O Lord, and answer me, and shew this people that Thou art Lord God; and let their hearts again be turned.—1 *Kings* xviii. 30, 36, 37.

QUARTET—(ANGELS.)

Regard Thy servant's prayer,
While angels bow before Thee,
And worlds around Thy throne
In strains of praise adore Thee.
O, help him in his need,
Thy gracious ear accord—
Jehovah, Sabaoth,
Creator, God, and Lord!

RECITATIVE—(ELIJAH.)

O Thou, who makest Thine angels spirits; Thou, whose ministers are flaming fires: let them now descend!—*Psalm* civ. 4.

CHORUS—(THE PEOPLE.)

The fire descends from heaven! the flames consume his offering!

Bow down, bow down! on your faces fall, adoring! The Lord is God: He is the Lord our God. Alone He is God: and we will have no other God, but God the Lord!—1 *Kings* xviii. 38, 39.

RECITATIVE—(ELIJAH.)

Take all the priests of Baal; and let not one of them escape ye : bring them down to Kishon's brook, and there let them be slain !

CHORUS—(THE PEOPLE.)

Take all the priests of Baal ; and let not one of them escape us ! Bring all and slay them !—1 *Kings* xviii. 40.

AIR—(ELIJAH.)

Is not His word like a fire : and like a hammer that breaketh the rock into pieces ?—*Jeremiah* xxiii. 29.

For God is angry with the wicked every day : and if the wicked turn not, the Lord will whet His sword. And He hath bent His bow and made it ready.—*Psalm* vii. 11, 12.

AIR.

Woe unto them who forsake Him ! destruction shall fall upon them, for they have transgressed against Him. Though they are by Him redeemed : yet they have spoken falsely against Him.—*Hosea* vii. 13.

RECITATIVE AND CHORUS—(ELIJAH, A YOUTH, AND THE PEOPLE.)

ELIJAH. O Lord, Thou hast overthrown Thine enemies and destroyed them ! Look down on us from heaven, O Lord ; regard the distress of Thy people ! Open the heavens and send us relief. Help, help Thy servant now, O God !

PEOPLE. Open the heavens and send us relief ! help, help Thy servant now, O God !—2 *Chronicles* vi. 26.

ELIJAH. Go up now, child, and look toward the sea. Hath my prayer been heard by the Lord ?

YOUTH. There is nothing.—1 *Kings* xviii. 43.
The heavens are as brass above me.—*Deut.* xxviii. 23.

Appendix E

Elijah. When the heavens are closed up because they have sinned against Thee: yet, if they pray and confess Thy name, and turn from their sin when Thou dost afflict them, then hear from heaven, and forgive the sin. Help, send Thy servant help, O God!

Chorus. Then hear from heaven and forgive the sin. Help, send Thy servant help, O God!—2 *Chronicles* vi. 26, 27.

Elijah. Go up again, and still look toward the sea.

Youth. There is nothing. The earth is as iron under me.—*Deuteronomy* xxviii. 23.

Elijah. Hearest thou no sound of rain? seest thou nothing arise from the deep?

Youth. No; there is nothing.

Elijah. Have respect to the prayer of Thy servant, O Lord my God!—2 *Chronicles* vi. 19.

Unto Thee will I cry, Lord my rock; be not silent to me: and Thy great mercies remember, Lord.—*Psalm* xxviii. 1.

Youth. Behold, a little cloud ariseth now from the waters! it is like a man's hand! The heavens are black with clouds and with wind: the storm rusheth louder and louder!—1 *Kings* xviii. 45.

The People. Thanks be to God for all His mercies.

Elijah. Thanks be to God! for He is gracious; and His mercy endureth for evermore!—*Psalm* cvi. 1.

CHORUS.

Thanks be to God! He laveth the thirsty land! The waters gather, they rush along; they are lifting their voices!

The stormy billows are high; their fury is mighty. But the Lord is above them, and Almighty!—*Psalm* xciii. 3, 4.

PART SECOND

RECITATIVE.

Elijah is come already; and yet they have known him not; but have done unto him whatsoever they listed.—*Matthew* xvii. 12.

AIR.

Hear ye, Israel; hear what the Lord speaketh: "Ah! hadst thou heeded My commandments!"

He to His people calleth; yet they regard not His voice, nor will they obey His call.

Yet to the righteous, saith the Lord, the Holy One of Israel; I—I am He that comforteth, and ye are mine.

Wake up, arise, Jerusalem!

Say, who art thou that despairest, and forgettest the Lord thy Maker; who hath stretched forth the heavens, and laid the earth's foundations?

Wake up, arise, Jerusalem!—*Isaiah* xlviii. 1, 18; xlv. 11; li. 12, 13, 17.

CHORUS.

"Be not afraid!" saith God the Lord. Be not afraid, for He is near; thy help is near!—*Isaiah* xli. 10.

Though thousands languish and fall beside thee, and tens of thousands around thee perish; yet still it shall not come nigh thee.—*Psalm* xci. 7.

RECITATIVE—(ELIJAH.)

Yet, Ahab, thou hast not kept the commandments of the Lord thy God; but hast done evil to provoke Him to anger, above all that were before thee; as if it had been a light thing for thee to walk in the sins of Jeroboam. Thou hast made a grove and an altar for Baal, and served him, and worshipped him: thou hast killed the righteous, and also taken possession. And the Lord shall smite all Israel, as a reed is shaken in the water: and He shall give Israel up; and thou shalt know He is the Lord.—1 *Kings* xvi. 30, 31, 32, 33.

(THE QUEEN.)

Dost thou now govern the kingdom of Israel, while Elijah's power is greater than the king's?

The gods do so to me, and more, if by to-morrow, about this time, I make not his life as one of them he caused to be destroyed at the brook of Kishon; whom he by the sword hath slaughtered.—1 *Kings* xxi. 7; xix. 2.

He hath transgressed, slay him! He hath prophesied against this city, as ye have heard with your ears!—*Jeremiah* xxvi. 11.

He also closed the heavens; and called down a famine upon the land.—1 *Kings* xviii. 10.

So go ye forth to every nation and every kingdom, and seek Elijah; and seize on him, slaughter him; do unto him as he hath done.—*Ecclesiastes* xlviii. 3, 2.

CHORUS.

Do unto him as he hath done: he hath transgressed, slay him! So go ye forth; seize on him, slaughter him!

RECITATIVE AND AIR—(ELIJAH.)

Though stricken, they have not grieved!—*Jeremiah* v. 3.

Tarry here, my servant, and I will go a day's journey into the wilderness.—1 *Kings* xix. 3, 4.

It is enough, O Lord; now take away my life; for I am not better than my fathers. I desire to live no longer; now let me die; for my days are vanity.—*Job* vii. 16.

I have been very jealous for the Lord God of Hosts; for the

children of Israel have broken Thy covenant, thrown down Thine altars, and slain Thy prophets with the sword ; and I, even I only am left : and they seek my life to take it away.—1 *Kings* xix. 10.

It is enough, O Lord ; now take away my life !

RECITATIVE.

Under a juniper tree he sleepeth.* Protected by angels of the Lord ; who encamp around all them that fear Him.—*Psalm* xxxiv. 7.

* 1 *Kings* xix. 5.

DUET—(Angels.)

Lift thine eyes unto the mountains, from whence cometh thy help.

For it cometh from the Lord, the maker of heaven and earth. He hath said ; thy foot shall not be moved : for thy shepherd will not slumber.—*Psalm* cxxi. 1, 3.

CHORUS—(Angels.)

He, watching over Israel, slumbers not, nor sleeps.—*Psalm* cxxi. 4.

Shouldst thou, walking in grief, languish—He will quicken thee.—*Psalm* cxxxviii. 7.

RECITATIVE—(Elijah and an Angel.)

Angel. Arise, Elijah ; for thou hast a long journey before thee.

Elijah. I have been very jealous for the Lord, the God Sabaoth ; for the children of Israel have broken His covenant, thrown down His altars, and slain His prophets with the sword ; and I, even I only am left, and they seek my life.—1 *Kings* xix. 7, 10.

Appendix E

AIR.

O rest in the Lord, wait patiently for Him, and He shall give thee thine heart's desires.

Commit thy way unto Him, and trust in Him ; and fret not thyself because of evil doers.—*Psalm* xxxvii. 1, 7.

CHORUS—(ANGELS.)

He that shall endure to the end shall be saved.—*Matthew* xxiv. 13.

RECITATIVE.

ELIJAH. Hear me speedily, O Lord ; my spirit faileth ; hide not Thy face from me : my soul is thirsting for Thee, as a thirsty land !—*Psalm* cxliii. 7, 6.

ANGEL. Arise now, get thee without ; stand on the mount before the Lord ; for there His glory will appear and shine on thee.

Thy face must be veiled, for he draweth near.—1 *Kings* xix. 11.

CHORUS.

And behold, the Lord passed by ! And a mighty wind rent the mountains around, brake in pieces the rocks, brake them before the Lord ; but the Lord was not in the tempest.

And behold, the Lord passed by ! And the sea was upheaved, and the earth was shaken ; but the Lord was not in the earthquake.

And after the earthquake there came a fire ; but the Lord was not in the fire.

And after the fire there came a still small voice, and in that still voice, onward came the Lord.—1 *Kings* xix. 11.

QUARTET AND CHORUS—(ANGELS.)

Holy, holy, holy is God the Lord—the Lord Sabaoth ! Now His glory hath filled all the earth.—*Isaiah* vi. 3.

RECITATIVE—(ELIJAH.)

O Lord, I have heard of Thee; but mine eye now seeth Thee.—*Job* xlii. 5.

My heart therefore is glad, my glory rejoiceth, and my flesh also shall rest in hope.—*Psalm* xvi. 9.

AIR.

For the mountains shall depart, and the hills be removed; but Thy kindness shall not depart from me, neither shall the covenant of Thy peace be removed.—*Isaiah* liv. 10.

CHORUS.

Then did Elijah the prophet break forth like a fire; his word appeared as light in darkness. Mighty kings by him were overthrown. He stood on the Mount of Sinai, and heard the judgments of the future, and in Horeb its vengeance.—*Ecclesiastes* xlviii. 1, 6, 7.

And when the Lord would take him away to heaven, behold! there came a fiery chariot, with fiery horses; and he went by a whirlwind to heaven.—2 *Kings* ii. 1, 11.

AIR.

Then shall the righteous shine forth as the sun in their heavenly father's realm.—*Matthew* xiii. 43.

Joy on their head shall be for everlasting, and all sorrow and mourning shall flee away for ever.—*Isaiah* li. 11.

RECITATIVE.

Elijah walked with God, and he was not, for God took him to heaven; and he was seen no more!—*Genesis* v. 24.

Behold! the Lord will send you Elijah the prophet, before the coming of the great and dreadful day of the Lord.

And he shall turn the heart of the fathers to the children, and the heart of the children unto their fathers, lest I come and smite the earth with a curse.—*Malachi* iv. 5, 6.

CHORUS.

But thus saith the Lord : I have raised one from the north : he shall come, and from the rising of the sun, he shall call upon my name, and come on princes.

Behold my servant and mine elect, in whom my soul delighteth.

On him the Spirit of God shall rest : the spirit of wisdom and understanding, the spirit of might and counsel, the spirit of knowledge and of the fear of the Lord.—*Isaiah* xli. 25 ; xlii. 1 ; xi. 2.

QUARTET.

O ! every one that thirsteth, come ye to the waters : come unto Him, and your souls shall live for ever !—*Isaiah* lv. 1, 3.

CHORUS.

Unto Him that is abundantly able to exceed all, even all that we can ask or think :—

Now all glory be unto Him through all ages, and for evermore. AMEN.—*Ephesians* iii. 20.

Index

Index

Index

Index

X

Index

THE END

PRINTED BY
WILLIAM CLOWES AND SONS, LIMITED,
LONDON AND BECCLES.